So *Many* Versions?

So *Many* Versions?

Twentieth Century English Versions of the Bible

Sakae Kubo & Walter Specht

ZONDERVAN PUBLISHING HOUSE OF THE ZONDERVAN CORPORATION GRAND RAPIDS, MICHIGAN 49506

SO *MANY* VERSIONS?

Contents

Abbreviations

AB	Amplified Bible
ASV	American Standard Version
BLE	Bible in Living English
JB	Jerusalem Bible
KJV	King James Version
LB	Living Bible
LXX	Septuagint
MLB	Modern Language Bible (Berkeley)
MS(S)	manuscript, manuscripts
NAB	New American Bible
NASB	New American Standard Bible
NEB	New English Bible
NIV	New International Version
NJV	New Jewish Version
NT	New Testament
NWT	New World Translation
OT	Old Testament
RSV	Revised Standard Version
TEV	Today's English Version
vs(s).	verse, verses

Acknowledgments

Appreciation is expressed to the following publishers for permission to use selections from the Bible translations for which they hold copyright:

THE AMERICAN BIBLE SOCIETY. *Today's English Version of the New Testament.* Copyright © American Bible Society 1966, 1971.

WILLIAM COLLINS SONS AND COMPANY, LTD. *Barclay's New Testament* by William Barclay. Copyright © 1968, 1970 by William Collins Sons and Company, Ltd. Quoted by permission of William Collins + World Publishing Co., Inc., Cleveland, Ohio.

CONFRATERNITY OF CHRISTIAN DOCTRINE. *The New American Bible.* Copyright © Confraternity of Christian Doctrine 1970.

DARTON, LONGMAN & TODD, LTD and DOUBLEDAY & COMPANY, INC. *The Jerusalem Bible.* Copyright © 1966 by Darton, Longman & Todd, Ltd.

DIVISION OF CHRISTIAN EDUCATION, NATIONAL COUNCIL OF CHURCHES OF CHRIST IN THE UNITED STATES OF AMERICA. *The Revised Standard Version of the Bible,* copyright 1946, 1952, © 1971, 1973; and the *Revised Standard Version Common Bible,* copyright © 1973 by The Division of Christian Education, National Council of the Churches of Christ in the United States of America.

HARPER AND ROW PUBLISHERS, INC. and HODDER AND STOUGHTON, LTD. *The New Testament,* A New Translation by James Moffatt. Copyright © 1964 by James Moffatt. Used by permission of Harper and Row, Inc. and Hodder and Stoughton, Ltd.

HARPER AND ROW PUBLISHERS, INC. and JAMES CLARKE AND COMPANY, LTD. *Weymouth's New Testament in Modern Speech* by Richard Francis Weymouth, as revised by J. A. Robertson. By permission of Harper and Row Publishers, Inc. and James Clarke and Company, Ltd.

THE JEWISH PUBLICATION SOCIETY OF AMERICA. *Torah* (Jewish Publication Society Bible). Copyright © 1962, 2nd rev. ed. © 1974, The Jewish Publication Society of America.

Introduction

There is need for a comprehensive evaluation of current versions of the Bible. Although there are good treatments of the history of the English Bible, they cannot give detailed treatment of every translation, especially recent ones. Moreover, new translations are constantly appearing and such books need updating from time to time. This book is an attempt to fill this gap. It is not possible to discuss every version but we have selected what we consider to be the most important ones on the basis of their use today. However, we have included in the appendix as complete a list of twentieth-century Bibles with annotations as we could compile.

There are several significant trends that we notice in twentieth-century Bible translations. One of the most significant is the abandonment of the King James Version tradition in the "official" Bibles—the Protestant *New English Bible* and the Jewish Publication Society Bible. Catholic Bibles likewise no longer follow the Rheims-Challoner tradition. Future "official" Bibles will undoubtedly follow this trend.

Another significant change is the almost complete dominance of the use of the best Greek text in the NT, especially in recent translations. While there is no unanimity in the use of a specific Greek edition, the text used is superior to those of the previous centuries. In the OT, the Masoretic text is still basic but is challenged by ancient versions and the biblical MSS of the *Dead Sea Scrolls*.

Among Catholic translations, the significant change has been in the use of the original languages rather than the Vulgate

13

as the base for translation. In this respect, Ronald Knox's translation came a bit too soon. In Catholic Bibles also there is a noticeable reduction of specifically Catholic notes and explanations.

The incorporation of the principles of linguistics is a new trend that probably will influence future translations as it has already the TEV. The translation of Bibles for those with limited English background is influenced by the dominance of English in the Western as well as the Third World. A trend that is advanced especially in France is developing in this country with the adoption of the Common Bible. In the future, Catholics and Protestants will move beyond the adoption of a mutually acceptable RSV and will work together in the translation of a completely new Common Bible, although even now Protestants and Catholics use each other's Bibles freely, without official objection, since their most recent translations are quite similar.

In the evaluation of these versions, it is well to keep in mind the reasons for the continual publication of new translations. No translation of the Bible can ever be considered final. Translations must keep pace with the growth in biblical scholarship and the changes in language. It may be helpful to list the three main reasons for new versions of the sacred text.

The first reason is that the discovery of older and better manuscripts for both Testaments enables the scholar of today to have a sounder text of the original to translate. Several outstanding Greek MSS of the NT have come to light in this century. The oldest of these were written on papyrus. One of the most important collections of biblical papyrus MSS was acquired in 1930/31 by Chester Beatty and is now in the Beatty museum in a suburb of Dublin. Three of these were NT codices. One contained portions of 30 leaves of an estimated original 220 of the four Gospels and Acts dated in the first half of the third century. Another, dated around 200, has 86 leaves of an original 104 of 10 of Paul's Epistles. The third comprises 10 of an estimated original 32 leaves of the Book of Revelation from the middle or latter part of the third century.

More recently, about 1956, another collection of papyrus MSS of the NT came into the hands of M. Martin Bodmer, a Genevan bibliophile and humanist. They are now in the Bodmer Library of World Literature at Cologny, a suburb of Geneva. Among them was a papyrus codex MS known as Bodmer Papyrus II, containing most of the Gospel of John, and dated by the editor, Victor Martin, Professor of Classical Philology at Geneva, about 200 A.D. Another MS in the group contains the earliest-known copies of Jude and 1 and 2 Peter. The editor, Michel Testuz, dates it in the third century. A third codex contains the oldest-known copy of Luke and one of the earliest of John. The editors, Victor Martin and Rodolphe Kasser, date it between A.D. 175 and 225. It would be difficult to overestimate the textual importance of these newly acquired witnesses for the wording of the NT. Besides these, the most important early MSS known before the twentieth century were not fully utilized by the major translations.

For the OT there are the world famous *Dead Sea Scrolls* discovered in 1947 and since. The biblical scrolls among them are so sensationally significant because they have carried our knowledge of the Hebrew Bible back by 1,000 years. Before their discovery, apart from a few scraps, the oldest Hebrew MSS known were dated toward the end of the ninth century A.D. But now there are MSS to be dated as early as the first century B.C. These discoveries have their bearing on the conclusion of scholars regarding the original wording of the sacred Scriptures.

In the second place, along with the discovery of these earlier MSS, there has developed a better understanding of the meaning of these original languages. This is largely due to the wonderful archaeological discoveries of the past century. As an illustration of this significant point, there are the discoveries of nonliterary papyri that have shown what many of the Greek words used by NT writers meant in daily life. For the study of the OT languages there is an abundance of written documents such as the Amarna Tablets, the Lachish Letters, the Jewish-Aramaic papyri, and the Canaanite tablets found at Ugarit, to name but a few. All of these have given scholars a better understanding of what the languages of the Bible really mean. Such knowledge must be reflected in better translations.

Earlier translations such as the KJV did not have the advantage of these tremendous discoveries. The KJV was dependent upon late MSS of the Middle Ages, which had been corrupted as they were copied and recopied by hand through the ages. Translators today have access to MSS that are in some cases less than a century removed from the autographs. As a result, today we have translations that are more in harmony with what the apostles actually wrote. New understandings of the original languages through achaeological discoveries have helped to shed light on obscure passages and have aided us in understanding some passages better than they were understood before.

Finally, one of the major reasons for the revisions of the English Bible is the tremendous change constantly taking place in the English language. Languages are living and constantly changing. Many words become obsolete. Others change their meaning with the passing of time. Even in the Revised Versions, both English and American, words are used that are foreign to modern readers.

These are good and compelling reasons for producing new translations of the Bible. Perhaps, however, some will feel that there is a glut of translations on the market today. There are more than the people can digest. Some feel it is time to call a halt to the work of translation for a while until we absorb the flood of recent translations. At any rate, we hope that this volume will help in the evaluation of the many Bibles on the market today.

Perhaps something should be said about paraphrase and translation. As it is ordinarily used, the word "paraphrase" refers to a freely rendered restatement of a passage in a clearer form in the same language without altering its meaning. In using this word for Bible translation from one language to another, it has come to connote a rather free translation in which phrases are added or omitted and often fidelity to the meaning is thus sacrificed. Dr. Eugene Nida, in an article in the *Bible Translator* (1 [July, 1950], 97-106), deplores the distinction between translation and paraphrase since it fails to take into consideration that in some instances the only way to translate is to paraphrase. He gives the example "bowels of mercies," which should be translated as "compassion" or "tender compassion." However, Nida admits that that type of paraphrasing is exceptional rather than usual. What Nida fails to consider in his article is that this term is not used for those translations that commonly "paraphrase" certain idioms or phrases. The usual meaning of "translation" is not opposed to using "paraphrase" in the kind of example Nida gives. What is meant by paraphrase is that the translator takes undue liberties throughout in adding, omitting, and altering the original in such a way that often the equivalence in meaning is not transferred. This does not mean that a mere slavish literalism to the form of the original is a good translation. Usually, in fact, such "faithful" translations are not translations at all. There is no quarrel with Nida's principles of translation from the point of view of dynamic equivalence but only with his attempt to identify "paraphrase" with "translation," not with respect to certain idioms alone but to the whole range of translation. There is a useful distinction that these words still make when used in this sense.

The word "paraphrase" also fittingly describes what Nida objects to—that which he calls "cultural translation" in distinction from "linguistic translation."[1] Beekman and Callow refer to Jordan's *"Cotton Patch" Version*, which substitutes contemporary Southern peoples, places, and parties for the biblical ones. For example, Corinth becomes Atlanta in 1 Corinthians 1:1 and Jews become "whites" and Gentiles, "Negroes."[2] They also refer to Captain J. Rogers's translation of the seaman's version of Psalm 23: "The Lord is my Pilot; I shall not drift," etc.[3] Such examples are dynamic equivalence with a vengeance. All responsible translators will avoid such renderings.

Besides being opposed to lack of fidelity to historical references as in the above instances, Beekman and Callow are also against the same regarding didactic references. The latter refer to "commands, illustrations, parables, and similitudes." However, when wrong or zero meaning results from the maintenance of a word, fidelity to meaning "takes precedence over fidelity to the historical nature of the imagery," and thus a substitution may be justified.[4] Even here great care must be exercised.

---

1. Eugene Nida, *The Theory and Practice of Translation* (New York: Adler, 1969), p. 13.
2. John Beekman and John Callow, *Translating the Word of God* (Grand Rapids: Zondervan, 1974), p. 35.
3. Ibid., p. 41.

Sometimes a translation becomes a mini-commentary, since explanations of words or expressions are placed in the text without indicating that these were not a part of the original text. Some of these go beyond making explicit in the receptor language what was implicit in the original. Barclay does this type of thing in his translation. For instance, Matthew 9:17 reads, "Neither is new wine put into old wineskins" in the RSV, but Barclay has "No more do people pour new *fermenting* wine into old wineskins *that have lost their elasticity.*" Is this legitimate or not? Has Barclay placed in the text what should have been placed in the notes? How about his translation of Matthew 10:38: "Can you be submerged in the sea of troubles in which I must be submerged?" for "Are you able to drink the cup that I drink, or to be baptized with the baptism with which I am baptized?" Here the translator has taken over the role of a commentator and sets forth his commentary as a translation. This is the danger of paraphrases that are put forth as or considered translations. The free quality makes it easy for the translator to insert interpretations or other clarifying matters into the text. There is a place for such paraphrases as aids to the better understanding of Scripture if they are so identified. In this sense they stand between a true translation, which transfers the meaning of the original as accurately as possible, and a commentary, which gives a full-scale interpretation.

As much as possible, therefore, the translator must be faithful to his text while at the same time faithful to the receptor language. Historical and cultural references should not be altered. Notes can be used to explain what may not be clear to the reader while at the same time the translation should be in the idiom and structures of the language into which the Scriptures are translated. This is not always an easy task, but we should not open the door to too free renderings through the general identification of translation with paraphrase. It is true that the basic distinction is whether a translation is faithful or not, i.e., whether it

> transfers the meaning and the dynamics of the original text. . . .
> The expression, *transfers the meaning,* means that the trans-

---

4. Ibid., pp. 36, 37.

lation conveys to the reader or hearer the information that the original conveyed to its readers or hearers. The message is not distorted or changed; it has neither unnecessarily gained nor lost information. The expression, *the dynamics,* means that (1) the translation makes a natural use of the linguistic structures of the *RL* [receptor language] and that (2) the recipients of the translation understand the message with ease.[5]

The key words in the above definition are "it has neither *unnecessarily* gained nor lost information." The crux of the problem is right at that point. Take Barclay's translation of Matthew 9:17 concerning new wine. He has actually clarified the meaning of the text. Is this legitimate translation or has he exceeded the bounds of translation? In our view, although he has clarified the meaning, he has not translated accurately. He has become a commentator. How much may a translator add and still be faithful? What may be added are only those things that are necessary to the accurate transference of the original into the linguistic structure of the receptor language. In his translation above, Barclay has exceeded this limitation. He has not merely made changes to suit the *linguistic* structure of the receptor language. What he has done, in fact, was to add content beyond that of the original. Such additions, if necessary, should be made in the notes.

Where we have differed with the translators, it has not been because they have used paraphrases, which may be necessary and legitimate, but because they have not been accurate in the transference of the meaning of the original into the structure of English.

---

5. Ibid., pp. 33, 34.

1

Early Modern Speech Versions

The Reformers of the Protestant Reformation gave great impetus to the truth that the Bible belongs to the common man. The Bible was not intended for scholars alone, but for common, ordinary men and women. It was this concept that led to translations in the vernacular. In the latter part of the fourteenth century, John Wycliffe, the first translator of the complete Bible into English, intended his version for ordinary people and put it in plain, pithy language. In the revised edition of this Bible, John Purvey wrote in the preface:

> Though covetous clerks are mad through Simony, heresy and many other sins, and despise and impede Holy Writ as much as they can, yet the unlearned cry after Holy Writ to know it, with great cost and peril to their lives. For these reasons and others a simple creature hath translated the Bible out of Latin into English.

In 1516 the first published Greek NT was edited by Erasmus. In the preface, this humanist wrote:

> I totally disagree with those who are unwilling that the Holy Scriptures, translated into the common tongue, should be read by unlearned. Christ desires His mysteries to be published abroad as widely as possible. I could wish that even all women should read the Gospel and St. Paul's Epistles, and I would that they might be read and known not merely by the Scots and the Irish but even by the Turks and the Saracens. I wish that the farm worker might sing parts of them at the plough, and that the weaver might hum them at the shuttle, and that the traveller might beguile the weariness of the way by reciting them.

In the sixteenth century William Tyndale risked his life to

translate the Scriptures and died as a martyr in 1538. What was it that inspired him to undertake such a dangerous and daring work? In his note, "W. T. to the Reader," preceding his translation of the Pentateuch, he stated,

> Which thing only moved me to translate the New Testament. Because I had perceived by experience, how that it is impossible to stablish the lay people in any truth, except the scripture were plainly laid before their eyes in their mother tongue, that they might see the process, order, and the meaning of the text.

The KJV of 1611 contained a lengthy preface entitled "The Translators to the Readers," which reveals the guiding purposes, attitudes, and methods of the translators of that great version. It states that the task of translating is one

> which helpeth forward to the saving of soules. Now what can be more available thereto, than to deliver God's booke unto God's people in a tongue which they can understand? . . . How shall men meditate in that which they cannot understand? How shall they understand that which is kept close in an unknown tongue? . . . Translation it is that openeth the window, to let in the light; that breaketh the shell, that we may eat the kernel; that putteth aside the curtains, that we may looke into the Most Holy Place; that removeth the cover of the well, that we may come by the water. . . . Indeede without translation into the vulgar tongue, the unlearned are but children at Jacob's well (which was deepe) without a bucket or something to draw with. . . .

Unfortunately, the very version prefaced by these noble words is no longer speaking the language of the common man. To the average man of today the language of the KJV seems strange and foreign. There is therefore danger that the Bible may seem to modern man to be something out of date and irrelevant. This has been recognized now for nearly a century. Hence, toward the end of the nineteenth and the beginning of the twentieth century a movement arose calling for translations of the Bible in modern English.

This movement was strengthened by the discoveries of large quantities of papyri in Egypt particularly at about the turn of the century and later. These papyri have illuminated every aspect of the life of the Greek-speaking people of the ancient world in which the NT was written. They have revolutionized the study of NT Greek, for they have shown that in the main the NT was written in the vernacular Greek of common people. The NT documents are written in a plain, simple style to meet the needs of ordinary men and women. Should it not then be translated in the same kind of English? This is the argument of the translators of the modern-speech versions.

Four of the modern-speech versions of the early twentieth century are of special significance and must be considered here because of their merit and because of the influence they exerted on the *Revised Standard Version*. They are: *The Twentieth Century New Testament*, Weymouth's *The New Testament in Modern Speech*, Moffatt's *A New Translation of the Bible*, and Smith and Goodspeed's *The Bible, An American Translation*.

THE TWENTIETH CENTURY NEW TESTAMENT

One of the pioneer modern speech versions, *The Twentieth Century New Testament*, was reprinted in 1961 in a new paper cover edition by the Moody Press of Chicago. The preface of the new edition states:

> *The Twentieth Century New Testament* is a smooth-flowing, accurate, easy to read translation that captivates its readers from start to finish. Born out of a desire to make the Bible readable and understandable, it is the product of the labors of a committee of twenty men and women who worked together over a period of many years to construct, we believe under divine surveillance, this beautifully simple rendition of the Word of God.

In 1933 the records of the secretary of this group of translators were deposited for safe-keeping in the John Rylands Library in Manchester by perhaps the last survivor of the committee. Without these papers we would probably never have known the story of the courageous people who put in fourteen years of difficult labor to produce this version. Prof. Edward Robinson, the Rylands librarian, kindly gave Prof. Kenneth W. Clark of Duke University access to these records. From them he reconstructed the story of the version, which he published as an article entitled, "The Making of the Twentieth Century New Testament," in the *Bulletin of the Rylands Library* of September, 1955.

The story begins in 1891 when the editor of the *Review of Reviews*, W. T. Stead, received two letters from writers unknown to each other, expressing the desire to have a translation that would make the meaning of the Bible plain to youth and uneducated people. One of these was Mrs. Mary Ann Kingsland Higgs of Greenacres, Oldham (near Manchester), the wife of a Congregational minister. Besides training four children of her own, she was a leader and teacher of youth groups in the churches her husband pastored. She had become disturbed when she discovered that youth did not understand the traditional idiom of the KJV nor that of the Revised Version, and wrote to Mr. Stead regarding her problem. She also made an attempt to solve the problem by beginning her own idiomatic translation of the Gospel of Mark.

The writer of the other letter was Ernest de Mérundol Malan, a signal and telegraph engineer of Newland, Hull, and a grandson of the famous Swiss Reformed clergyman, César Malan. Mr. Malan also had four children and followed the custom of reading the Bible to them. In this bilingual family it became evident to the father that the modern French version of Lassere was better understood by his children than the traditional English Bible. So he, too, wrote about his problem to the editor of the *Review of Reviews*. Mr. Stead put Mr. Malan and Mrs. Higgs in touch with each other, and they began to collaborate on the translation of the Gospel of Mark. As their work progressed, they expanded their plan to include the other Gospels and Acts and solicited the help of other translators.

Stead printed a notice calling for "co-workers in the task of translating the Gospels and Acts of the Apostles into our everyday speech." As a result, a number of like-minded people responded, and the group of translators grew to twenty. Since they never met together as a group, it was necessary for them to collaborate by mail. Malan, just thirty-three years of age, was the driving spirit behind the project and acted as the secretary of the committee. He requested that each member send an autobiographical sketch that would serve as an introduction to the others. Fifteen of these sketches were preserved in the records, and they give us a vivid picture of the kind of people engaged in this task. Ranging in age from nineteen to sixty-three, they lived in various parts of the British Isles. They represented a wide range in education, in occupation, and in religious affiliation. About half were ministers or ex-ministers, and the rest included housewives, businessmen, and school-teachers. Denominationally, they included Anglicans, Methodists, Presbyterians, Congregationalists, and Baptists. The one thing they all seemed to have had in common was poor health. Most of them, too, represented large families. They were also caught up in the social and intellectual ferment that shook Victorian Britain in the late nineteenth century.

Malan took the main responsibility in organizing the translation work, financing the project, and publishing the finished product. His plan for the work was so well thought out and organized that it may be regarded as standard procedure for group translating. The original committee of twenty was divided into five groups, each with an assigned portion of the NT to translate. Within each group, individuals were given certain sections to render. Each translation was circulated among the group members for criticism and suggestions. Then each group was to interchange and criticize the translation of every other group. Each group assigned one of its members to serve on the revision committee. The revisers made changes only on the basis of a two-thirds vote. There was then an English Committee selected to review and improve the English idiom of the translation. Finally, the translation was published in three parts. It was a tentative edition to allow for further criticism and changes before the final edition was published.

As the work progressed, twelve more translators were added to the committee, but unfortunately we know nothing about them, as their autobiographies were not requested. Three scholars of note were also brought in as advisors: G. G. Findlay of Headingley College, Leeds; James Rendel Harris, of Cambridge; and Richard F. Weymouth, retired Headmaster of Mill Hill School.

The "tentative edition" was published in three parts between 1898 and 1900. After careful revision work, the permanent edition was published anonymously in 1904 in London and New York. It contained an anonymous preface written by

Edward Deacon Girdlestone, the oldest member of the group. Girdlestone had also suggested the title *The Twentieth Century New Testament*. He gives as the purpose of the translation "to enable Englishmen to read the most important part of their Bible in that form of their own language which they themselves use." He expressed the fear that the retention of the Scriptures in a form of English no longer in common use "is liable to give the impression that the contents of the Bible have little to do with the life of today."

In the printing of the new translation some modification in the order of the books in the NT was made in the direction of chronological arrangement. The NT begins with Mark, regarded as the oldest of the Gospels. Between Acts and Paul's Letters is the Epistle of James. Paul's Letters are printed in the following order: 1 and 2 Thessalonians, Galatians, 1 and 2 Corinthians, Romans, Colossians, Philemon, Ephesians, Philippians, 1 and 2 Timothy, Titus, and Hebrews. The rest of the books follow in this order: 1 and 2 Peter; Jude; 1, 2, and 3 John; and Revelation. Each document is preceded by a brief introduction.

The Moody reprint of 1961 restores the traditional order of the books and leaves out the introductions. Unfortunately, the splendid preface by Girdlestone gives way to a new short one. In the text of the translation itself around seventy-five changes are made. Some of these are apparently intended to benefit American readers. Substitutions are given for "shillings," "pounds," "farthings," "quarters," "barrister," and "the Governor of the Gaol." The 1904 edition consistently rendered the Greek word "gehenna" as "the Pit." All but two of these are changed to "Hell" in the Moody reprint. Perhaps Matthew 5:22 and 18:9 simply escaped the eye of the editor. The 1904 edition consistently rendered the Greek "hades" as "Place of Death." With the exception of Revelation 6:8 and 20:13, 14, these are all changed in the reprint to "Hades," which is not in keeping with the aim of the original translators "to exclude all words and phrases not in current English." In describing Jesus' death on the cross in Mark 15:37, 39 and Luke 23:46, the translators say simply that He "expired." This is an exact rendering of the Greek, and there is no warrant for changing it, as the reprint does, to "dismissed His spirit." Nor is the reprint's "dismissed His spirit" in Matthew 27:50 an improvement over the translator's "gave up his spirit." A similar Greek phrase is found in the Septuagint of Genesis 35:18 for Rachel's death.

Nevertheless the Moody Press has done a real service in making available this fine pioneer in modern speech English. With Weymouth, it shares the honor of inaugurating the era of modern speech versions. The following samples will illustrate the simplicity and clarity of the translation:

Matthew 11:27-30
Everything has been committed to me by my Father; nor does any one fully know the Son, except the Father, or fully know the Father, except the Son and those to whom the Son may choose to reveal him. Come to me, all you who toil and are burdened, and I will give you rest! Take my yoke upon you, and learn from me, for I am gentle and lowly-minded, and "you shall find rest for your souls"; for my yoke is easy, and my burden is light.

John 1:4, 5
That which came into being in him was Life;
And the Life was the Light of Man;
And the Light shines in the darkness,
And the darkness never overpowered it.

Philippians 3:20, 21
But the State of which we are citizens is in Heaven; and it is from Heaven that we are eagerly looking for a Saviour, the Lord Jesus Christ, who, by the exercise of his power to bring everything into subjection to himself, will make this body that we have in our humiliation like to that body which he has in his Glory.

WEYMOUTH'S NEW TESTAMENT

Richard Francis Weymouth (1822-1902) was a distinguished classical scholar who in 1868 received the first Doctor of Literature degree offered by the University of London. From 1869 to 1886 he was headmaster of Mill Hill School, London, operated by nonconformists. He was a Baptist layman who was profoundly interested in the NT. In 1862 he published an edition of the Greek NT, presenting the text on which the majority of nineteenth-century editors agreed. In footnotes he indicated where the Received Text (Textus Receptus) or more recent editors disagreed with the text he established on the basis of the majority consensus. He called his edition *The Resultant Greek Testament.*

Evidently his work with the boys in the Mill Hill School impressed upon his mind the need for a modern speech version of the NT. When he retired at Brentwood, a town in Essex some twenty miles northeast of London, he proceeded to make such a translation of his *Resultant Greek Testament.* Although he completed the MS, ill health and finally his death in 1902, prevented him from seeing it through the press. This task he entrusted to his friend, Ernest Hampden-Cook, a Congregational minister, who served as resident secretary for the Mill Hill School from 1891 to 1896. Hampden-Cook also revised the translation, inserted the paragraph headings, and wrote some of the notes. He had been one of the translators of *The Twentieth Century New Testament,* and it was doubtless through his influence that Weymouth served as an advisor to that group of translators.

Weymouth called his translation "The New Testament in Modern Speech, an Idiomatic Translation into Every-day English. . . ." In the preface he outlines his aims and methods as a translator. He had no desire, he wrote, to supplant the standard English versions, and no wish that his version be used for public reading in church. Rather he hoped to supplement the other versions by furnishing, as he put it, "a succinct and compressed running commentary." He tried to the best of his ability to ascertain the meaning of every passage, and then to state that meaning as accurately and naturally as he could in present-day English. He also dreamed that his version might make some contribution to the new standard English Bible.

In his English he sought to avoid the use of colloquialisms on the one hand, and the language of English "society" on the other. He sought to clothe the thoughts of the NT in language that was modern, but at the same time dignified and reverent. As a Greek scholar he gave careful attention to points of grammatical accuracy. He tried, for example, to reproduce in translation the various nuances of the Greek tenses.

The text of the translation is arranged in paragraphs, with chapter and verse divisions given in the margin. Quotation marks are used extensively. However, quotations from the OT are printed in capital letters. The footnotes are extensive. For the most part, they seek to justify or explain the renderings given, though some deal with the MS readings followed.

Several editions of this translation have been published. The first appeared in 1903. The second, appearing in 1907, corrected misprints and removed "a few infelicities in the English of the translation." The editor sought for improvements with the note: "Criticisms of this translation, and suggestions with regard to future editions, will be welcomed. . . ." Further corrections and changes were made in the third edition. But the first major overhaul was made in the fourth edition, published in 1924, the work of "several well-known New Testament scholars." In the fifth edition the editor, James Alexander Robertson of Aberdeen, supplied numerous notes, some "illustrating the text," some "being of a geographical or historical character, and others aiming at expounding the teaching of the New Testament, and at the explanation of difficulties." This edition was published in 1929, with a number of reprints since. It was printed in the United States by the Pilgrim Press in Boston, and later by Harpers.

Among the "infelicities" in the English of Weymouth was the rendering of the Greek phrase meaning eternal life by "the life of the ages." Apparently Weymouth failed to appreciate the Semitic background of the phrase. It is really an eschatological conception meaning the life of the coming age, which, however, according to John, is made available to believers here and now. The revisers of the translation in the fourth edition changed "the life of the ages" to "eternal life."

The rendering of the Lord's Prayer will give some idea of the nature of this translation:

> Matthew 6:9-13
>
> Our Father in heaven, may Thy name be kept holy; let Thy Kingdom come; let Thy will be done, as in heaven so on earth; give us to-day our bread for the day; and forgive us our shortcomings, as we also have forgiven those who have failed in their duty towards us; and bring us not into temptation, but rescue us from the Evil one.

A comparison of 1 Thessalonians 4:13-17 as given in the second and fifth editions will also exhibit some of the more striking changes made by later revisers:

Now, concerning those who from time to time pass away, we would not have you to be ignorant, brethren, lest you should mourn as others do who have no hope. For if we believe that Jesus has died and risen again, we also believe that through Jesus God will bring with Him those who shall have passed away. For this we declare to you on the Lord's own authority—that we who are alive and continue on earth until the Coming of the Lord, shall certainly not forestall those who shall have previously passed away. For the Lord Himself will come down from heaven with a loud word of command, and with an archangel's voice and the trumpet of God, and the dead in Christ will rise first. Afterwards we who are alive and are still on earth will be caught up in their company amid clouds to meet the Lord in the air.

—Second Edition

Now, concerning those who fall asleep we would not have you ignorant, brethren, lest you should mourn, as do the rest who have no hope. For if we believe that Jesus died and rose again, in the same way also through Jesus God will bring with Him those who have fallen asleep. And this we declare to you on the Lord's own word—that we who are alive and survive until the Coming of the Lord will have no advantage over those who have fallen asleep. For the Lord Himself will come down from heaven with a loud summons, with the voice of an archangel, and with the trumpet of God, and the dead in Christ will rise first. Afterwards we who are alive and survive will be caught up along with them in the clouds to meet the Lord in the air.

—Fifth Edition

THE MOFFATT BIBLE

James Moffatt (1870-1944) was a brilliant Scottish scholar who was born and educated at Glasgow. He received a Master of Arts degree with honors in classics from Glasgow University in 1890 and took his theological degree from the Free Church College of Glasgow. Following his ordination, he served as a minister of the United Free Church for some fifteen years. During this time he continued his scholarly pursuits. In 1901 he published *The Historical New Testament,* an original translation of the New Testament documents arranged in their chronological order according to the critical literary theories of his time. This won for him a Doctor of Divinity degree from St. Andrews University, which had never previously conferred the degree on so young a man. He was Professor of Greek and NT Exegesis at Mansfield College, Oxford, from 1911 to 1915, and upon his departure Oxford conferred the Doctor of Divinity degree upon him. He was professor of

Church History at the United Free College of Glasgow from 1915 to 1927, and at Union Theological Seminary in New York from 1927 to 1939.

In 1913 he published his first edition of *The New Testament: A New Translation*. As the name implies, it was an entirely fresh rendering and not a revision of *The Historical New Testament*. In the preface he stated his aim "to translate the New Testament exactly as one would render any piece of contemporary Hellenistic prose." He endeavored to divorce himself from all previous versions and produced a strikingly independent modern speech translation, brilliant and stimulating. Unfortunately, he used as his base the Greek text of Hermann von Soden, in which textual critics see many defects. For example, he translates Matthew 1:16 as: "... Joseph (to whom the virgin Mary was betrothed) the father of Jesus, who is called 'Christ.'" This rendering is, of course, flatly contradicted by the story of the virgin birth in verses 18 to 25. In some 130 instances he departed from von Soden's Greek text. In quite a number of these instances such modern Greek editions as Westcott-Hort, Nestle-Aland, and the United Bible Societies would agree with his conclusions. One striking reading in which some recent translations have followed him gives the name of the notorious prisoner released in place of Jesus Christ as "Jesus Bar-Abbas" (Matt. 27:17).

Moffatt at times accepted readings of the so-called "Western" type, which most modern editors have not adopted as original. In Matthew 25:1, for example, on the basis of a few Greek and Latin MSS, he has the ten maidens with their lamps go out to meet the bridegroom *and the bride*. At Jesus' baptism, according to Luke 3:27, a voice from heaven exclaims, according to Moffatt: "Thou art my son, the Beloved, *to-day have I become thy father*." The last clause is probably an earthly adaptation of the baptismal endorsement to Psalm 2:7. In Acts 16:30 a "Western" reading is adopted that adds a vivid touch to the story of Paul and Silas' release from prison. It was only "after securing the other prisoners" that the Philippian jailer took the missionaries out of prison and asked, "Sirs, what must I do to be saved?" At Ephesus, Paul, according to the reading accepted in Acts 19:9, taught "every day from eleven to four in the lecture-room of Tyrannus."

Moffatt often adopts readings that have little MS support. But beyond that, he has accepted around thirty conjectural emendations, without MS support. The reading in John 19:29, "so they put a sponge full of vinegar on a spear," rather than "on hyssop," rests on a conjectural emendation, though one medieval MS has that reading. There is no MS evidence for dropping from the text the words of 1 Timothy 5:23, "Give up being a total abstainer; take a little wine for the sake of your stomach and your frequent attacks of illness." Moffatt says they are "either a marginal gloss or misplaced." In James 4:2 he accepts Erasmus' conjecture and reads "you covet," rather than "you kill." But one of the most striking was the suggestion of J. Rendel Harris that "Enoch" had dropped out of 1 Peter 3:19, which Moffatt renders, "It was in the Spirit that Enoch also went and preached to the imprisoned spirits. . . ."

Moffatt also felt at liberty to rearrange the materials in the NT. He frequently changes the order of verses, supposedly restoring them to their "original position." The Gospel of John has suffered more than any other book in the NT from this attempted "restoration." John 3:22-30 is transposed to its supposedly "true position" between 2:12 and 2:13. John 7:15-24 is placed in "its original position" after John 5:47. John 11:5 is placed between vss. 30 and 31. John 12:45-50 is placed in the middle of vs. 36. Chapters 15 and 16 are "restored to their original positions in the middle of 13:31." Finally, in chapter 18, vss. 19 to 24 are placed between vss. 14 and 15.

In 1924 Moffatt startled the English-speaking world with the publication of his *The Old Testament: A New Translation,* in two volumes. He states that this fresh translation was designed "to present the books of the Old Testament in effective and intelligible English." Moffatt regarded the traditional text as "often desperately corrupt." Hence "nearly every page" of his translation, he tells us, "contains some emendation of the text." At times he felt that the text was too defective to be restored, and he simply omitted such words and inserted dots (. . .). Except in such compound titles as "the Lord of hosts" he, like the French, translated YHWH, the sacred name of God, as "The Eternal."

Moffatt did even more rearranging of the materials within the documents of the OT than he had in the New. One is startled to read as the first words of Genesis a sort of subtitle derived from Genesis 2:4a: "This is the story of how the universe was formed." Both the transfer of these words from chapter 2 and their translations are open to question. The expression "these are the generations (or descendants of)" occurs ten times in Genesis, dividing the book into ten sections. Furthermore, the Hebrew title of many of the Hebrew books is derived from the beginning words. The Hebrew title for "Genesis" means "in the beginning," clearly indicating that the book began as our standard translations have it. This unwarranted re-editing of the documents, together with the all-too-free use of emendations is the greatest weakness in Moffatt's translation.

The complete Moffatt Bible was published as a single volume in 1926. Many editions of it came from the press in subsequent years. Moffatt then put out his "Revised and Final Edition" in 1935. He asserted in the preface that almost every sentence of his translation had been restudied. He wrote, "It is a revision as thorough as I can make it; and I mean it to be final."

The Moffatt Bible certainly makes for interesting reading. The language is fresh and colorful. A few examples will serve to illustrate this.

Among other things, a bishop must not be "addicted to pilfering" (Titus 1:7). On the cross Jesus was offered "a drink of wine mixed with bitters" (Matt. 27:34). Concerning the town of Meroz, which refused to take part in the battle against the Northern Canaanites, Moffatt translated, "Curse Meroz, the Eternal's angel cries, blast her burghers with a curse!" (Judg. 5:23). Mourners are to be given "coronals for coronachs" (Isa. 61:3). Moses' mother put him in "a creel made of papyrus reeds, daubed . . . over with bitumen and pitch" (Exod. 2:3). Amos accuses the "careless citizens" of Samaria of "lolling on their ivory diwans, sprawling on their couches, dining off fresh lamb and fatted veal, crooning to the music of the lute . . . lapping wine by the bowlful . . . with never a single thought for the bleeding wounds of the nation" (Amos 6:4-6). Rezin and Pekah are called "two fag-ends of flickering torches" (Isa. 7:4). Paul speaks of the danger of young widows "gadding about from one house to another—and not merely idle but gossips and busybodies, repeating things they have no right to mention" (1 Tim. 5:13). Christ was slain "by hanging on a gibbet" (Acts 5:30; 10:40). The righteous man finds his joy in God's law, "poring over it day and night" (Ps. 1:2). Jesus said, "Do not pray by idle rote like pagans, for they suppose they will be heard the more they say; you must not copy them" (Matt. 6:7, 8). Again He declared, "Till heaven and earth pass away, not an iota, not a comma, will pass from the Law until it is all in force" (Matt. 5:18).

The exotic sound (to American ears) of some of Moffatt's vocabulary is to be attributed, at least in part, to his Scottish background. He lists *bagpipes* as among the musical instruments played at the dedication of Nebuchadnezzar's image (Dan. 3:10, 15). In Jesus' parable of the vineyard, the master summons his *bailiff* to pay the workers (Matt. 20:8). The Tertullus who represented the Jews in accusing Paul was a *barrister* (Acts 24:1). *Cairn* is used several times for a monument of stones (Gen. 31:48, et al.). "There was a rich man who had a *factor*" who mismanaged his property (Luke 16:1). Joseph's master put him in *gaol* (Gen. 39:20). Jerusalem's leaders "are like *harts* that find no pasture" (Lam. 1:6). The lover of Canticles says, "I will *hie* me to your scented slopes" (Song of Sol. 4:6). Isaiah predicts, "Then there shall be a *highroad* between Egypt and Assyria" (19:23; cf. 11:16). When David danced he wore "a linen *kilt* round his middle" (2 Sam. 6:14; 1 Chron. 15:27). Micah accused his compatriots of "crushing *yeomen* and their homes, *smallholders* and their livings" (2:2).

The Moffatt Bible achieved great popularity, and was used as the basic text for *The Moffatt Commentary*. Moffatt achieved his goal of making the Bible "more interesting" and "less obscure."

An American Translation

One of the most eloquent advocates of modern speech versions was Edgar Johnson Goodspeed (1871-1962) of the University of Chicago as the following sample paragraph indicates:

> If the purpose of New Testament translation is to bring what the New Testament writers meant to convey directly and vividly before the modern American reader, then it should not

be necessary for him to detour through a course in sixteenth century English, such as is necessary for the understanding of even the simpler parts of the New Testament. (*New Chapters in New Testament Study,* p. 113)

On February 24, 1920, Goodspeed presented a paper on the subject to the New Testament Club of the University of Chicago. He discussed and freely criticized the three leading modern speech versions of the time: *The Twentieth Century New Testament,* Weymouth, and Moffatt. There followed a discussion period in which one of Goodspeed's colleagues, Dr. Shirley Jackson Case, drily remarked that if the NT professor saw so many flaws in these earlier versions, perhaps he should produce one of his own. Amid the laughter that followed at Goodspeed's expense, there was one young man present who took the suggestion seriously—Guy M. Crippen of the University of Chicago Press. After a sleepless night, Crippen presented the idea to the editor of the Press, Gordon G. Laing, who wrote the professor, inviting him to make the translation. Goodspeed was at first disposed to brush the request aside. "Every translation of a masterpiece is a failure," he mused. "Why add another?" At lunch, however, he read Laing's letter to his wife, who encouraged him to consider the request seriously. He therefore tried his hand at rendering Mark and eventually accepted the invitation. No man in America was better equipped by background and training for such a task.

Goodspeed soon learned that he could do only fifteen or sixteen verses a day. Concerning his experience, he said:

> The most difficult thing, I found, was to forget the old translations, King James and especially the Revised Versions, English and American, which I found I knew better than I did King James. The familiarity we all have with the English Bible was my greatest obstacle. For of course I did not wish merely to reproduce that but to give my version something of the force and freshness that reside in the original Greek. I wanted my translation to make on the modern reader something of the impression the New Testament must have made on its earliest readers, and to invite the continuous reading of the whole book at a time. That was what I was striving for. (*As I Remember,* p. 162)

From the very beginning the professor kept in mind not merely the use of his NT in private reading and study but also its reading in public. "It is difficult for me," he said, "to conceive a translation of the New Testament designed only for private meditation and study since every part of it so unmistakably addresses not the solitary Christian but the Christian public, religiously a most significant feature of the book. Religion is a social experience!" (Ibid., p. 160). He proceeded to try out his translation in public. When called upon to speak in the Divinity School Chapel, he would read a few pages from his new version, and he found the students listening with rapt attention. In his own home before the evening sing on Sundays, he would read the Scripture lesson from his own translation. It was therefore geared to public reading from the very first.

Goodspeed felt "that the most appropriate English form for the New Testament is the simple, straightforward English of everyday expression." He wanted to produce "a version with something of the ease, boldness, and unpretending vigor which mark the original Greek." He conceived of his task as, first, to grasp what the several NT writers meant to say, and then to cast that thought in simple, clear, present-day English (Preface, p. iii).

He avoided the use of "thee" and "thou" even when Deity was addressed. He called his new version *An American Translation*. It was to be an American translation by an American scholar for American readers in their own vernacular. "For American readers, especially, who have had to depend so long upon versions made in Great Britain," he declared, "there is room for a New Testament free from expressions which, however familiar in England and Scotland, are strange to American ears" (Ibid.).

Goodspeed based his translation on the Greek text of Westcott and Hort. In a half dozen places he departed from this text. Three of these are conspicuous: the reading "on a pike" for "upon hyssop" in John 19:29; "Lybians" for "Libertines" (i.e., freedmen) in Acts 6:9; and the insertion of "Enoch" in 1 Peter 3:19.

This new translation was published by the University of Chicago Press in 1923. It also appeared in serial form in the Chicago *Evening Post* and in twenty-four other newspapers throughout the United States and Canada. For a time there was considerable opposition from many quarters to this modern speech version, but it was also widely acclaimed. America has not produced a better modern-speech version.

The following are a few samples of its renderings:

Matthew 5:3

Blessed are those who feel their spiritual need, for the Kingdom of Heaven belongs to them!

Matthew 5:17, 18

Do not suppose that I have come to do away with the Law or the Prophets. I have not come to do away with them but to enforce them. For I tell you, as long as heaven and earth endure, not one dotting of an *i* or crossing of a *t* will be dropped from the Law until it is all observed.

1 Corinthians 1:17-25

For Christ did not send me to baptize, but to preach the good news—but not with fine language, or the cross of Christ might seem an empty thing. For to those who are on the way to destruction, the story of the cross is nonsense, but to us who are to be saved, it means all the power of God. For the Scripture says "I will destroy the wisdom of the wise, I will thwart the shrewdness of the shrewd!" Where now is your philosopher? Your scribe? Your reasoner of today? Has not God made a fool of the world's wisdom? For since in God's providence the world with all its wisdom did not come to know God, God chose, through the folly of the gospel message, to save those who had faith in him. For Jews insist upon miracles, and Greeks demand philosophy, but we proclaim a Christ who was crucified—an idea that is revolting to Jews and absurd to the heathen, but to those whom God has called, whether they are Jews or Greeks, a Christ who is God's power and God's wisdom. For God's folly is beyond the wisdom of men, and God's weakness is beyond their strength.

Philippians 2:5-11

Have the same attitude that Christ Jesus had. Though he possessed the nature of God, he did not grasp at equality with God, but laid it aside to take on the nature of a slave and become like other men. When he had assumed human form, he still further humbled himself and carried his obedience so far as to die, and to die upon the cross. That is why God has so greatly exalted him, and given him the name above all others, so that in the name of Jesus everyone should kneel, in heaven and on earth and in the underworld, and everyone should acknowledge Jesus Christ as Lord, and thus glorify God the Father.

Within a matter of weeks following the publication of Good-speed's NT, the University Press approached him regarding a similar treatment of the OT. Doctor Goodspeed referred the Press to Prof. J. M. Powis Smith of the OT department. In the OT translation, Prof. Smith associated with him three graduates of Chicago who were competent and highly trained experts in Hebrew and related languages. They were Theophile J. Meek of the University of Toronto, Alexander R. Gordon of McGill University, and Leroy Waterman of the University of Michigan. Smith acted as the editor.

This translation was based on the traditional Hebrew text. The editor wrote, "Our guiding principle has been that the official Masoretic text must be adhered to as long as it made satisfactory sense. We have not tried to create a new text; but rather to translate the received text wherever translation was possible" (Preface, p. xii). The passages where changes in the text were made on the basis of ancient versions, or what they called "scientific emendation," were listed in the appendix of the separate printing of the OT in 1927. The extent of these changes is quite disturbing.

Special attention was given to the poetic portions of the OT. The translation sought to bring "into clear light many of the hidden beauties of Hebrew poetry." Poetic form was given to these passages.

The language is modern, though in the OT "thou," "thee," and "thy" have been retained where the second personal pronoun occurs in words addressed to God. The editor set forth this guiding principle:

> The translator to do his best work must be in sympathy with his subject matter and be able to put himself into mental and spiritual contact with its authors.... On the other hand, a translation should read well. It should be in a vocabulary and style appropriate to the thought which it is designed to express. If the original be dignified, impressive, and eloquent, those qualities must not be lacking in the translation; if it be trivial, commonplace, and prosaic, the translation must take on the same character. The content of the Old Testament is, with little exception, upon a high literary plane. The language of the translation, therefore, cannot be allowed to fall to the level of the street.... (Ibid., p. xiv)

In 1931 Goodspeed's NT and the Smith's OT were combined

to form *The Bible—An American Translation*. Though a few changes were made, the translations were essentially the same as when published as separate volumes. In 1938 Goodspeed also made a translation of the Apocrypha. In 1939 this translation was included with the OT and NT to form *The Complete Bible: An American Translation*.

The four versions discussed in this chapter are important as inaugurators of the era of modern speech versions in the twentieth century. They helped to accustom the English-reading public to the Sacred Scriptures in modern English. In addition, each of these translations has an intrinsic merit of its own and is still being used. They are all noteworthy also because of the contribution they made to the RSV. Two of the translators, Goodspeed and Moffatt, served on the NT committee for the RSV while Leroy Waterman was on the OT committee. James Moffatt acted as secretary for both committees until his death in 1944.

2
The Revised Standard Version

For more than two centuries the King James Version (KJV) dominated the Protestant churches of the English-speaking world. During the nineteenth century, however, the demands for revision became increasingly strong. Finally, on February 10, 1870, Bishop Wilberforce (of Winchester) submitted a resolution to the Upper House of the Convocation of Canterbury that a committee be appointed to study the advisability of a revision of the Bible. The following May, a Revision Committee of fifty-four members was formed, representing not only the Church of England, but nearly all the evangelical bodies as well: Baptist, Congregational, Methodist, and Presbyterian. An American Committee of thirty men was selected in 1871 to go over the work of the English revisers and to offer suggestions. In 1881 *The Revised Version of the New Testament* was published, and the publication of *The Revised Old Testament* followed in 1885.

The recommendations of the American Committee were carefully considered by the English revisers, but only those that were approved by a two-thirds vote by the British Committee were incorporated in the text. The remaining readings and renderings preferred by the American Committee were published in an appendix. The Americans, on their part, agreed to give their support to the Revised Version, and not to issue an edition of their own for a period of fourteen years.

This agreement expired in 1901, and the American Committee in the meanwhile had had adequate time to prepare its edition. This was published in August, 1901, and bore the subtitle "Being the Version Set Forth A. D. 1611 Compared with

the Most Ancient Authorities and Revised A. D. 1881-1885."
Then followed this significant addition: "Newly Edited by the
American Revision Committee, A. D. 1901. Standard Edition."
From this title page is derived its name: *The American Standard
Version* (ASV). This version represented the best biblical learn-
ing of its time.

Nevertheless, the English Revised Version and its American
counterpart had serious defects. The principles laid down for
the guidance of the revision committees were too conservative.
The committees were instructed, for example, to make as few
changes as possible in the text of the KJV, consistent with
faithfulness to the original. A two-thirds vote was required
before a change could be made. And the wording of such
changes was to be limited as far as possible to the language
of the KJV and earlier versions. This meant that the language
was not really modernized.

Furthermore, the Revised Versions strove for consistency in
rendering. They sought to render a given word in the original
by the same English word consistently, regardless of its context.
In their view, faithfulness to the original demanded a meticulous word-by-word rendering. They attempted a precise rendering of the tenses and the article. Often in the NT they even
followed the order of the Greek words rather than the word
order that is natural to English. The result is that the Revised
Versions are stiff, pedantic, and unidiomatic. They lack the free
literary charm of the KJV. Hence, there soon arose demands
for another, more thorough revision.

The italicized words in the following statements from the
ASV will illustrate its use of antiquated words, foreign to the
modern reader, or an archaic usage of common words.

"And they shall be an *abhorring* unto all flesh" (Isa. 66:24).

"The Holy Spirit testifieth . . . that bonds and afflictions *abide*
me" (Acts 20:23).

"The day of Jehovah is great and very terrible, and who can
abide it" (Joel 2:11).

"The *abjects* gathered themselves together against me" (Ps.
35:15).

"He had thirty sons; and thirty daughters he sent *abroad*, and
thirty daughters he brought in from *abroad* for his sons"
(Judg. 12:9).

"It was nothing *accounted* of in the days of Solomon" (1 Kings 10:21).

"Come, and I will *advertise* thee what this people shall do to thy people in the latter days" (Num. 24:14).

"Being *affectionately desirous* of you" (1 Thess. 2:8).

"Solomon made *affinity with Pharaoh*" (1 Kings 3:1).

"*Opening* and *alleging* that it behooved the Christ to suffer" (Acts 17:3).

"He sendeth an *ambassage,* and asketh conditions of peace" (Luke 14:32).

"And all they that cast *angle* into the Nile shall mourn" (Isa. 19:8).

"In everything ye *approved* yourselves to be pure in the matter" (2 Cor. 7:11).

"He *assayed* to join himself to the disciples" (Acts 9:26).

"Their own doings *beset* them about" (Hosea 7:2).

"Though thou shouldest *bray* a fool in a mortar with a pestle" (Prov. 27:22).

"*Cause* that it be read also in the church of the Laodiceans" (Col. 4:16).

"Not in *chambering* and wantonness" (Rom. 13:13).

"Jacob was *wroth,* and *chode* with Laban" (Gen. 31:36).

"And *consorted* with Paul and Silas" (Acts 17:4).

"And *contemned* the counsel of the Most High" (Ps. 107:11).

"And Pilate, wishing to *content* the multitude, released unto them Barabbas" (Mark 15:15).

"But Martha was *cumbered* about much serving" (Luke 10:40).

"And the *dam* sitting upon the young" (Deut. 22:6).

"But *doting* about questionings and disputes of words" (1 Tim. 6:4).

"And he would *fain* have filled his belly with the husks" (Luke 15:16).

"As many as desire to make a *fair show* in the flesh" (Gal. 6:12).

"And in covetousness shall they with *feigned* words make merchandise of you" (2 Peter 2:3).

"As though they would lay out anchors from the *foreship*" (Acts 27:30).

"Not only to the good and gentle, but also to the *froward*" (1 Peter 2:18).

"So as no *fuller* on earth can whiten them" (Mark 9:3).

"It is good for thee to enter into life *maimed* or *halt*" (Matt. 18:8).

"His strength shall be *hunger-bitten*" (Job 18:12).

"Not only of the *lading* and the ship, but also of our lives" (Acts 27:10).

"They *left* the horsemen to go with him" (Acts 23:32).

"They had no *leisure* so much as to eat" (Mark 6:31).

"Every *lusty* man and every man of valor" (Judg. 3:29).

"They *mar* my path" (Job 30:13).

"A man that beareth false witness...is a *maul* and a sword" (Prov. 25:18).

"He shall not stand before *mean* men" (Prov. 22:29).

"Look ye out the best and *meetest* of your master's sons" (2 Kings 10:3).

"Lest haply your hearts be *overcharged* with surfeiting, and drunkenness, and cares of this life" (Luke 21:34).

"For with me thou shalt be in *safeguard*" (1 Sam. 22:23).

"And *scrabbled* on the doors of the gate" (1 Sam. 21:13).

"Delicate living is not *seemly* for a fool" (Prov. 19:10).

"Better is a dinner of herbs...than a *stalled* ox" (Prov. 15:17).

"Your words have been *stout* against me" (Mal. 3:13).

"Or having a *wen*" (Lev. 22:22).

"If they bind me with seven green *withes*...then shall I become weak" (Judg. 16:7).

In 1928 the copyright of ASV, which had been held by Thomas Nelson and Sons, was transferred to the International Council of Religious Education. This body is an association of the educational boards of forty major Protestant denominations of the U.S. and Canada. This council renewed the copyright and established an American Standard Bible Committee of scholars to be the custodian of the text of ASV with authority to undertake further revisions as deemed advisable. In 1937 the International Council of Religious Education voted to authorize a new revision. The action stated:

There is need for a version which embodies the best results of modern scholarship as to the meaning of the Scriptures, and expresses this meaning in English diction which is designed for use in public and private worship and preserves those qualities which have given to the King James Version a supreme place in English literature. We therefore define the task of the American Standard Bible Committee to be that of the revision of the present American Standard Bible in the light of the results of modern scholarship, this revision to be designed for use in public and private worship, and to be in the direction of the simple, classic English style of the King James Version.

Thirty-two scholars served on the committee charged with making the revision. Dean Luther Weigle of Yale Divinity School acted as chairman, and James Moffatt of Union Theological Seminary was the secretary until his death in 1944. He was succeeded by Fleming James, dean emeritus of the School of Theology, the University of the South (Tennessee). In addition to the committee, there was an advisory board of fifty representatives of cooperating denominations. The committee was divided into two sections, one dealing with the OT, the other with the NT. The details of the principles and the procedures followed are given in two pamphlets, with chapters written by various members of the committee: *An Introduction to the Revised Standard Version of the New Testament* (1946), and *An Introduction to the Revised Standard Version of the Old Testament* (1952).

The RSV NT was published in February, 1946. The preface does not undertake to set forth the lines along which the revision was made. But it does again emphasize the need for the revision in these words:

Let it be said here simply that all the reasons which led to the demand for revision of the King James Version one hundred years ago are still valid, and are even more cogent now than then. And we cannot be content with the Versions of 1881 and 1901 for two main reasons. One is that these are mechanically exact, literal word-for-word translations, which follow the order of the Greek words, so far as this is possible, rather than the order which is natural to English; they are more accurate than the King James Version, but have lost some of its beauty and power as English literature. The second reason is that the discovery of a few more ancient manuscripts of the New Testament and of a great body of Greek papyri dealing with the everyday affairs of life in the early centuries of the Christian era, has furnished scholars with new resources, both for seeking to recover the original text of the Greek New Testament and for understanding its language. (pp. v-vi)

Regarding the Greek text underlying the NT, one of the translators, F. C. Grant, has written:

> With the best will in the world, the New Testament translator or reviser of today is forced to adopt the eclectic principle: each variant reading must be studied on its merits, and cannot be adopted or rejected by some rule of thumb, or by adherence to such a theory as that of the "Neutral Text." It is this eclectic principle that has guided us in the present Revision. The Greek text of this Revision is not that of Westcott-Hort, or Nestle, or Souter; though the readings we have adopted will as a rule, be found either in the text or the margin of the new (17th) edition of Nestle (Stuttgart, 1941). (*An Introduction to the Revised Standard Version of the New Testament,* p. 41)

The RSV OT is based on the consonants of the traditional Masoretic Hebrew and Aramaic text. In the main, the vowels supplied by the Masoretes between the sixth and ninth centuries A.D. were also followed. Occasionally, however, different vowels were used when the translators were convinced that a more probable reading would be obtained. The revisers were also convinced that the consonantal text had frequently suffered in transmission. Hence, use was made of ancient versions and the available material from the Qumran MSS in an endeavor to restore the original reading. In thirteen passages in Isaiah readings were adopted from the Isaiah scroll of the Qumran library. In seven of the thirteen instances the reading has the support of one or more of the ancient versions (Isa. 14:30; 15:19; 45:2; 49:24; 51:19; 56:12; 60:19), such as the Greek, Syriac, Latin, and Aramaic Targums. Numerous other readings supported by one or more of these versions or, for the Pentateuch, the Samaritan recension, were also accepted. Several substantial additions to the text in various places were thus made. For example, "Let us go out to the field" is inserted in Genesis 4:8, and "Why have you stolen my silver cup?" in Genesis 44:4. In Judges 16:13, 14 the revisers restored some fifteen words from the Greek which they felt had dropped out of the Hebrew text. Substantial material was also added to the traditional text of 1 Samuel 10:1 and 14:41. Psalm 145 is an alphabetical acrostic psalm, but the Hebrew text lacks the lines beginning with the letter *nun.* The RSV has added these two lines from the Greek at the end of vs. 13. (For other additions, see 2 Sam. 17:3; 1 Kings 8:12, Song of Sol. 3:1.)

But there still remained passages in which the revisers felt that neither the traditional Hebrew text nor the ancient versions had preserved the original reading. In such instances they resorted to a conjectural reconstruction. Footnotes indicate these by the abbreviation *Cn,* followed by a translation of the traditional Hebrew text. Conservative scholars feel that the RSV has been too free in resorting to these supposed corrections, as well as in too frequently following the ancient versions.

More than a score of years have passed since the complete RSV was published, and the version has had a wide circulation. A large number of denominations have officially adopted it for use in worship. It seems, therefore, unnecessary to quote samples from it. However, it may be helpful to call attention to some of its main features. To begin with, it is not a new translation, but a revision of earlier standard English versions. As such it seeks to preserve the best of the earlier versions while at the same time substituting modern English for antiquated language. Nevertheless, it still conforms to the general pattern and often the exact wording of Tyndale's version of the sixteenth century. The revisers strove for simplicity yet dignity in rendering. The goal of the translators of KJV in 1611 was the goal of the RSV committee: "Truly (good Christian Reader) we never thought from the beginning, that we should need to make a new translation, nor yet to make a bad one a good one ... but to make a good one better."

The text of prose passages in the RSV is arranged in sense paragraphs as in the ASV, instead of being broken up into separate verses as in the KJV. The system used in the KJV tends to destroy all sense of connection between the verses and gives the impression that each is a separate unit standing by itself. The first complete English Bible to use verse divisions was the *Geneva Bible* of 1560. Rabbi Nathan is credited with devising the present verse numbers for the OT in 1448. The verse divisions for the NT were made by the scholar-printer, Robert Stephanus, for his Greek-Latin NT of 1551. They constitute a useful reference tool and are essential for a concordance.

The verse numbers are printed throughout the paragraphs of the RSV in smaller type at the top of the line.

The RSV has continued and extended the practice of the ASV in printing poetic passages in poetic form. The metrical nature of ancient Semitic poetry is better understood today than it was when the KJV was produced. One of its characteristics is accentual meter. This means that each line contains a certain number of accents or beats. A more striking characteristic is its parallelism of members. The basic unit of Hebrew poetry is a line followed by a second (or, at times, by a third), which complements it by restating it (synonymous parallelism), contrasting with it (antithetic parallelism), or further developing or completing it (synthetic or step parallelism). The RSV has sought to reproduce the accentual meter in its renderings and has arranged the lines in couplets or triplets. But it has gone further and sought to arrange the poetic passages in stanzas. Approximately 40 percent of the OT is in poetic form. This includes not only the poetic books—Job, Psalms, Proverbs, parts of Ecclesiastes, the Song of Solomon, and Lamentations— but major portions of many of the prophetic books as well. In addition, there are poetic passages in the Pentateuch and the historical books.

In contrast to the OT, the RSV does not arrange much of the NT in poetic form. In the Gospels it seems to be limited to quotations from poetic portions of the OT and a very few sayings of Jesus. But it is generally recognized today that much of Jesus' teaching was cast into the mold of Semitic poetry and could well be printed as poetry. The hymns or poetic passages of the first two chapters of Luke are in poetic form. Some of the songs of the Apocalypse are also printed as poetry.

With regard to the tetragrammaton, the ineffable divine name, rendered "Jehovah" in the ASV OT, the revisers returned to the practice of the KJV in rendering it LORD (or, under certain circumstances, GOD). This harmonizes with the long-established synagogue practice of reading the letters YHWH as *Adonai,* meaning "Lord," as well as the Septuagint Greek rendering *Kyrios* (Lord), and the Vulgate *Dominus.*

THE RSV APOCRYPHA

In October, 1952, the General Convention of the Protestant

Episcopal Church requested that the Division of Christian Education of the N.C.C.C., U.S.A. organize a committee to revise the English translation of the Apocrypha. Accordingly, the General Board of the N.C.C.C. authorized the appointment of a group of scholars to make and publish The Revised Standard Version of the Apocrypha.

The Apocrypha were included in all the sixteenth-century English versions, including the KJV of 1611. The English Revised Version of the document was published in 1894. As is well known, there is a wide difference of opinion regarding the status of these books among Christian bodies.

Roman Catholics regard them, with the exception of 1 and 2 Esdras and the Prayer of Manasseh, as inspired and canonical Scripture, and call them "Deuterocanonical." The Fourth Session of the Council of Trent on April 8, 1546, decreed that these books "entire and with all their parts" are "sacred and canonical" and pronounced an anathema on anyone who "knowingly or deliberately" rejects them. Though denied canonicity and authority, 1 and 2 Esdras and the Prayer of Manasseh are included in Latin MSS of the Vulgate, and are printed as an appendix to the Bible in later editions.

The Church of England, the Lutheran churches, and the Zurich Reformed churches hold that these books are useful, but not canonical. In Luther's German translation of the Bible, these books are segregated between the OT and NT, with the title: "Apocrypha, that is, books which are not held equal to the sacred Scriptures, and nevertheless are useful and good to read." The Swiss Reformer Oecolampadius stated in 1530: "We do not despise Judith, Tobit, Ecclesiasticus, Baruch, the last two books of Esdras, the three books of Maccabees, the additions to Daniel; but we do not allow them divine authority with the other." Article Six of the famous Thirty-nine Articles of the Church of England (1562) states that these books are read "for example of life and instruction of manners," but the Church does not use them "to establish any doctrine."

The position of the Calvinistic and other Reformed churches is clearly stated in the Westminster Confession of Faith (1647): "The books commonly called Apocrypha, not being of divine inspiration, are no part of the Canon of the Scripture; and therefore are of no authority in the Church of God, nor to be any otherwise approved, or made use of, than any other human writings." However, even the Protestants who take this last position have come to realize these documents have an immense historical value. They serve to bridge the 400-year gap between the Testaments, and aid the reader in understanding the social, political, and religious background of the NT. They are intensely interesting and significant literary documents of an important period in religious history.

The publication of *The Apocrypha of the Old Testament, Revised Standard Version,* on September 30, 1957, was therefore welcomed by Christians of many faiths. The appearance of these books constituted an important step in the direction of finding a version acceptable to both Catholics and Protestants.

RSV Catholic Edition

In 1965 a Catholic edition of the RSV NT, prepared by the Catholic Biblical Association of Great Britain with the approval of the Standard Bible Committee, was published. A "List of Changes" made in the text for this edition is given in Appendix Two. The minimal number of changes made consist of two kinds: those having to do with the underlying Greek text and those giving a different translation of the Greek. The first consisted in restoring the sixteen passages found in the Received Text that the RSV had placed in footnotes. This included such passages as the long ending of Mark (16:9-20), the story of the woman taken in adultery (John 7:52-8:11), and the Lucan account of Peter running to the tomb (Luke 24:12). In each instance, the RSV has a footnote stating, "Other ancient authorities add. . . ." The Catholic edition restores the passage and has in the footnote, "Other ancient authorities omit. . . ." The second type of change consists in giving a different translation. Joseph in Matthew 1:19 does not resolve to "divorce" Mary quietly but "to send her away quietly." The "brothers" of Jesus (Matt. 12:48f.; Mark 3:31ff.; Luke 8:19ff.; John 7:34) are "brethren," based on the belief that they were not real brothers—"the Greek word or its Semitic equivalent is used for varying degrees of blood relationship." The angel Gabriel's greeting to Mary is "Hail, full of grace," instead of "Hail, O favored one" (Luke 1:28). "Who," rather than "which," is used in referring to the Holy Spirit (Rom. 5:5; 8:11; Eph. 1:14). The marginal translation is preferred in Romans 9:5, "Christ, who is God over all, blessed for ever." Appendix One consists of "Explanatory Notes" of various passages as required by Canon Law. The large majority of these notes are acceptable to Protestants and are helpful. Of course, Protestants would take exception, in part at least, to the interpretation of Matthew 16:18, 19.

The Catholic edition of the entire Bible was published in 1966. No changes were made in the RSV text of the OT. All of what Protestants call the Apocryphal books, except 1 and 2 Esdras and the Prayer of Manasseh, are included as integral parts of the canon. The order of the books follows that found in the Latin Vulgate, except that the additions to Esther are incorporated in that book. There are twenty-three pages of "Explanatory Notes."

The publication of the *RSV Catholic Edition* marks a new day in ecumenical relations. The RSV, with a few modifications, provides a translation of the Word of God that all English-speaking Christians can share. Although the problem of the OT canon remains, Protestants and Catholics have largely come to an agreement on the translation of accepted books. This means that in theological discussions both can appeal to the same authoritative text. Dialogue between them is therefore greatly facilitated. It is worthy of note also that the *Oxford Annotated RSV Bible* with the Apocrypha received the *Imprimatur* of Cardinal Cushing, Archbishop of Boston, in 1965.

The RSV Bible Committee is a continuing committee, with authority to make revisions in the text of the RSV when it is deemed advisable. A number of changes were made in the text in 1959 as the result of criticisms and suggestions from various readers. These include changing the rendering "married only once" (1 Tim. 3:2, 12; 5:9) to "the husband of one wife." In Job 19:26 "without my flesh I shall see God" was changed to "from my flesh I shall see God." "Loaf" in Matthew 7:9 and 1 Corinthians 10:17 is changed to "bread." The Roman centurion's exclamation is now given as in the KJV: "Truly this was the Son of God!" not "a son of God" as previously (Matt. 27:54; Mark 15:39). The translation of 1 Corinthians 15:19 and John 16:23 is also improved.

The second edition of the RSV NT was copyrighted in 1971. Again suggestions and criticisms from individuals and from two denominational committees were carefully studied. Attention was also given to textual and linguistic studies that had been made since 1946. As the result, a few changes in the underlying Greek text were made. The most conspicuous of these was the restoration to the text of two notable passages previously given only in footnotes: the longer ending of Mark (16:9-20) and the story of the woman taken in adultery (John 7:53-8:11). The blank space separating them from the rest of the text calls attention to them, and footnotes give information regarding the textual problems involved. Two passages in Luke are also restored to the text (Luke 22:19b-20; 24:51b) while another (Luke 22:43, 44) is removed and placed as a footnote. New notes calling attention to significant textual variations in MSS are added in a few places (e.g., Matt. 9:34; Mark 3:16; 7:4; Luke 24:32, 51).

A number of changes in the wording of the translation were also made, resulting in greater clarity. In 2 Corinthians 3:5, 6, "competent" and "competence" are substituted for "sufficient" and "sufficiency": "Not that we are competent of ourselves to claim anything as coming from us; our competence is from God, who has made us competent to be ministers of a new covenant. . . ." In Matthew 12:1 "heads of grain" is more American than "ears of grain." "Move from here to there" (Matt. 17:20) sounds more up-to-date than "Move hence to yonder place." In 2 Corinthians 5:19 instead of "God was in Christ reconciling the world to himself" the Second Edition reads: "In Christ God was reconciling the world to himself" (Luke 22:29). "I assign to you, as my Father assigned to me, a kingdom" is given in place of "As my Father appointed a kingdom for me, so do I appoint for you." These examples illustrate the kinds of changes made.

THE COMMON BIBLE

Not only is the RSV Bible Committee a continuing committee, but it has been internationalized by members from Great Britain and Canada, as well as from the U.S.A. It now also includes Catholics as well as Protestant members. In the interest of Ecumenism the committee in 1973 published the RSV *Common Bible* with the Apocrypha/Deuterocanonical Books. It appeared during the "Week of Prayer for Christian Unity" in England in February, and during Lent in the U.S.A. It has international endorsement by Roman Catholics, Greek Orthodox, and Protestants.

To facilitate the use of the RSV as a common Bible, this edition arranged the OT apocryphal books in two groups: (1) the Deuterocanonical Books, which are accepted by Catholics as Scripture, and (2) 1 and 2 Esdras and the Prayer of Manasseh, are not regarded as authoritative by the Roman Catholic Church, but included in the Greek Canon of Scripture. In the preface the position of the various Christian bodies with respect to the Apocrypha is clearly explained. (pp. viii-xi)

The publication of *The Common Bible* is indeed a significant event in the history of the English Bible. It is a new day when Catholics, Greek Orthodox, and Protestants can all use the same translation. *The Common Bible* marks the end of controversy regarding the authoritative English text to be employed in dialogue.

A significant paragraph closes the preface to the RSV. It is worth quoting:

> The Bible is more than a historical document to be preserved. And it is more than a classic of English literature to be cherished and admired. It is a record of God's dealing with men, of God's revelation of Himself and His will. It records the life and work of Him in whom the Word of God became flesh and dwelt among men. The Bible carries its full message, not to those who regard it simply as a heritage of the past or praise its literary style, but to those who read it that they may discern and understand God's word to men. The Word must not be disguised in phrases that are no longer clear, or hidden under words that have changed or lost their meaning. It must stand forth in language that is direct and plain and meaningful to people today. It is our hope and our earnest prayer that this Revised Standard Version of the Bible may be used by God to speak to men in these momentous times, and to help them to understand and believe and obey His Word.

3

The Knox Translation

It is difficult, almost impossible, for permissive, flabby, twentieth-century Christians to understand Christians of the sixteenth century who were willing not only to die for their faith but, what is stranger still, to kill for their faith. It was in that climate that William Tyndale translated the Bible into English for the Protestants. For this he ultimately paid with his life. Since the Bible was of central importance to the Christian faith, how it was translated could determine to a certain extent the direction of that faith. Should the Greek verb *metanoeō* be translated "repent" or "do penance"? The theological implications were weighty. Semantics, therefore, was tremendously important. Not only were battles fought over the words in the translation but also over the notes appended to the translation. What could not be written into the translation was written in the footnotes. This was usually an attack against the Catholics or the Protestants, depending on who did the translation.

The Catholics in England were placed at great disadvantage when the Protestant Bible was translated. Armed with the Bible in English, the Protestants could quickly turn to it in a dispute and simply read the passage. The unfortunate Catholic had no English Bible and had to translate on the spot. Even in teaching their own parishioners, the Catholic priests were handicapped. William Allen, a leading Catholic of the time who also assisted Gregory Martin in producing the Rheims-Douai translation, sensed this predicament when he wrote:

> Catholics educated in the academies and schools have hardly
> any knowledge of the Scriptures except in Latin. When they

are preaching to the unlearned and are obliged on the spur of the moment to translate some passage into the vernacular they often do it inaccurately and with unpleasant hesitation because either there is no vernacular version of the words, or it does not occur to them at the moment. Our adversaries however, have at their finger tips from some heretical version all those passages of Scripture which seem to make for them, and by a certain deceptive adaptation and alteration of the sacred words produce the effect of appearing to say nothing but what comes from the Bible. This evil might be remedied if we too had some Catholic version of the Bible, for all the English versions are most corrupt.... If His Holiness shall judge it expedient, we ourselves will endeavor to have the Bible faithfully, purely, and genuinely translated according to the edition approved by the Church, for we already have men most fitted for the work. (*Letters and Memorials of Cardinal Allen,* pp. 64, 65, as quoted in Hugh Pope, *English Versions of the Bible,* p. 250.)

The NT (called the Rheims NT) was published in 1582 and the OT (called the Douai OT) was published in 1609/10, even though it was translated before the NT. Unlike the Protestant Bible, which was based on the Greek and Hebrew, this Catholic version was based on the Latin Vulgate. However, like the KJV, the Rheims-Douai version possessed a strange fascination and continued to be the Bible for Catholics through the years (in revised form, primarily that of Bishop Challoner). The King James tradition also continues on into the RSV. Not until the publication of the NEB (1961, 1970) do we have a fresh, *official* translation of the Protestant Bible. However, there have been many fresh translations that were privately produced.

The revised form of the Rheims-Douai version was the only Catholic Bible to have official approval until the translation of Monsignor Knox's NT in 1945. The latter did not displace the former, but they were both approved versions for Great Britain. The OT was published in 1948 but, unlike the NT, was not approved as an official version. Knox's translation was received with great acclaim when it appeared. It had broken the shackles of the tradition of the Rheims-Douai version, which was essentially a sixteenth-century translation in spite of its revisions. *Time* (Feb. 11, 1952, p. 41) called Ronald Knox "the man who made the great twentieth-century translation of the Bible." At the time it may have seemed so, but events since have shown that it was only the beginning of freer translations and his use of the Vulgate even for a Catholic translation has been unfortunate. He translated too soon.

Ronald Knox was born into the home of an Anglican priest, educated at Eton and Oxford, was a brilliant student of classics, and a writer of vigorous prose and detective novels. At the age of twenty-nine, he. became a convert to Catholicism. In 1939 he began his work of translating the Bible into English. One can appreciate his writing ability, with its witticisms and forceful illustrations, by reading *Trials of a Translator,* a collection of several of his articles dealing with his translation. He follows Belloc's principle of translation in asking himself, not "How shall I make this foreigner talk English?" but "What would an Englishman have said to express the same?" He criticizes the KJV as "essentially a word-for-word translation, no less than the Septuagint, no less than the Vulgate. 'For the Pharisees and all the Jews, except they wash their hands, eat not, holding the tradition of the elders'; is that English idiom? 'For the Nazis, and all the Germans, except they say Heil Hitler! meet not in the street, holding their lives valuable'; is that English idiom?" (pp. 75, 76).

Knox's forte is his literary ability. After one reads *Trials of a Translator,* however, one feels that he is somewhat restricted in translation. His translation for his day was new and fresh but there are very few memorable translations in the NT. Take for example his translation of Romans 12:1,2:

> And now, brethren, I appeal to you by God's mercies to offer up your bodies as a living sacrifice, consecrated to God and worthy of his acceptance; this is the worship due from you as rational creatures. And you must not fall in with the manners of this world; there must be an inward change, a remaking of your minds, so that you can satisfy yourselves what is God's will, the good thing, the desirable thing, the perfect thing.

Nevertheless, one feels the vigor of his prose in certain portions of the OT by his inversion of subject and verbs and by his elimination of conjunctions and articles. Notice these features in this passage from Nahum 2:3, 4:

> Bright flash that enemy's shields, warriors of his go clad in scarlet; dart like flame his chariots as he goes to the attack,

dizzily sways charioteer. How jostle they in the streets, those chariots, hurtle they in the open market-place; dazzle they like flame of torches, like the lightning that comes and goes!

One is surprised, therefore, that Knox with his taste for literature did not translate the poetic parts of the Bible according to Hebrew parallelism. He gives as one reason the need to be practical. He means by this two things. He felt he needed to conserve paper because of the paper shortage at the time. Prose would take less space than poetry, so this would mean quite a saving of paper. He also means that by saving space it would make it easier for people to carry the Bible around with them. It would not be so cumbersome. But his real reason is that his translation might read like an original writing, not a translation. He says, "What the reader wants, I insist, is to get the illusion that he is reading, not a translation but an original work written in his own language. And to our notions of poetic composition, these remorseless repetitions are wholly foreign when you have read a page or two on end, they begin to cloy" (p. 40).

One is further surprised to find that when Knox has dispensed with Hebrew parallelism, he nevertheless maintains the use of acrostics. This is found in Psalms 24, 33, 110, 111, 118, 144; Proverbs 3:10-31; and Lamentations 1-4. There are different types of acrostics. In Psalm 24, each of the verses begins with a consecutive letter of the alphabet. In Psalms 110 and 111, the acrostic pattern is in the form of two letters in the verse, the first beginning the verse in capital and the second in the second half of the verse in lowercase. Thus A and b are found in verse 1 and C and d in verse 2, etc. The letters are always printed in boldface so they stand out. In Psalm 118, the first letter of each sentence in the first paragraph begins with A, the first letter of each sentence of the second paragraph begins with B, etc. These devices must have taxed the ingenuity of the translator. A few examples of acrostic types follow:

Psalm 24:1-3
All my heart goes out to thee, O Lord my God. **B**elie thou never the trust I have in thee, let not my enemies boast of my downfall. **C**an any that trust in thee be disappointed, as they are disappointed, who wantonly forsake the right?

Psalm 110:1-3

All my heart goes out to thee, Lord, in thanksgiving, before the assembly where the just are gathered. Chant we the Lord's wondrous doings, decreed to fulfill all his purposes. Ever his deeds are high and glorious, faithful he abides to all eternity.

Psalm 118:1-3

Ah, blessed they, who pass through life's journey unstained, who follow the law of the Lord! Ah, blessed they who study his decrees, make him the whole quest of their hearts! As for the wrong-doers, they leave his ways untrodden.

As we have mentioned earlier, the text of Knox's translation is the Vulgate, but it was the edition authorized by Pope Clement VIII in 1592. He felt bound to this particular edition even when he knew it could very well be wrong. For example, Acts 17:6 reads, "These that have turned the world upside down are come hither also." This was the way it originally read even in the Vulgate. But the Latin words for "world," *orbem*, later was changed to "city," *urbem*, a change easy to make, as anyone can see. But, stubbornly, Knox translates it as "state," since "that is how the thing stands in every Vulgate in the world nowadays, and it is no part of the translator's business to alter, on however good grounds, his original" (*Trials of a Translator*, p. 2). For the same reason he has included 1 John 5:7, 8 which are not found even in the best Latin MSS. Because it is a secondary version, as F. F. Bruce says, "No one will go to his version for help in determining the precise sense of the original." (*The English Bible: A History of Translations* [New York: Oxford University Press, 1961], p. 204.)

The use of the Vulgate has led also to the Latin form of the names of the books—a usage the *Jerusalem Bible* has abandoned. This is somewhat confusing to Protestants. Such names as Paralipomena, Osee, Abdias, Sophonias, and Aggaeus may not be decipherable. The Apocrypha are also included, scattered throughout, since they are a part of the Catholic Bible.

In a contemporary translation it is strange that quotation marks are not used to set off direct speech and that "thou" and "thee" are retained throughout as the second-person pronouns. John Reumann also points out certain Latinisms, such as "perdition" for "destruction" in Matthew 7:13 and "charity" for "love" in 1 Corinthians 13. Reumann decries an "amalgamation of the antique and the modern," such as "swaddling clothes"; "all must give in their names"; "his espoused wife"; and "in her pregnancy" in the Christmas story. (*The Romance of Bible Scripts and Scholars* [Englewood Cliffs, N.J.: Prentice-Hall, Inc., 1965], pp. 207, 210.)

The footnotes are generally of the explanatory type, but some go further to emphasize Catholic doctrine. For example, in connection with Matthew 1:25 ("he had not known her when she bore a son") we find this note: "The text here is more literally rendered 'He knew her not till she bore a son'; but the Hebrew word represented by 'till' does not imply that the event which might have been expected *did* take place afterwards.... So that this phrase does not impugn the perpetual virginity of our Lady." In connection with Matthew 12:46-50, where Jesus' brothers are mentioned, Knox adds, "Since it is impossible for anyone who holds the Catholic tradition to suppose that our Lord had brothers by blood, the most common opinion is that these 'brethren' were his cousins; a relationship for which the Jews had no separate name." In explanation of 1 Corinthians 3:10-15, he adds this note: "At the same time, we are to recognize that many whose actions in this world have had little value, will themselves escape condemnation, though only by passing through the fires of Purgatory." No connection, however, is made with the Virgin Mary in Genesis 3:15 and Revelation 12.

In checking the text of Knox, we find, generally speaking, that it is very similar to the KJV, which is to say it is not of good quality. Some differences are its omission of "for thine is the kingdom and the power and the glory forever. Amen" in Matthew 6:13; "nor the Son" in Matthew 24:36; and "even as Elias did" in Luke 8:54. Concerning Mark 16:9-20, which Knox includes in the text, he appends this note: "And in a few of our existing manuscripts these last twelve verses are wanting, which fact (together with the abruptness of their style) has made some critics think that they were added from another source. But they are evidently a primitive account, and there is no reason why we should not ascribe their inclusion here to St. Mark." Knox's practice in dealing with the text and his persistence in using the poor text of Vulgate manuscripts do not recommend him as a text critic. Patrick Skehan, a

Catholic OT scholar, after careful examination of Knox's practice in textual matters, says concerning the OT translation that
"the use made of the Septuagint is thoroughly disappointing
and inadequate" and that "in his judgment such reference to
MT has in fact served very little purpose" (*Theological Studies*
X [1949], 326). He is referring to Knox's claim of making
"constant reference to the Masoretic text." Skehan further adds
that Knox's treatment of the Vulgate itself "as a text is un-
critical to a remarkable extent."

Knox has been freer in the OT than in the New. Notice
the following translations:

Genesis 1:1-5
God, at the beginning of time, created heaven and earth. Earth
was still an empty waste, and darkness hung over the deep;
but already, over its waters, brooded the Spirit of God. Then
God said, Let there be light; and the light began. God saw the
light, and found it good, and he divided the spheres of light
and darkness; the light he called Day, and the darkness Night.
So evening came, and morning, and one day passed.

Exodus 20:3-7
Thou shalt not defy me by making other gods thy own. Thou
shalt not carve images, or fashion the likeness of anything in
heaven above, or on earth beneath, or in the waters at the
roots of earth, to bow down and worship it. I, thy God, the
Lord Almighty, am jealous in my love; be my enemy, and
thy children, to the third and fourth generation, shall make
amends; love me, keep my commandments, and mercy shall
be thine a thousandfold. Thou shalt not take the name of the
Lord thy God lightly on thy lips; if a man uses that name
lightly, the Lord will not acquit him of sin.

Psalm 23 [24]
The Lord owns earth, and all earth's fulness, the round world,
and all its inhabitants. Who else has built it out from the sea,
poised it on the hidden streams?
    Who dares climb the mountain of the Lord, and appear in
his sanctuary? The guiltless in acts, the pure in heart; one
who never played fast and loose with his soul, by swearing
treacherously to his neighbour. His to receive a blessing from
the Lord, mercy from God, his sure defender; his the true
breed that still looks, still longs for the presence of the God
of Jacob.
    Swing back the doors, captains of the guard; swing back,
immemorial gates, to let the King enter in triumph! Who is

this great King? Who but the Lord, mighty and strong, the Lord mighty in battle? Swing back the doors, captains of the guard; swing back, immemorial gates, to let the King enter in triumph! Who is this great King? It is the Lord of Armies that comes here on his way triumphant.

Hebrew parallelism is abandoned. The familiar "For three transgressions . . . and for four" of Amos has become "Thrice forfeit . . . and forfeit once again."

Knox did break new ground by a fresh translation instead of revising Douai-Rheims. His NT was officially approved along with that of Rheims, and this was quite a progressive step. However, the optimistic claims for his translation from our vantage point are not as valid today. For since Knox, we now have Catholic Bibles consistently based on the original languages and using contemporary speech. *The Jerusalem Bible* and *The New American Bible* will eclipse Knox, since they have most of his virtues without his weaknesses and disadvantages.

4
Phillips' Translation

What started out as one pastor's attempt to make the NT understandable to a London youth group eventually turned out to be Phillips' translation of the NT. It was because the young people "couldn't make head or tail" of the Authorized Version that J. B. Phillips felt led to the work of translation. And it was because he happened to send his first translation (Colossians) to C. S. Lewis, who encouraged him to go on, that Phillips' *Letters to Young Churches* (1947) was published. C. S. Lewis' reaction to Phillips' first attempt was "It's like seeing an old picture that's been cleaned. Why don't you go on and do the lot?" When he had completed the Pauline Epistles, Phillips was encouraged by people from various parts of the world to go on to the Gospels. He was reluctant to do this, since people might object to his paraphrasing the actual words of Jesus. He completed the Gospels in 1952, the Acts *(The Young Church in Action)* in 1955, and the Book of Revelation in 1957. The entire NT was published in 1958, *Four Prophets* in 1963, and the revised NT in 1973.

The great popularity of this version lies in its freshness of style and its readability. The NT reads as if it were originally written in twentieth-century English. It does not read like a translation at all. True, there are places where Phillips has not succeeded as well as in the major part of his work and where Britishisms hinder some understanding, but these are few and far between. As a whole, he succeeds admirably. This success is due to the care he took in avoiding "translator's English" and in trying out his translations with his friends.

But Phillips was concerned not only about his readers, he

was also concerned about his authors. He wanted to write as if he were in their shoes. He says, "For myself I have taken the bold step of trying to imagine myself as the original writer, whether he be the careful and precise Matthew, the sturdy, blunt Mark, the sympathetic, undertsanding Luke, or the more profound and mystically-inclined John." (*Bible Translator*, IV [1953], 55)

Any translation that attempts to translate not merely words but ideas and seeks to bridge the gap between the ancient past and the present faces many problems. How far should one go? Amounts of money, measures, and weights may be relatively easy to translate, but does one modernize "Greet . . . with a holy kiss" with "Shake hands," or "sandals" with "shoes," or "girding one's loins" with "tighten one's belt"? What about ideas that are foreign to our modern culture? One can see how translation might imperceptibly merge into interpretation. Perhaps Phillips has chosen the better part by avoiding both the literalism that cannot be considered a translation at all and a radical modernization that would require the complete rewriting of a book like Hebrews and Revelation. Nevertheless, Phillips tends to overmodernize and is sometimes inconsistent. In his revised edition (1973) Phillips has corrected some of these weaknesses. His major improvement is the use of a better Greek text and more precision and accuracy in the translation of the text. The revised translation is placed in brackets when quoted with that of the first edition. Where no indication is given, the translation is the same in both editions. A more detailed account of the 1973 edition will follow later.

There are some excellent features in this translation. The paragraph form with section headings is excellent for reading and understanding, though for those who want to check any specific verse, it presents a difficulty, since only the first verse of each section is numbered. In the new edition no verse numbers appear at all, making it even more difficult to check. The best feature, of course, is the translation itself.

William Smalley (*Bible Translator* XVI [1965], 165-170) has made a comparative study of Phillips and the NEB on Romans 12. He finds Phillips superior in vss. 1-3, 9, 10, 17-21. One unforgettable verse, which Smalley calls "one of the most powerful renderings in the whole New Testament," is Phillips' Romans 12:2: "Don't let the world around you squeeze you into its own mold, but let God remold your minds from within...." ["... but let God re-make you so that your whole attitude of mind is changed...."] The KJV already had an excellent translation with "conform" and "transform" but lacks the vigor of Phillips. One would appreciate Phillips more if comparison were made throughout with the KJV. Some exceptionally good translations of Phillips are the following:

Matthew 5:5
Happy are those who claim nothing, for the whole earth will belong to them!

Matthew 7:29
For his words had the ring of authority.

Romans 3:20
No man can justify himself before God by a perfect performance of the Law's demands—indeed it is the straight-edge of the Law that shows us how crooked we are.

Romans 5:20, 21
Now we find that the Law keeps slipping into the picture to point the vast extent of sin. Yet, though sin is shown to be wide and deep, thank God his grace is wider and deeper still! The whole outlook changes—sin used to be the master of men and in the end handed them over to death; now grace is the ruling factor, with righteousness as its purpose [with its purpose making men right with God] and its end the bringing of men [them] to the eternal life of God [to eternal life] through Jesus Christ our Lord.

Romans 7:7-11
It now begins to look as if sin and the Law were very much the same thing [were the same thing]. Can this be a fact? Of course it cannot. But it must in fairness [om. in fairness] be admitted that I should never have had sin brought home to me but for the Law. For example, I should never have felt guilty of the sin of coveting if I had not heard the Law saying "Thou shalt not covet." But the sin in me, finding in the commandment an opportunity to express itself, stimulated all my covetous [om. covetous] desires. For sin, in the absence of the Law, has no chance to function technically as 'sin' [has not life of its own]. As long, then, as I was without the Law I was, spiritually speaking [om. spiritually speaking], alive. But when the commandment arrived, sin sprang to life and I "died." The commandment, which was meant to be a

direction to life, I found was a sentence to death. The commandment gave sin an [its] opportunity, and without my realizing what was happening [what it was doing], it "killed" me.

Romans 8:18, 19

In my opinion whatever we may have to go through now is less than nothing compared with the magnificent future God has planned [has in store] for us. The whole creation is on tiptoe to see the wonderful sight of the sons of God coming into their own.

Romans 12:1, 2

With eyes wide open to the mercies of God, I beg you, my brothers, as an act of intelligent worship, to give him your bodies, as a living sacrifice, consecrated to him and acceptable by him. Don't let the world around you squeeze you into its own mold, but let God remold your minds from within [re-make you so that your attitude of mind is changed], so that [thus] you may [will] prove in practice that the plan of God for you is good, meets all his demands and moves toward the goal of true maturity [the will of God's good, acceptable to him and perfect].

Romans 12:6-8

Through the grace of God we have different gifts. If our gift is preaching, let us preach to the limit of our vision. If it is serving others let us concentrate on our service; if it is teaching let us give all we have to our teaching; and if our gift be stimulating of the faith of others let us set ourselves to it. Let the man who is called to give, give freely; let the man who wields authority think of his responsibility [man in authority work with enthusiasm]; and let the man who feels sympathy for his fellows act cheerfully [his fellows in distress help them cheerfully].

Romans 12:14-21

And as for those who try to make your life a misery, bless them. Don't curse, bless. Share the happiness of those who are happy, and the sorrow of those who are sad. Live in harmony with one another [each other]. Don't become snobbish but take a real interest in ordinary people. Don't become set in your own opinions. Don't pay back a bad turn by a bad turn, to anyone. Don't say, "It doesn't matter what people think," but [om. Don't ... but] see that your public behavior is above criticism. As far as your responsibility goes, live at peace with everyone. Never take vengeance into your own hands, my dear friends: stand back and let God punish if he will. For it is written: "Vengeance belongeth unto me: I will recompense." [add, saith the Lord] And these are God's words [And it is also written]: "If thine enemy hunger, feed him; if he thirst, give him to drink: For in so doing thou shalt heap coals of fire upon his head." Don't allow yourself to be overpowered with [by] evil. Take the offensive—overpower evil by [with] good!"

Romans 15:1, 2

We who have strong faith ought to shoulder the burden of the doubts and qualms of others and not just to go our own sweet way. Our actions should mean the good of others—should help them to build up their characters [We should consider the good of our neighbor and help to build up his character].

1 Corinthians 2:6

We do, of course, speak "wisdom" among those who are spiritually mature, but it is not what is called wisdom by this world, nor by the powers-that-be, who soon will be only the powers that have been.

In spite of the excellence of this translation, some word of caution needs to be voiced. In an excellent article (in *Bible Translator* [1959], 135-143) Robert Bratcher points out the vulnerability of this translation—its lack of faithfulness in translating the text. Phillips translates Matthew 6:2, "Don't hire a trumpeter" where the Greek simply says, "Sound no trumpet." The idea that someone else is to do the trumpeting for the one who gives alms is not stated and therefore it should not have been translated in the above manner. Perhaps the phrase "the bread we need" [add, "for the day"] in Matthew 6:11 is justifiable, since it translates the idea of the Greek word whose meaning is not altogether clear but is usually translated "daily" or "morrow."

"Brush your hair" was a bit too free for "anoint your head" (Matt. 6:17). Thus Phillips in the new edition has gone back to "anoint your head." The same is true for "This is the essence of all true religion" (Matt. 7:12), a translation for "For this is the law and the prophets." The new edition reads, "This is the meaning of the Law and the Prophets." "You have worked on the side of evil" (Matt. 7:23) is not exactly what Jesus said ("you evildoers"). Phillips adds "comfortably" in Matthew 15:35 but the Greek original does not have this word. In Matthew 16:18 Phillips adds "the rock" after Peter, an addition many will consider interpretive rather than a translation. The forcefulness of Jesus' expression "for your hardness of heart" is lost by Phillips' "It was because you knew so little of the meaning of love" (Matt. 19:8). "Mosquito" for "gnat" (Matt. 23:24) seems to take away from the comparison. "Where he can weep and wail over his stupidity [where there will be tears and bitter regret]" (Matt. 25:30) is too interpretive and loses the force of "gnashing their teeth." "Talitha cumi" and "Ephphatha" become "in Aramaic" followed by the translation (Mark 5:41; 7:34). "Utterly astounded" is not the same as Phillips' "scared out of their wits" (Mark 6:51). "Spoils your faith" for "causes you to sin" is too generalized (Mark 9:42). "Rubbish heap" (Mark 9:43) for "hell" (gehenna) is weak. "Don't bully people" is less forceful to an American than "Rob no one by violence" (Luke 3:14).

Phillips writes much more than the text says in Luke 7:33, 34, "For John the Baptist came in the strictest austerity and you say he is crazy. Then the Son of Man came, enjoying life [food and drink], and you say, 'Look, a drunkard and a glutton, a bosom friend of the tax collector and the outsider!'" To avoid being explicit about the greeting by a kiss, Phillips in the first edition translated Luke 7:45, "There was no warmth in your greeting," but he has changed this to "You gave me no kiss of welcome." "He rejoiced in the Holy Spirit" (Luke 10:21) was distorted by Phillips to "Jesus himself was inspired with joy," but this too he later rendered more accurately as "Jesus' heart was filled with joy by the Holy Spirit." "How many of my father's hired servants" (Luke 15:17) is changed to "Why, dozens of my father's hired men."

"For God's sake" (Mark 5:7), "To hell, with you and your money" (Acts 8:19), "May he be damned" and "be a damned soul" (Gal. 1:9) are unfortunate translations. "Practical and spiritually-minded" for "full of the Spirit and of wisdom" (Acts 6:3) is too free. "Speaking in foreign tongues" (Acts 10:46) is interpretive, as is also NEB's "speaking in tongues of ecstasy." "From cultured Greek to ignorant savage" (Rom. 1:14) is too strong for "to Greeks and non-Greeks, to the wise and to the foolish." "For Christ means the end of the struggle for righteousness-by-the-Law" (Rom. 10:4) is commentary rather than translation. "Greet one another with a holy kiss"

(Rom. 16:16) is translated, "Give one another a hearty handshake all round for my sake [in Christian love]," but it is questionable if this is a proper modern equivalent.

Phillips recognizes many of his earlier translations as being too free and has made more accurate translations in his new edition. He had translated "when he appears" (1 John 3:2) as "if reality were to break in," but saw that this was indefensible and thus revised it to read as above. In earlier editions Ephesians 1:1 read, "to all faithful Christians at Ephesus (and other places where this letter is read)" but now the words in parentheses have been omitted. We see the same in 1 John 3:2 where he had translated, "Oh, dear children of mine (forgive the affection of an old man!), have you realized it?" Actually all this translated the one word, "Beloved." In the new edition, this sentence is omitted and "my dear friends" is substituted for it.

In a careful study of 1 Corinthians 1, the following deviations from the original were observed. We compare it with RSV, which in these verses is faithful to the original.

	RSV	Phillips
1:2	to those sanctified in Christ Jesus	to those whom Christ [add Jesus] has made holy
1:2	together with all those in every place who call on the name of our Lord Jesus Christ	to all true believers in Jesus Christ
1:4	because of the grace of God which was given you in Christ Jesus	for what the gift of grace in Jesus Christ [Christ Jesus] has meant to you
1:5	that in every way you were enriched in him with all speech and all knowledge	he has enriched your whole lives, from the words of your life to the understanding in your hearts
1:7	so that you are not lacking in any spiritual gift	And you have been eager to receive his gifts
1:8	who will sustain you to the end	He will keep you steadfast in the faith to the end
1:10	by the name of our Lord Jesus Christ	by all that Christ [our Lord Jesus Christ] means to you
1:12	each of you says	each making different claims
1:17	to baptize	to see how many I could baptize [primarily to baptize]
1:17	lest the cross of Christ be emptied	for I have no desire to rob the cross

1:18 to those who are perishing ... who are being saved	to those who are involved in this dying world ... who are being saved from that death
1:20 Where is the wise man? Where is the scribe? Where is the debater of this age?	For consider, what have the philosopher, the writer and the critic of this world to show for all their wisdom?
1:21 For since, in the wisdom of God, the world did not know God through wisdom, it pleased God through the folly of what we preach to save those who believe	For it was after the world in its wisdom had failed to know God, that he in his wisdom chose to save all who would believe by the "simple-mindness" of the gospel message
1:30 He is the source of your life in Christ Jesus	Yet from this same God you here received your standing in Jesus Christ

There are certain of Phillips' translations that, although not wrong, seem incongruous in such a modern speech version. Some of these are too literary, whereas others are too colloquial. In the first group are the following: "the entail of sin and death" (Rom. 5:12), "magnificent denouement" [revelation] (Col. 3:4), "palpable frauds" (Titus 1:16), "express purpose of liquidating [undoing] the devil's activities [work]" (1 John 3:8), "invidious distinctions" (James 2:9), "inevitable disintegration" (2 Peter 1:4), "he is dilatory" (2 Peter 3:8), "slightest prevarication" (1 Peter 2:22), "serried ranks of witnesses" (Heb. 12:1). In the second group are these: "the whole assembly was at sixes and sevens" (Acts 19:32), "too high and mighty" (Rom. 1:26), "parting shot" (Acts 28:25).

There are also certain inconsistencies. In Matthew 5:40 "coat" and "overcoat" ["cloak"] are used, but for the same words "coat" and "shirt" are used in Luke 6:29. In Acts 12:8 and Matthew 10:10 "sandals" is used, but elsewhere "shoes." Monetary terms are used rather loosely. In Matthew 25:14 a "talent" is $1,000 [one thousand pounds] but in Mark 6:37, 200 denarii is translated "ten dollars" ["twenty pounds"] and in Mark 14:5, 300 denarii is "thirty dollars" ["thirty pounds"].

In addition to the above unsuitable translations, there are others that could be improved. The expression "little faith" (Matt. 6:30; 14:31) is not proper English. "Cornfields" (Matt. 12:1) and "ears of corn" (Luke 6:1) are good English but the American needs to retranslate "corn" into "grain." In reference to Simon in Matthew 10:4, "the patriot" is a bit mild for "the Zealot." "Look of earth and sky" (Luke 12:56) is not the way that thought is expressed by Americans. For an American, the expression "foxes have earths" (Matt. 8:20) sounds peculiar. "Play actors" is more obscure than "hypocrites" (Matt. 23:13, 15). "Protest" does not seem to be the right word in Luke 9:5. "Thieves' kitchen" (Luke 19:45) is not an American expression. Perhaps Phillips should have studied English as used elsewhere as carefully as he studied British English if he expected his translation to be used in the entire English-speaking world. The common denominator has not been reached in the above instances.

In the first edition, after the Epistle he appended the name of the writer except for 2 Thessalonians, Hebrews, and 2 Peter. It should be understood, however, that these names are not found at this place after any of the letters in the original. He has now omitted these. Bratcher notes that "he curiously omits a translation of *ho presbuteros* 'the elder' in 2 John 1, but more than makes up for it in 3 John 1, where he translates the same *ho presbuteros* by 'John the Elder!'" Phillips has now corrected these by adding "the Elder" in 2 John 1 and omitting "John" in 3 John 1.

Another weakness of Phillips' translation was the Greek text he used. In his *Letters to Young Churches* he indicates that his Greek text was the same as that for the Revised Version of 1881. Unfortunately, this text is not the best by today's standards. He has now changed to the United Bible Societies' Greek text. But unfortunate still is his treatment of Mark 16: 9-20 and John 7:53-8:11. The latter is kept in the traditional position without any differentiation, with only an asterisk referring to a note, and the former is differentiated only by the subject heading which reads "An ancient appendix" and the addition of an alternative reading. There is only a brief unsatisfactory note with the shorter ending: "An alternative ending found in certain manuscripts following verse 8." The UBS text has much fuller explanations at both places and omits the second passage from its traditional position, placing it at the end of the Gospel of John. The UBS text brackets Luke 24:12 but Phillips does not. The same is true for Luke 24:36cd. John

5:3b, 4 is omitted by UBS but Phillips includes it in parentheses. UBS has "hyssop" in John 19:29 but Phillips continues to translate it as "spear." UBS double-brackets Luke 22:19b, 20 but Phillips translates it without any signs. UBS single-brackets Matthew 12:47 but Phillips does not.

There are certain passages where the original is ambiguous and may be translated in different ways. We present a few of these. Phillips is printed on the right:

Mark 15:39
The son of God (RSV)

a son of God

John 1:9
The true light that enlightens *every man was coming into the world* (RSV)

That was true light [,] which shines upon every man *as he comes* [, which was now coming] *into the world*

John 1:11
he came to his *own home;* and his *own people* (RSV)

He came into his *own creation* [world], *and his own people . . .*

Romans 9:5
to them belong the patriarchs and of their race, according to the flesh, is the *Christ.* God who is over all be blessed for ever (RSV)

The patriarchs are theirs, and so too, as far as human descent goes, is Christ himself, *Christ who is God* over all [Christ who is over all. May God be], blessed for ever

1 Corinthians 7:36
But if any man think that he behaveth himself uncomely toward *his virgin* (KJV)

But if any man feels he is not behaving honorably toward the *woman he loves . . .* (Compare with NEB)

Hebrews 2:7
Thou didst make him for a *little while lower* than the angels (RSV)

Thou madest him *a little lower* than the angels

Hebrews 10:20
by the new, living way which he has opened for us through the curtain, *the way of his flesh* (NEB)

by a fresh and living Way, which he has opened up for us by himself passing through the *curtain, that is, his own human nature*

Revelation 12:17
which keep the commandments of God and *have* the testimony of Jesus Christ (KJV)

Those who keep the commandments of God and *bear* their witness to Jesus

Revelation 19:10

For the testimony of Jesus is the   (This witness to Jesus inspires
  spirit of prophecy (RSV)   all prophecy.)
  (Compare with NEB)

The second edition is the same as the first edition except for two significant changes. John 1:9 now reads, "That was the true light, which shines upon every man, which was now coming into the world"; and Romans 9:5 reads: "The patriarchs are theirs, and so too, as far as human descent goes, is Christ himself, Christ who is over all. May God be blessed for ever. Amen." There is one slight change in John 1:11 where "creation" has been changed to "world."

There is not much distinction in Phillips' translation of Hebrews and especially Revelation. This results no doubt from the difficulty of translating the ideas represented in these books, since they are foreign to this modern age.

Because of the tremendous popularity of this version, it deserves careful scrutiny. We have pointed out some of the weaknesses above so that the reader may be aware of these as he uses this version. Concerning its style, there is unanimity in favor of its excellence. Bratcher's evaluation here is typical: "Of its merits we can only add our voice to the chorus of praise. . . ."

This version was never intended to be used for scholarly and careful exegesis and should not be used for this purpose but for private use as a second Bible. Everyone can use it with great profit and like C. S. Lewis will sense over and over, "It's like seeing an old picture that's been cleaned!"

PHILLIPS' REVISED EDITION (1972)

There are several reasons Phillips gives for undertaking a revised version. In his own words:

> The most important by far was the fact, which perhaps I had been slow to grasp, that "Phillips" was being used as an authoritative version by Bible Study Groups in various parts of the world. . . . This passion of mine for communication. . . has led me sometimes into paraphrase and sometimes to interpolate clarifying remarks which are certainly not in the Greek. But being now regarded as "an authority," I felt I must curb my youthful enthusiasms and keep as close as I possibly could to the Greek text. Thus most of my conversationally-worded additions in the Letters of Paul had to go. Carried away some-

times by the intensity of his argument or by his passion for the welfare of his new converts I found I had inserted things like, "as I am sure you realise" or "you must know by now" and many extra words which do not occur in the Greek text at all. . . .

There was a further reason for making the translation not merely readable but as accurate as I could make it. It has been proposed that a Commentary on the Phillips translation should be undertaken. I felt it essential that the scholars who would contribute to such work should have before them the best translation of which I am capable. I certainly did not want them to waste time in pointing out errors which I had in fact by now corrected!

The last, but not least important, reason for making a fresh translation was to check the English itself. . . . Rather to my surprise only a few alterations were necessary, and this showed me that the ordinary English which we use in communication changes far more slowly than I had imagined. (Introduction, pp. viii, ix)

Another reason for the new edition, though he does not give this as one, is the opportunity to use a better Greek text. He had earlier based his translation on the Greek text used by the English Revised Version but for this edition he changed to the United Bible Society Greek text of 1966.

In his introduction, Phillips calls this new edition "a new translation" and "a wholly new book," although he admits that he retained "some considerable parts of the former translation." The jacket indicates that "more than two thousand improvements and corrections" were made. What do we really find in this new Phillips?

First of all, there are a considerable number of minor changes: in matters of punctuation, some words formerly capitalized (e.g., "Gentiles") are now lowercase and vice versa; "toward" is changed to "towards"; "kneeled" becomes "knelt." Quotations from the OT are no longer italicized. Verse numbers are not indicated at all (not even for major divisions). English spellings of words are kept in the American edition. Words are more frequently hyphenated (e.g., "first born" is now "first-born").

Some books have been revised only slightly. In the first three chapters of Revelation, not counting the minor changes noted above, only the following alterations were noticed: "martyred" was changed to "killed" (2:13) and "purified" to "refined" (3:18).

Considerable changes were noted in Colossians, the first book translated by Phillips. Approximately 160 major and minor changes were noted. Not including changes due to the text, the majority of changes are the omission of expressions not in the Greek and the retranslation of those portions that appeared to be more interpretive than necessary. The following are examples of expressions that are omitted: "I want you to know by this letter that" (1:3); "very much" (1:7); "As a matter of fact" (1:8); "As you live this new life" (1:11); "we must never forget that" and "that is, in the kingdom of light" (1:13).

The following are modifications made to come closer to the Greek text: the addition of "we have heard that" (1:4); "boundless resources" changed to "glorious power" (1:11); "by his Son alone" changed to "by him" (1:14); "whether spiritual or material" changed to "whether heavenly or earthly" (1:16); "which is composed of all Christian people" changed to "which is the Church" (1:18); "Life from nothing began through him, and life from the dead began through him, and he is, therefore, justly called the Lord of all" changed to "He is the Beginning, the first to be born from the dead, which gives him pre-eminence over all things" (1:18); and "by virtue of the sacrifice of the cross" changed to "making peace by virtue of Christ's death on the cross" (1:20).

In checking the Gospel of Matthew, we noted fewer changes than in Romans or Colossians though more than in Revelation. Most were slight changes. Romans did not have as many changes as Colossians, but the same type of changes were noted. Complete retranslations were made in 7:22, 23 and 8:11. Major changes were made in 3:29; 11:25, 36; 12:3; 14:4; 15:4, 16, 27.

Phillips claims that "this new edition is in fact a new translation from the latest and best Greek text published by the United Bible Societies in 1966." Our observations above do not indicate that it is a "new translation." We have not checked every instance of deviation between the former Greek text used and the present one. No doubt, there is real improvement here. However, in checking certain crucial passages, we have not found the changes significant.

Over all, one must say that the new Phillips is an improvement over the old, especially in regard to the Greek text and greater accuracy in translation. However, it is basically the same Phillips. In some verses, one will not find the spiciness of the old but in its place a more accurate translation, more faithful to the Greek. A moderately conservative introduction for each book has been added.

FOUR PROPHETS (1963)

At the urging of many, J. B. Phillips turned his translational skill to a portion of the OT (Amos, Hosea, Isaiah 1-35, and Micah, arranged in that order). He had made a popular and successful translation of the NT, but since his "knowledge of Hebrew was rather sketchy" and the problems of translating the Hebrew were great, he was reluctant to try it. He realized the difference between translating Greek and translating Hebrew. First of all, Hebrew expresses much in few words—"message after message is packed full of power, and expressed with a terrifying economy of words." Second, he rediscovered that while Greek had difficulties, Hebrew had greater difficulties, such as the untranslatable play on words and the defective text. Third, while he could translate the NT into ordinary English, Hebrew did not lend itself to this approach. As he expresses it, "It is wildly unsuitable for the transferring into English of the dignified utterance or the passionate pleading of these ancient men of God. There is little hint in any of them of a conversational, let alone a colloquial, style. They were speaking in the name of the Lord and, like King James' translators 2,000 years later, both they and their later editors thought that only the highest language could do justice to the oracles of the Most High." Fourth, Hebrew idioms and thought are more distant to us than those of Greek.

Phillips chose these four prophets because they did their work at a crucial time in the history of God's people and because they "pierce through a great many falsities (including religious falsities)."

In addition to the translator's preface, a general historical background written by E. H. Robertson serves as introduction for all the prophets, and an introduction is provided by the translator for each of the books. In contrast to his usage in the NT, each verse is numbered, making it much easier for one to locate a particular verse. Subject headings are provided, as in the NT. Two maps are provided at the end, one of "the world surrounding the four prophets" and one of Palestine. Unlike Knox, Phillips has kept the Hebrew poetic form of parallelism.

The translation is rather free at times; at other times it is much like the RSV, which seems to have influenced Phillips quite heavily, although Phillips is fairly independent where textual difficulties appear. Because of the different original languages, it is difficult to compare this translation with that of his NT. In the latter he is quite free, especially in bridging the gap between the past and present in the translation of ideas instead of words. In the former he seems to have been somewhat restricted in this respect, although he translates Isaiah 5:27, "Not a belt is loose, not a shoe-string broken" for "Not a waistcloth is loose, not a sandal-thong broken."

Hebrew is concrete rather than abstract, but the concrete images of the Hebrew do not always communicate to a Western mind. Therefore we find Phillips usually translating by giving the meaning of the image, and this has the effect of making the picturesque prosaic. Sometimes he uses a Western figure for a simple description in Hebrew. Sometimes he substitutes a Western figure for a Hebrew figure.

Notice the following examples where the meaning of the image is given (the first is Phillips, followed by the more literal translation of the RSV): "break the power" for "break the bow" (Hosea 1:5); "pass which is bright with promise" for "door of hope" (Hosea 2:15); "the land is withered" for "the land mourns" (Hosea 4:3); "like a bow which never shoots straight" for "like a treacherous bow" (Hosea 7:16); "I will destroy the power of the house of Hazael" for "I will send a fire upon the house of Hazael" (Amos 1:4); "made justice a bitter jest" for "turn justice to wormwood" (Amos 5:7); "the starry universe" for "Pleiades and Orion" (Amos 5:8); "cries of woe" for "alas! alas!" (Amos 5:16); "who only lives while he breathes" for "in whose nostrils is breath" (Isa. 2:22); "will never be able to shake themselves free" for "cannot remove your necks" (Micah 2:3). Some of the changes are not really necessary, however, since the Hebrew is not always obscure to the English reader.

The following examples show how Phillips has used a Western figure for a plain description in the Hebrew: "nursed the anger in his heart" for RSV's "his anger tore perpetually" (Amos 1:11); "wash the paint from her face" for "put away her harlotry from her face" (Hosea 2:2); "lick their lips" for "greedy" (Hosea 4:8); "rotten to the core" for "sinful" (Isa. 1:4); "hand in glove with thieves" for "companions of thieves" (Isa. 1:23); "raise their necks in pride" for "shall not walk haughtily" (Micah 2:3).

The following examples show how Phillips has used a Western figure for a Hebrew one: "grind the faces of the poor" for "trample the head of the poor" (Amos 2:7); "like a lonely watch-tower" for "like a besieged city" (Isa. 1:8); "turn my face away" for "hide my eyes" (Isa. 1:15); "Let them be led by the nose" for "babes shall rule over them" (Isa. 3:4); "noses in the air" for "outstretched necks" (Isa. 3:16); "green growth" for "branch" (Isa. 4:2).

Occasionally Phillips has added explanatory expansions that are sometimes helpful, sometimes unnecessary. In Amos 5:4 after "Bethel" he has added "House of God," which is the meaning of the word Bethel. Instead of the simple "I am like a moth to Ephraim" of the RSV, Phillips has "I am the moth which rots the fabric of Ephraim" in Hosea 5:12. In Isaiah 2:12 "the Lord of hosts has a day" is expanded by Phillips to "the Lord of hosts has a day of reckoning."

Phillips' translation is very free at times. Usually the translation is acceptable but it is sometimes questionable. "The words of Amos ... which he saw concerning Israel" becomes "These are the words of Amos when he saw the truth about Israel" (Amos 1:1). "For three transgressions ... and for four" becomes "Because of outrage after outrage" (Amos 1:3). "When the Lord first spoke through Hosea" becomes "While Hosea was waiting" (Hosea 1:2). "As the Lord lives" becomes "My God" (Hosea 4:15). "New moon" becomes "any month" (Hosea 5:7). "Hear, O heavens" becomes "Let the heavens hear" (Isa. 1:2). "And the mountains will melt under him and the valleys will be cleft" becomes "Beneath him the mountains melt and flow into the valleys" (Micah 1:4). "For from the hire of a harlot she gathered them, and to the hire of a harlot they shall return" becomes simply "For the price of her unfaithfulness pays for her betrayal!" (Micah 1:7). Micah seems to have been translated most freely. Especially is this true of Micah 1:10-15 where there is a play on words in the Hebrew. To bring out this force Phillips has added quite a bit to the text. Compare Phillips with the RSV which follows:

Phillips

So then, in Gath where tales are told, breathe not a word!
In Acco, the town of Weeping, shed no tear!
In Aphrah, the house of Dust, grovel in the dust!
And you who live in Shaphir, the Beauty-town, move on, for your shame lies naked!
You who live in Zaanan, the town of Marching, there is no marching for you now!
And Beth-ezel, standing on the hillside, can give no foothold in her sorrow,
The men of Maroth, that town of Bitterness, wait tremblingly for good,
But disaster has come down from the Lord, to the very gate of Jerusalem!
Now, you who live in Lachish, the town far-famed for horses,
Take your swiftest steeds, and hitch them to your chariots!
For the daughter of Zion's sin began with you,
And in you was found the source of Israel's rebellion.
So give your farewell dowry to Moresheth of Gath!
The houses of Achzib, that dried-up brook, have proved a delusion to the kings of Israel,
And once again I bring a conqueror upon you, men of Moresheth,
While the glory of Israel is hidden away in the cave of Adullam.

RSV

Tell it not in Gath,
    weep not at all;
in Beth-le-aphrah
    roll yourselves in the dust.
Pass on your way,
    inhabitants of Shaphir,
    in nakedness and shame;
Inhabitants of Zaana
    do not come forth;
the wailing of Beth-ezel
    shall take away from you its standing place.
For the inhabitants of Maroth

> wait anxiously for good,
> because evil has come down from the LORD
>   to the gate of Jerusalem.
> Harness the steeds to the chariots,
>   inhabitants of Lachish;
> you were the beginning of sin
>   to the daughter of Zion,
> for in you were found
>   the transgressions of Israel.
> Therefore you shall give parting gifts
>   to Moresheth-gath;
> the houses of Achzib shall be a deceitful thing
>   to the kings of Israel.
> I will again bring a conqueror upon you,
>   inhabitants of Mareshah;
> the glory of Israel
>   shall come to Adullam.

Some of the differences are due to a defective text, but most of the changes are due to expansion on the part of Phillips to try to convey the play on words.

Phillips has some excellent translations. Among them are the following:

> Therefore when the corn is ripe I shall take it away, And when the wine is ready, I will take it back. And when the wool and flax are ready to clothe her, I will snatch them away (Hosea 2:9).

> Your hands are dripping with blood (Isa. 1:15).

> Once a home of righteousness, now a haunt of murderers (Isa. 1:21).

> Her leaders dispense justice—at a price, Her priests teach—what they are paid to teach, And her prophets see visions—according to the fees they receive (Micah 3:11).

Others have mentioned Amos 3:12b; 6:4; 7:2; Isaiah 5:26-30; 28:4; and 30:16 as superb examples of his work.

Scholars who are looking for an accurate translation will not be completely happy with Phillips' production. Neither was it intended to be used for study purposes. It takes too many liberties to be so used. Phillips, however, has given us a readable translation of these prophets and many will find new understandings of their messages through his work.

5

The Modern Language Bible

The Modern Language Bible (MLB) is a new edition of the Berkeley Version, with an updating and improvement of the OT and a major revision of the NT by a group of scholars. It is therefore also known as *The New Berkeley Version in Modern English.* The Berkeley Version came into being as the result of the vision of a Dutch-born American, Gerrit Verkuyl. For many years he served with the Board of Christian Education of the Presbyterian Church, U.S.A. He had a growing conviction of the need for a translation of the Bible in modern English. He wrote, "As thought and action belong together so do religion and life. The language, therefore, that must serve to bring us God's thoughts and ways toward us needs to be the language in which we think and live rather than that of our ancestors who expressed themselves differently." (Preface to Berkeley NT, p. iii)

Verkuyl was in many ways a remarkable man. Over twenty-one years of age when he came to America in March, 1894, he worked as a farm hand in California. He had yet to learn English and gain an education. At Park College, Missouri, where he received his Bachelor of Arts degree in 1901, his interest in Greek was aroused while he was a freshman. He received his Bachelor of Divinity degree from Princeton Theological Seminary in 1904, with NT as his specialty. A NT fellowship enabled him to study in Europe, where he received his Doctor of Philosophy degree from the University of Leipzig in 1906. He did additional graduate work in Berlin.

His work with the Presbyterian Board of Christian Education brought him into contact with children and youth all over the United States, and the need for a translation in up-to-date language was impressed on his mind. He was kept so busy in writing, lecturing, and teaching, however, that for many years he did not find time to carry out his dream of producing such a version. But in 1936 he began working on his translation in earnest. In the following year he moved to Berkeley, California, and two years later resigned from the Board of Christian Education to devote his full time to the project. The finished product was published in 1945 as the Berkeley Version of the New Testament, its name coming from the city of Berkeley, California.

Four years later the Zondervan Publishing House invited him to undertake the OT as well. A staff of twenty scholars under Verkuyl's chairmanship did the work, and in 1959 the complete Berkeley Version in Modern English was published. Then in 1969 the revised edition known as *The Modern Language Bible* came from the Zondervan Publishing House, which had obtained the rights of publication to the Berkeley Version.

Verkuyl "aimed at a translation less interpretive than Moffatt's," he declared, "more cultured in language than Goodspeed's, more American than Weymouth's and freer from the King James Version than the Revised Standard." He based his NT translation on the eighth edition of the Greek text of Tischendorf, though he consulted other texts such as Nestle's. In deference to readers familiar with the KJV, he added to this text in parentheses such words, clauses, and passages as are found in the Received Text, but which, in the opinion of most textual critics, rest on insufficient manuscript evidence to be considered as an original part of the documents. He felt that to leave out such passages would be an offense to "these little ones," the designation he used for such devout Bible readers. In the revision of his NT in the MLB these passages are enclosed in brackets (see Matt. 6:13; 12:47; 17:21; 21:44; 23:14, et al.). In each instance there is a footnote usually worded thus: "The words enclosed in brackets are not found in the majority of the most reliable ancient manuscripts." The footnote for John 5:3b-4 reads, "The manuscript evidence for the words in vss. 3 and 4 that are enclosed in brackets is so slight that it is virtually certain that they were not in the original Greek text." Similarly, a footnote to Acts 8:37 states, "So many reliable ancient manuscripts omit v. 37, here enclosed in brackets, that it is practically certain that it was not part of the original text." The question then may well be raised: Should any words that we are reasonably certain were not in the original text be printed in the translated text, even in brackets?

The MLB, furthermore, is not entirely consistent in putting in all the additions found in the Received Text. The KJV of Matthew 19:9 after the words "Whosoever shall put away his wife, except it be for fornication, and shall marry another, committeth adultery" adds "and whoso marrieth her which is put away doth commit adultery." But this last clause is not in the MLB even in brackets. Likewise the last clause of the KJV of Mark 9:49, "and every sacrifice shall be salted with salt," is not given in the MLB. The same is true for "blessed art thou among women" in the KJV of Luke 1:28. Other phrases in the KJV of the Gospels not given in the MLB include "and they that were with him" (Luke 8:45); "even as Elias did" (Luke 9:54); "written ... in letters of Greek, and Latin, and Hebrew" (Luke 23:38); "and of an honeycomb" (Luke 24:42).

For the most part, the translators of the OT endeavored to render the traditional Hebrew text just as it reads. However, when they were convinced the text had suffered in transmission, they did not hesitate to correct or emend it. But the instances of such corrections are far less numerous than in most recent English or American versions. In three passages in Isaiah they accepted the reading of the famous Isaiah Scroll of the Qumran Community (Isa. 14:4; 45:8; 56:12). There are footnotes to fifteen other passages, calling attention to other variant readings in the Isaiah Scroll that they did not adopt. In Genesis 44:4 they inserted the question "Why have you stolen my silver cup?" in parentheses with the footnote "The Septuagint translation contains this brief sentence which seems quite in place." In Song of Solomon 3:1 there is no footnote to indicate that the last line, "I called him, but he did not answer," is lacking in the Hebrew and was supplied from the Septuagint. In Exodus 8:23 the MLB, like the KJV and RSV, follows the Septuagint in translating, "I will make a distinction between My people and your people," rather than the Hebrew, which has "I will put redemption between my people and your people." No footnote, however, advises the reader that a change has been made. Likewise, there is no footnote to indicate that the reading "Edom" and "troops of Edom" in 2 Samuel 8:12, 13 comes from the Greek, whereas the Hebrew has "Syria" and "Syrians." Nor is there a footnote to 1 Samuel 6:18 to show that the translation "the great stone in the field of Joshua" does not correspond to the Hebrew. (See also Job 5:5; 32:9; 37:7; 1 Kings 19:3; Neh. 6:16; Zech. 3:15; Ps. 68:23; Micah 6:16; et al.)

The MLB purports to be a completely new translation and not a revision of earlier versions. The translators sought, above all, to be faithful to the original Hebrew, Aramaic, and Greek. They were on guard against paraphrase, for, as Verkuyl puts it, "That leads so readily to the infusion of human thought with divine revelation, to the confusion of the reader" (Preface). This means that the MLB is fairly literal. Verkuyl states, "As far as possible this is a complete translation of every word in the Bible" (ibid.). At the same time, an effort was made to use English "according to its choicest current usage." In the earlier edition the language, particularly in the NT, was often unidiomatic and, at times, wooden. Fortunately, the NT has been thoroughly revised, resulting in marked improvement. In general, the present edition is accurate, clear, and simple.

Like the RSV, the text is divided into paragraphs. The verse numbers are given throughout in small superscript type. The Psalms, most of Proverbs, some of Ecclesiastes, Song of Solomon, Lamentations, most of Joel, and the third chapter of Habakkuk are printed in poetic form. Surprisingly, the sublime poetry of Job is printed as prose. The same applies to the large poetic portions of Isaiah and other prophets.

Quotation marks are used throughout the Bible. The second personal pronouns—"Thou" in the nominative, "Thy" ("Thine") in the possessive, and "Thee" in the objective—are retained in language addressed to Deity (1 Kings 8:23-53; Ezra 9:6-15; Dan. 8:14-19; Matt. 6:9, 10, et al.). Otherwise the version follows modern usage in using "you" and "your" for the second personal pronoun.

One of the distinctive features of this version is the capitalization of pronouns referring to Deity, including references to Jesus, even when He was an infant (Matt. 2:11; Luke 2:21ff.).

In the OT there does not seem to be complete consistency in dealing with divine names. The tetragrammaton, YHWH, is rendered "Jehovah" in Exodus 3:15 and Psalms 8:1, 9; YAHWEH, in Hosea 12:5; and "the LORD" in Amos 5:8.

This name came to be regarded by the Jews as too sacred to be pronounced. Hence in the synagogues down to the present day "Adonai," i.e., "Lord," is substituted for it. Scholars today generally regard the correct pronunciation as "Yahweh," but often the late medieval form "Jehovah" is still used for it. Usually in the MLB and the RSV, the name is rendered LORD, spelled with small capital letters. In Ezekiel 2:4 the Hebrew has the combination *Adonai Yahweh,* which the MLB gives as LORD God. One would expect, rather, LORD GOD. In Psalm 45:11 one finds LORD but one would expect Lord, as the original has *Adonai.*

There is no uniformity in dealing with place names involving the tetragrammaton. In Genesis 22:14 occurs the transliteration "Jehovah-Jireh," with the footnote: "Meaning, The Lord will provide." In Exodus 17:15 the place name is translated, "The LORD my Banner," with the footnote: "Jehovah Nissi." In Judges 6:24 a similar name, "Jehovah-Shalom," is given as "Adonai-shalom," with the note "The Lord is peace." Finally, Ezekiel 48:35 states, "And the name of the city henceforth shall be THE LORD IS THERE," with the note giving the transliterated form: "YAHWEH SHAMMA."

Of interest also are the dates given, beginning with Genesis 12. This continues Dr. Verkuyl's work in the NT of which he says, "To the best of our ability we have tried to determine the dates of events, of sayings, and of writings." The dates given in the NT are certainly not far off. But the dates given for Abraham's call and other events in Genesis are, to say the least, debatable.

Another characteristic feature of the MLB is its explanatory footnotes, or as the title page puts it, "Informative Notes to Aid the Understanding of the Reader." From the very beginning of his work as a translator, Verkuyl felt the need for explanatory notes. "When I began my translating," he said, "I did not know that Weymouth had supplied footnotes; but

I did know that there was need for them, if only to avoid interpreting within the text, as Moffatt so often does."

The footnotes are of various kinds. Some have to do with the text, as noted above. Others give explanation of proper names. For example, a note to Matthew 1:16 deals with four Marys in the NT. Notes to Matthew 2:1 advise us that "Bethlehem is situated five or six miles south of Jerusalem," that "Herod the Great, who ruled from 37-4 B.C., was the father or ancestor of other Herods," and that the wise men were "Magi, from *magus* meaning *great,* a Persian title that was used for teachers and wise men, in this instance astrologers." In succeeding notes there are explanations of the scribes, Pharisees, Sadducees, etc. Obviously this kind of information is helpful to the average Bible reader.

Occasionally there are also notes of a linguistic nature. Matthew 5:22 reads, "Whoever speaks abusively of his brother is liable before the Sanhedrin." A note states, "The Aramaic word *rhaka* used here in the original text means *empty, worthless.*" A note to Matthew 5:48, "You then, are to be perfect," explains, " 'Perfect' is from the Greek *teleios* meaning *complete, mature.*" Matthew 13:27 has a note explaining, "The Greek word *doulos* means *slave* and is so translated here and in many places throughout the NT...." On the same page a note to vs. 8 states, "The Greek word here rendered 'world' *kosmos,* means primarily *orderly arrangement.* It also denotes *universe, world,* and inhabitants of the earth...."

Still other notes are of an interpretive nature, often involving theology. Genesis 6:2 speaks of intermarriage between the "sons of God" and the "daughters of men." A note explains: "Some have it that this refers to fallen angels, but there is no Scripture evidence that they could become men with body and soul; nor, if they could, would wicked men be called 'sons of God.' We believe that the sons of Seth's family married daughters of Cain's family; that the home thus became ungodly and children grew up without relating life to God." A note to Isaiah 58:13 is also illustrative of this type: "The appointed Sabbath is holy ground. To observe the day cheerfully is a test of the people's fidelity to the Lord. The Sabbath is as a sanctuary, not to be trodden upon with irreverent feet." According to the footnote on 1 Peter 3:19, Christ's preaching to "the spirits in prison" means, "It was by the Holy Spirit that Christ preached through Noah to men of his day who are now in prison because they rejected the message." One other illustration must suffice: A note to Ephesians 4:22 explains "old nature" as "literally 'the old man,' all that the Christian is apart from Christ. In vs. 24 it is 'the new man' (lit.), that is, what the believer is in his new birth through Christ." Generally speaking, Protestants have felt that the Bible should be allowed to speak for itself apart from interpretive notes.

There are other notes of a homiletic or devotional nature. Genesis 3:8 speaks of the sound of God walking in the garden in the cool of the day. A note suggests, "The hour of twilight remains a choice season for spiritual recreation—quiet communion." Concerning Adam's blaming Eve for giving him the forbidden fruit (vs. 12), a footnote comments, "Blaming someone else is as old as humanity; it shows lack of repentance." Finally, the explanation of the rainbow in Genesis 9:15 is the basis for the covenant: "To the worshipper of God, the rainbow still says: 'God is faithful; trust Him.' "

The translators of the MLB approached their task from the stance of conservative evangelicals. This is reflected in their approach to messianic prophecies. In the preface Verkuyl has said, "We are in tune with the 'Authorized Version' of 1611 in fidelity to the Messianic Promise, first made as soon as man had sinned, renewed to Abraham, Isaac and Jacob, narrowed to Judah's offspring and later to David's descendants." A footnote to Genesis 3:15 declares that this verse contains the "first promise of the Redeemer, Victor over sin and Satan." In the verse the capitalization of the pronoun "He," referring to the offspring of the woman, makes this messianic interpretation evident: "*He* will crush your head and you will crush his heel." The failure to capitalize "his" is perhaps an oversight. Genesis 49:10 reads, "The scepter shall not depart from Judah, nor the leader's staff from between his feet until Shiloh comes and Him the peoples shall obey." A footnote states, "Pointing, we believe, to Messiah." Balaam's prediction, "A star shall come up out of Jacob, a Scepter shall rise out of Israel" (Num. 24:17), is interpreted in a note as, "The coming Messiah. The star has long been the symbol of royalty and imperial greatness."

Several psalms are interpreted messianically. Psalm 2 carries the title "The Lord and His Anointed Are Supreme," and a note points out that the Hebrew for "Anointed" is *Messiah*. The seventh verse is particularly significant (note the capitalization):

> I will tell the decree:
> The Lord said to Me, Thou art My Son;
> This day have I begotten Thee.
>   (See also vss. 8, 9, 12.)

Concerning Psalm 22, a note explains, "This is one of the striking Messianic psalms, depicting marked details of the sufferings of Christ." A note interprets "the angel of the Lord" in Psalm 34:7 as "The Redeemer, of the New Testament." In Psalm 45 we are informed, "The one addressed is, man plus, God among men, the Godman." Concerning the king who is to revere God "while the sun endures," a note tells us that "As this goes beyond human attainments, we consider it Messianic" (Ps. 72:5). Another note says, "How accurate a picture the poet draws of the Messiah's character! This King is more than human." A note to Psalm 89:27 states, "Neither David nor any other mortal could literally be God's first-born; but Christ, David's offspring could." Another note to vs. 36 says, "In Christ the covenant with David was amply fulfilled." Psalm 110 is also interpreted as messianic.

While the term "servant" in Isaiah is used "with elasticity," it refers especially to the Messiah, particularly in such passages as Isaiah 42:1-4 (note the capitalization of the third-person personal pronouns); 49:5-7; and, above all, 52:13-53:12, picturing the Servant's sufferings. A note also tells us that "The speaker in chaps. 61 and 62, is the Great Deliverer." A messianic interpretation is furthermore given to Daniel 9:24-27: "From the going forth of the message to restore and rebuild Jerusalem until the coming of a Prince, a Messiah, there are seven weeks and sixty-two weeks" (v. 25). "But after the sixty-two weeks Messiah shall be slain, although there is nothing against Him" (v. 26). The "He" of vs. 27 is also the Messiah: "In a week He shall make the covenant to prevail for many, and in the middle of the week He will cause sacrifice and offering to cease."

The MLB is, in general, a simple, clear, and accurate rendering in contemporary English. The thorough revision given the work of Verkuyl has resulted in a far more satisfactory translation than the original Berkeley New Testament. Textually, one could wish that readings found in the KJV that have poor support in the Greek MSS had been placed in footnotes rather than included in the text in brackets. Other prominent variant readings that never found a place in the KJV could also have been included in footnotes, unless the evidence in their favor demands they be included in the text.

The Old Testament translation represents the work of twenty scholars who combined competence with reverence for the sacred text. These translators, however, apparently labored independently rather than as a committee. No doubt the rendering could have been further refined by more interchange and by direct confrontation between the translators in committee sessions.

Nevertheless, the MLB is a work of high quality and stands as a monument to evangelical scholarship. It is a useful tool to compare with other versions in the study of the Word of God.

6
The New World Translation and The Bible in Living English

Denominational versions are fortunately rare. Such versions are generally usable only by the group that sponsored the translation. Some earlier Protestant and Catholic translations also fall into this group, especially with their biased and one-sided notes. *The Common English Version* of the American Bible Union (Baptist) of 1862 underlined its point of view by such translations as "John the Immerser" and "when he saw many of the Pharisees and Sadducees coming to his Immersion." The most biased of such is *The New World Translation* (1961) of the Jehovah's Witnesses.

Not only does the word "Jehovah" recur in the OT (as it did also in the ASV), but it is introduced 237 times into the text of the NT and 72 times in the footnotes. There is absolutely no basis for the translation of the Greek original by the word "Jehovah." By the way, the word "Jehovah" is an artificially created form resulting from the consonants of the name of God transliterated YHWH and the Hebrew vowels of the word for Lord, *Adonai*. This resulted from the fact that Jews refrained from uttering the name of God and usually substituted in its place the word *Adonai*. Thus the vowels of this latter word were placed with the consonants of YHWH so that the reader would know he should read *Adonai* instead. Most English Bibles follow the Jewish practice of translating YHWH as LORD, except when YHWH is preceded by the word *Adonai* in which case it is translated GOD, since *Adonai* itself is translated Lord.

The translators arbitrarily decide when the word "Lord" in the Greek should be rendered "Jehovah" and when it should be left as "Lord." While they sometimes use the title "Lord" with reference to Jesus—for example, in 1 Corinthians 12:3, "Nobody can say: 'Jesus is Lord!' except by the holy spirit," and 2 Corinthians 4:5, "For we are preaching, not ourselves, but Christ Jesus as Lord"—at other times they translate it as "Jehovah" even when the reference to Jesus is clear. This is the case in Acts 19:20 where the NWT reads, "Thus in a mighty way the word of Jehovah kept growing and prevailing," even though they had earlier translated the parallel thought by the words "and the name of the Lord Jesus went on being magnified" (Acts 19:17). The expression "the Spirit of the Lord" is always translated "The spirit of Jehovah," and yet in the NT it sometimes refers to the Spirit of God and sometimes to the Spirit of Christ. Such a use even occurs within one verse, Romans 8:9: "But you are not in the flesh, you are in the Spirit, if the *Spirit of God* really dwells in you. Any one who does not have the *Spirit of Christ* does not belong to him" (RSV, italics ours). Here NWT translates, "God's spirit" and "Christ's spirit."

Especially objectionable is the NWT translation of John 1:1, "In [the] beginning the Word was, and the Word was with God, and the Word was a god." This is completely in harmony with the theology of Jehovah's Witnesses, since for them Christ is a created being. Therefore, He is to them not God but a god. It is true that the Greek does not have the article before "God" here. However, since in this verse in Greek *theos* (God) is a predicate noun and precedes the verb and subject, it is definite, since a definite predicate noun when it precedes the verb never takes an article in Greek. Some also see the anarthrous construction as emphasizing quality and translate *theos* as "divine." There is no justification for the Jehovah's Witnesses' translation.

There is no consistency in their translation of *theos* without the article. In the Gospel of John it is always written as "God"; that is, with a capital G (including, surprisingly, John 20:28), except in four instances. John 6:45 has a quotation from Isaiah 54:13. The Greek has a form of *theos* but the Hebrew has *Yahweh* and this has led to the NWT's use of "Jehovah." "God" is not in these verses. This is understandable but not an accurate translation of the Greek. In the three other instances *theos* without the article is translated "a god." The first instance of this is John 1:1 about which we have already commented. But this same translation is found in the following verses:

> John 1:18
> No man has seen God at any time; the only begotten god who is in the bosom position with the Father is the one that has explained him.

> John 10:33
> The Jews answered him: "We are stoning you, not for a fine work, but for blasphemy, even because you, although being a man, make yourself a god."

What the NWT translators have done with John 1:18 is very interesting. They could have selected two other MS readings, "the only one" and "the only son of God," but they steadfastly kept the text they were following and translated it "the only begotten god." The word for "only begotten" probably should be translated "only" and there is absolutely no reason for not translating *theos* as "God." As we have already mentioned, there is no consistency except that of dogmatic consistency in their translation of *theos* as "a god." They have not even been consistent in their dogmatism in the translation of John 20:38 where we would have expected, "My lord and my god!"

There are several passages where the names "God" and "Jesus Christ" are joined by a conjunction, with one article before the first name. The rule is that usually two nouns in such a grammatical structure refer to the same person or thing. However, in every case of this kind where the nouns "God" and "Jesus Christ" are found together, they are translated so as to make God and Jesus Christ separate persons. Compare, for example, the following translations of Titus 2:13:

> Looking for that blessed hope, and the glorious appearing of the great God and our Saviour Jesus Christ (KJV)

> awaiting our blessed hope, the appearing of the glory of our great God and Savior Jesus Christ (RSV)

> looking forward to the happy fulfilment of our hopes when the splendour of our great God and Saviour Christ Jesus will appear (NEB)

while we wait for the happy hope and glorious manifestation
of the great God and of our Savior Christ Jesus (NWT)

The first three translations are similar and make God and
Jesus Christ the same person, although it is ambiguous in KJV.
There is only a slight change in the NWT, but given the Witnesses' theological bias, it is sufficient to show that a clear distinction is made between the two by the repetition of the
preposition "of." This same tendency shows up in the NWT
translation of 2 Peter 1:1: ". . . the righteousness of our God
and [the] Savior Jesus Christ." The article is not present before Savior in the Greek text, but before God only; the translators added it to make the distinction.

With the same theological bias the NWT translates Colossians 1:16, 17 in the following way: ". . . because by means
of him all [other] things were created. . . . All [other] things
have been created through him. . . . Also, he is before all [other]
things and by means of him all [other] things were made to
exist." Needless to say, the words in the brackets are not in
the original but are added to imply "other than Christ himself,"
that is to say, Christ Himself was created but He created all
other things.

A more subtle translation with the same theological motiva-
tion is the NWT rendering of Philippians 2:6: ". . . who, although he was existing in God's form, gave no consideration to
a seizure, namely, that he should be equal to God." Compare
this with the translation of the JB: "His state was divine, yet
he did not cling to his equality with God." Or the RSV: ". . .
who, though he was in the form of God, did not count equality
with God a thing to be grasped." The NWT implies simply that
Jesus gave no consideration to being equal with God while the
others assert that He did not cling to His equality with God
but emptied Himself. There is a vast difference of meaning
and an important theological implication in these translations.

Still another theologically motivated characteristic is the
way "Holy Spirit" is printed. Since Witnesses do not believe
in the deity of the Holy Spirit, these words are never capitalized.
According to them, "The holy spirit is not a person or being,
and no scripture authorizes the conclusion that it is. It is the
active force of God with which he accomplishes his purpose.

The Scriptures are crystal clear on the subject." (*Awake!* June 22, 1955, p. 261)

Even though Jehovah's Witnesses believe the Lord's Supper was only a memorial service, this does not justify their translation of 1 Corinthians 11:24, 25: " 'This means my body which is in YOUR behalf. Keep doing this in remembrance of me! . . . 'This cup means the new covenant by virtue of my blood.' " The Greek verb used is "is" and should have been translated thus. Their concern for accuracy and literalism seems to be set aside whenever the literal text conflicts with their theological position.

Besides the examples noted above, there are other interpretive translations. Jehovah's Witnesses believe the dead have no conscious existence, but there is no justification for their translation of 1 Corinthians 15:29: "Otherwise, what will they do who are being baptized for the purpose of [being] dead ones? If the dead are not to be raised up at all, why are they also being baptized for the purpose of [being] such?" In the margin of their NT edition, there is a reference to Romans 6:4, which indicates they interpret this verse to mean that Paul is referring to the fact that the Christian dies with Christ at baptism. However one interprets this passage (and this interpretation is very unlikely), at least the passage should be translated accurately. The Greek word translated "for the purpose of" means more likely "in behalf of," "for," or "in place of." The addition of "being" is purely interpretive. KJV translates the phrase as "for the dead"; RSV and NEB as "on behalf of the dead."

Another interpretive translation, though without apparent theological bias, is made in 1 Corinthians 7:36: "But if anyone thinks he is behaving improperly toward his virginity, if that is past the bloom of youth, and this is the way it should take place, let him do what he wants; he does not sin. Let them marry." The first thing to be said about this verse is that no matter what translation one takes up, it will surely be an interpretation. It is almost impossible to translate this passage without interpreting it. Notice the words we have italicized in the following translations:

> But if any man think that he behaveth himself uncomely toward his *virgin,* if *she pass the flower of her age* (KJV)

If any one thinks that he is not behaving properly toward his *betrothed, if his passions are strong* (RSV)

But if a man has a *partner in celibacy* and feels that he is not behaving properly towards her, if, that is, his *instincts are too strong* for him (NEB)

However, it is difficult to justify "virginity" in NWT. The Greek word means "virgin" and the word for "virginity" is another word coming from the same root.

This special pleading in the NWT is its worst feature. Another weakness is the translation itself. The OT scholar, H. H. Rowley, writes—

The jargon which they use is often scarcely English at all, and it reminds one of nothing so much as a schoolboy's first painful beginnings in translating Latin into English. The translation is marked by a wooden literalism which will only exasperate any intelligent reader—if such it finds—and instead of showing the reverence for the Bible which the translators profess, it is an insult to the Word of God. (*Expository Times* 65 [1953-54]: 41-42)

Examples of these poor renderings abound:

Genesis 18:20, 21
Consequently Jehovah said: "The cry of complaint about Sodom and Gomorrah, yes, it is loud, and their sin, yes, it is very heavy. I am quite determined to go down that I may see whether they act altogether according to the outcry over it that has come to me, and, if not, I can get to know it."

Genesis 6:1-3
Now it came about that when men started to grow in numbers on the surface of the ground and daughters were born to them, then the sons of the [true] God began to notice the daughters of men, that they were goodlooking; and they went taking wives for themselves, namely, all whom they chose. After that Jehovah said: "My spirit shall not act toward man indefinitely in that he is also flesh."

Exodus 20:3
You must not have any other gods against my face.

Isaiah 1:13
Stop bringing in any more valueless grain offerings. Incense—it is something detestable to me. New moon and sabbath, the calling of a convention—I cannot put up with the [use of] uncanny power along with the solemn assembly.

Daniel 7:25

And he will speak even words against the Most High, and he will harass continually the holy ones themselves of the Supreme One.

Matthew 5:18

for truly I say to you that sooner would heaven and earth pass away than for the smallest letter or one particle of a letter to pass away from the Law by any means and not all things take place.

1 Corinthians 5:1

Actually fornication is reported among you, and such fornication as is not even among the nations, that a wife a certain [man] has of [his] father.

1 Corinthians 10:11

Now these things went on befalling them as examples, and they were written for a warning to us upon whom the ends of the systems of things have arrived.

The above examples are in harmony with the Witnesses' attempt to be as literal as possible, but when literalism obscures the meaning of the verse it has gone too far. To this obscurity they add such a nonliterary style as to repulse the reader. We do not want to imply that the entire translation is of the same poor quality as the above examples. However, there are enough renderings of this kind that were we to judge it simply on this basis, it would score very low.

There are other peculiarities in translation that should be noted. The use of "torture stake" for the cross and "impale" for crucify are two of these unfortunate examples. It is based on the belief of the Jehovah's Witnesses that the cross on which Jesus was crucified was a single stake. John Mattingly marshals the evidence to show the fallacy of the Witnesses' contention:

> Another unusual translation our unidentified committee gives us is that of Mt 10:38, "whoever does not accept this torture stake and follow after me is not worthy of me." Again all sorts of authorities are marshaled, this time to back their contention that Christ was "impaled" (Mt. 27:38 and al.). First it should be noted that "impale" is used in a sense not acknowledged by Webster's New International Dictionary (Unabridged, 1949). They do not mean the Oriental custom of thrusting a body down on a pointed stake. Rather they give an illustration from Justus Lipsius' *De Cruce*, showing a man affixed by nails to a single upright pole but with the hands

attached about a foot above his head on the one upright. It is not mentioned that Lipsius gives five different pictures in all and that he himself held in this same book for the traditional representation as true. They do lay great emphasis on the original meaning of "stauros" as a single upright pole. That this single upright pole was used for executions they prove by citing Roman literature. But there is a strange silence about the descriptions of the crucifixions of slaves at the beginning of the Christian era. Customarily the slaves were made to carry the *patibulum* or horizontal bar of their cross to the place of execution. So common was this form of crucifixion that the Roman authors use *patibulum* as synonymous with *crux* (Seneca, *De Vita Beata,* 19:3; *Epistola* 101:12. Tacitus, *Historiae,* IV, 3). To hold that Constantine introduced the traditional cross as a relic of his pagan worship of the sun god (p. 771) is unworthy of their evident scholarship. True the cross does not appear in the catacombs as a symbol of Christ before 312 A.D. Neither does their "torture stake"; nor later, for that matter. As for the Fathers, it is the traditional cross they describe. To cite only two witnesses; Irenaeus speaks of Christ's cross as having five ends, two longitudinal, two latitudinal, and a fifth on the support for the body of the victim (*Adversus Haereses,* II, 24, 4). He wrote before 200 A.D. Still earlier is the witness of the *Epistle of Barnabas,* X, 8. Here the writer speaks of the cross as having the shape of a Greek *Tau.* (*Catholic Biblical Quarterly* XIII [1951], 441)

What is gained by this insistence on the use of "torture stake" for "cross" and of "impale" for "crucify" is difficult to see. Surely there is nothing gained for the Witnesses' doctrinal position to risk these idiosyncrasies in translation.

Other features that characterize this translation are the names the translators give to the OT and the NT, their use of capitals to indicate the plural of the second person, their attempt to translate more accurately the Greek verbs, their Greek text base, and their complete dropping of the archaic second person pronouns such as thou, thy, thine, thee, and ye.

The Witnesses do not call the first division of the Bible the Old Testament or the second division the New Testament. Instead, they designate these parts respectively as The Hebrew-Aramaic Scriptures and The Christian Greek Scriptures, thus making a distinction in the language and perhaps an unintentional implication that the OT is not Christian.

While their attempt to distinguish between the singular and plural of the second person is commendable, it presents certain problems. The pronoun is capitalized in its entirety when it refers to the plural. This involves the verb when it is in the imperative. This makes for awkwardness in reading.

The attempt to indicate the force of the Greek verbs is good but is done at the expense of literary beauty. Note such translations as the following:

> Matthew 5:25
> Be about settling matters quickly with the one complaining against you at law.

> Matthew 5:44
> Continue to love YOUR enemies.

> Matthew 6:19
> Stop storing up for yourselves treasures upon the earth.

> Matthew 6:33
> Keep on, then, seeking first the kingdom and his righteousness.

One commendable feature of this translation is that it is based on a relatively good Greek text, mainly that of Westcott and Hort. This leads to the dropping of many late readings due to a tendency toward harmonization, especially in the Gospels. The spurious passages in 1 John 5:7, 8 is also omitted, whereas John 7:53-8:11, concerning the adulterous woman, is placed in the lower margin in smaller print and Mark 16:8 is followed by the longer and shorter conclusion both in smaller print with an introductory explanation.

The dropping of the archaic second person pronouns puts NWT in line with more modern translations.

Certain other interesting and peculiar translations appear. One of these is the translation of the Greek word usually translated "age" or "world." The NWT consistently translates it as "system of things." Surely no improvement, this practice merely adds to the woodenness and awkwardness of the translation. For example, take the following:

> Matthew 13:22
> this is the one hearing the word, but the anxiety of this system of things and the deceptive power of riches choke the word.

> Matthew 28:20
> And, look! I am with YOU all the days until the conclusion of the system of things.

Hebrews 1:2
and through whom he made the systems of things.

Hebrews 11:3
By faith we perceive that the systems of things were put in order by God's word.

2 Timothy 4:10
For Demas has forsaken me because he loved the present system of things.

The translation of the word *petra* as "rock-mass" every time it is used is unnecessary and awkward. Thus Romans 9:33 reads, "Look! I am laying in Zion a stone of stumbling and a rock-mass of offense..." and 1 Corinthians 10:4 says, "For they used to drink from the spiritual rock-mass that followed them, and that rock-mass meant Christ." In this day when rock mass has quite a different meaning, "spiritual rock-mass" may conjure up an entirely different image than what the text calls for.

"Holy ones" for "saints" is not any improvement. For example, Ephesians 1:1 reads, "Paul, an apostle of Christ Jesus through God's will, to the holy ones who are in Ephesus. . . ." "Inspired expression" for "spirit" cannot be justified in 1 John 4:1-3, 6. The Greek word is translated as "spirit" in 3:24; 4:13; and 5:6, 8 in the Epistle. There is no valid reason for this change.

An ultra-consistency has led to the translation of the Greek word *parousia* in every instance as "presence." The word has this meaning but surely in the majority of the cases, especially where it refers to the second advent, it should be translated "coming." One English word cannot always translate a particular Greek word accurately. A particular Greek word, as well as a particular English word, does not always have the same meaning. The context must determine its meaning. Unfortunately, the translator(s) of NWT did not have this flexibility.

There are certain peculiar translations in the NWT. Compare them with the RSV, which follows each passage:

> in which the *force of life was active* (Gen. 7:15)
> in which there was the *breath of life*
> And Jehovah began to smell a *restful odor* (Gen. 8:21)
> And when the Lord smelled the *pleasing odor*
> As for him, he will become a *zebra* of a man (Gen. 16:12)
> He shall be a *wild ass* of a man

As for me, look! my covenant is with you, and you will certainly become father of a *crowd of nations* (Gen. 17:4)
Behold, my covenant is with you, and you shall be the father of a *multitude of nations*

And Sarah kept noticing the son of Hagar the Egyptian, whom she had borne to Abraham, *poking fun* (Gen. 21:9)
But Sarah saw the son of Hagar the Egyptian, whom she had borne to Abraham, *playing with her son Isaac*

But this delight is in the law of Jehovah, And in his law he *reads in an undertone* day and night (Ps. 1:2)
but his delight is in the law of the LORD, and on his law he *meditates* day and night

Call out *full-throated;* do not hold back (Isaiah 58:1)
Cry *aloud*, spare not

Will *earthling man* rob God? (Mal. 3:8)
Will *man* rob God?

"*grease* your head" (Matt. 6:17)
"*anoint* your head"

"*Sacred secret*" (1 Cor. 2:7)
"*mystery*"

"*wild beast*" (Rev. 13:1)
"*beast*"

The text is arranged by sense paragraphs rather than individual verses like the KJV. This is a definite improvement. However, the use of ancient terms for weights, measures, money, and time is definitely a backward step.

Dr. Metzger's evaluation is that "on the whole one gains a tolerably good impression of the scholarly equipment of the translators." The translation at times is also good. However, the theological bias and the inconsistent quality of the translation neutralize the good elements within it.

THE BIBLE IN LIVING ENGLISH

When the Watchtower Bible and Tract Society published this new version, it was thought at first that it was a revised edition of its earlier *New World Translation*. However, this is not the case. It is an entirely new translation by one Steven T. Byington (1868-1957), who was not a Jehovah's Witness. He attended a Congregational church that later merged with another to form the United Church of Ballard Vale, Massachusetts. He obtained an A.B. in classics from the University of Vermont and later spent one year at Union Theological Seminary and a half year at Oberlin studying biblical languages. After his death, the Watchtower Bible and Tract Society of Pennsylvania received the publication rights for the translation and published it in 1972.

According to the translator, the purpose of this translation "is to put the Bible into living present-day English." His principles of translation can be seen from the following statements: "To say in my own words what I thought the prophet or apostle was driving at would not, to my mind, be real translation; nor yet to analyze into a string of separate words all the implications which the original may have carried in one word; the difference between conciseness and prolixity is one difference between the Bible and something else. So far as a translation does not keep to this standard, it is a commentary rather than a translation: a very legitimate and useful form of commentary, but it leaves the field of translation unfilled." He tends to be more literal than free, yet is not completely bound to the limitations of the translated language. "The test," he says, "is generally whether the English translated into Hebrew or Greek would have had to give what the Hebrew or Greek writer wrote."

It will seem strange that in pronouns addressed to God the BLE has "thou" in the NT but "you" in the OT. Byington's justification for this is "that the New Testament men had nearly the same feelings as we have about addressing God, but the Old Testament men, those of them who had most to say to God, such as Abraham, Moses, Elijah, Jeremiah, had not such feelings as lead us to give God a special pronoun."

One feature, at least, that led the Witnesses to publish this translation is the rendering of the name of God as "Jehovah." The translator recognizes that this name is due to a blunder but does not feel that the spelling and pronunciation are important. "What is highly important is to keep it clear that this is a personal name."

The translation is set forth in one column with the verse numbers on the left-hand margin. There are no subject headings, notes, or references. Marginal notes are found at the end of each book. These consist of alternative translations, the literal rendering, or alternative readings for the verse indicated. The designations "Old Testament" and "New Testament" are not found before each section, although the translator refers to these in his preface. This lack of designation is probably due to the influence of the Witnesses who do not use these terms. Two charts and two maps are found at the end of the Bible.

Spellings of some of the names of the books of the Bible and of some persons in the Bible are different from those we have become accustomed to and which Catholic Bibles also now use. For instance, we find the following: Hambakuk, Hoshea', Malaki, Sephaniah, Zecariah, Enoc, and Lamec.

The translator refers to the fact that the "old version" (KJV) contains "forged texts." He is quite aware of textual criticism as his reference to the OT text also indicates. In checking the text of the NT, we found that Byington used considerable freedom in his selection. He probably used a text like that of Nestle but did not follow it slavishly. Mark 16:9-20 is set off with this heading: A WRITING SAID TO BE BY ELDER ARISTON: THE VERSES ARE NUMBERED AS PART OF THE SIXTEENTH CHAPTER OF MARK. John 7:53-8:11 is placed at the end of the Gospel of John instead of in the traditional location and is set off from the last of the Gospel with a heading. Especially interesting is the choice of "Jesus Barabbas" instead of "Barabbas" in Matthew 27:16. He follows the NEB here. Also following the NEB, he has "on a pilum [javelin]" in John 19:29, instead of "hyssop," and omits Matthew 16:2b, 3. Luke 22:43, 44 and 23:34 are placed in brackets. In the "Explanation" at the beginning it is mentioned that "adjustments made by the Publishers are indicated by the use of square brackets." Does this mean that these verses were actually omitted by the translator but were added by the publishers? If that is the case, he has gone further than most translations, which keep these verses.

In checking a few of the "Marginal Notes to First Corinthians" the following observations were made. The note to 1:28 reads "*Lit.* supersede the somethings." Actually the Greek text reads "in order that he might bring to nothing things that are." The note on 2:4 reads "*Var.* with persuasion by wisdom of words." Nestle lists six other readings besides the one the translator chose to follow, but none of them reads as he has given. Also it is difficult to know by what principles he is selecting the variants he lists. Most of the notes give the literal form of the text.

While this translation is completely independent from the NWT, we made a comparison of the two. Since it is published by the Jehovah's Witnesses, we were especially interested in those passages where the characteristic biases of the NWT were evident. In the BLE, "Jehovah" is used in the OT but is not found in the NT. The word "God" is capitalized when referring to Jesus Christ, e.g., in John 1:1; 1:18; 6:45; 10:33. Where the NWT added the article "the" in brackets in Titus 2:13 and 2 Peter 1:1 and "other" in Colossians 1:16, 17, this translation does not, so that Jesus Christ can be identified with God in these passages. Furthermore, by its punctuation in Romans 9:5 it has clearly identified Christ as God: "Whose are the fathers, and from whom in the way of flesh comes the Christ, he who is over everything, God blessed forever—Amen!"

The designation "Holy Spirit" is capitalized, contrary to the NWT, and the words "cross" and "crucify" are used instead of "torture stake" and "impale."

The only apparent reason for the Witnesses' publishing this translation is the translator's use of "Jehovah" for God's name in the OT, unless they also want to tone down the idosyncrasies in their own translation.

The translation leans more to the literal side of the spectrum and is rather straightforward. We give two samples, one from the OT and one from the NT:

Genesis 3:1-5

And the snake was the shrewdest of all the wild beasts that God Jehovah had made; and it said to the woman, "A pity God said you were not to eat of all the trees in the garden." And the woman said to the snake, "Fruit from the trees in the garden we are to eat, but as to the fruit of this tree in the middle of the garden God said 'You are not to eat any of it, nor touch it, or you will die.'" And the snake said to the woman, "Die you would not; but God knows that on the day you eat of it your eyes will be opened and you will be like gods, knowing good and bad."

Matthew 5:17-20

"Do not suppose that I came to tear down the law or the prophets; I did not come to tear down but to fill up. For I tell you verily, till the heavens and the earth pass away, not the dot of an i nor the cross of a t in the law shall pass away, till everything is done. So whoever breaks one of the pettiest of those commandments, and teaches men so, shall be called petty in the Reign of Heaven; but whoever does them and teaches them shall be called great in the Reign of Heaven. For I tell you that unless your righteousness outdoes the scribes and Pharisees you shall not get into the Reign of Heaven"

The above samples point out some of the weaknesses of this translation. It lacks literary beauty and in some places it tends toward the novel. It is no surprise to discover these weaknesses in a translation made by one man who has no real professional training for the task. We list below some of these peculiar translations. The translation from the BLE will be given first, followed by that of the RSV.

Genesis

1:28 "bear empire over the fishes"—"have dominion over the fish"

2:4 "line of the heavens"—"generations of the heavens"

2:13 "Negroes' country"—"land of Cush"

3:7 "pinned fig-leaves together and made themselves belts" —"sewed fig leaves together and made themselves aprons"

3:15 "it bursting your head and you bursting its heel"—"he shall bruise your head, and you shall bruise his heel"

4:23 "For I have killed a man for my scratch, a child for my bruise"—"I have slain a man for wounding me, a young man for striking me"

6:14 "Make yourself a gopher-wood box"—"Make yourself an ark of gopher wood"

Exodus

20:3 "no other gods to face me down"—"no other gods before me"

In Leviticus new terms appear such as "sin-steer" for "sin offering," "lessons" for "testimony" (referring to the ark), "farina" for "fine flour," "welfare-sacrifice" for "peace offering," and "handsel-oblation" for "offering of first fruits."

Leviticus

2:4 "And when you present the oblation of a grain-offering baked in a baking crock, farina in ritual-matzoth shortened with oil and in sheet matzoth rubbed over with oil"—"When you bring a cereal offering baked in the oven as an offering, it shall be unleavened cakes of fine flour mixed with oil, or unleavened wafers spread with oil."

1 Samuel

17:38 "And Saul dressed David in his own brigandine"— "Then Saul clothed David with his armor"

17:40 "chose five pebbles out of the bed of the arroyo and put them in his shepherd's wallet, his yalkut"—"chose five smooth stones from the brook, and put them in his shepherd's bag or wallet"

2 Samuel

18:21 "the Negro"—"the Cushite"

Isaiah

1:18 "Come let us have it out"—"Come now, let us reason together"

8:6 "admire the hubbub of Rason"—"melt in fear before Rezin"

40:15 "a drop hanging on a bucket"—"drop from a bucket"

Daniel

12:4 "keep the things under a stopper and seal the book till an ultimate date"—"shut up the words, and seal the book, until the time of the end"

Matthew

4:21 "putting their nets to rights"—"mending their nets"

5:6 "because they shall have their meal"—"for they shall be satisfied"

5:11 "twit you and persecute you"—"revile you and persecute you"

5:37 "anything in excess of this is so much of bad"—"anything more than this comes from evil"

5:48 "be thorough as your heavenly Father is thorough"— "be perfect, as your heavenly Father is perfect"

9:29 "Have it as you have faith for"—"According to your faith be it done to you"

13:15 "for this people's wits are thickened"—"for this people's heart has grown dull"

13:57 "they were staggered at him"—"they took offense at him"

18:6 "ass-power millstone"—"a great millstone"

18:7 "Woe to the world for trippings-up! for the trippings-up have to come, yet woe to the man through whom the tripping-up comes"—"Woe to the world for temptations to sin! For it is necessary that temptations come, but woe to the man by whom the temptation comes!"

John

1:12 "gave the chance to become children of God"—"gave power to become children of God"

1:16 "out of his fullness all of us have had portions"—"from his fulness have we all received"

Romans

2:13 "not the audience of the law"—"not the hearers of the law"

6:5 "if we have come to be twinned with the likeness of his death"—"if we have been united with him in a death like his"

8:11 "through his Spirit your inmate"—"through his Spirit which dwells in you"

11:5 "there are leavings in accordance with the choice made by grace"—"there is a remnant, chosen by grace"

Hebrews

1:14 "servient spirits"—"ministering spirits"

2:16 "take up angels, methinks"—"surely it is not with angels that he is concerned"

4:13 "thrown flat on its back for his eyes"—"laid bare to the eyes of him"

9:14 "from the corpses of our deeds"—"from dead works"

11:2 "old-timers"—"men of old"

12:9 "our bodily fathers"—"earthly fathers"

Revelation

1:15 "green gold"—"burnished bronze"

2:16 "mouth-sword"—"sword of my mouth"

4:3 "jaspid stone and a sard"—"jasper and carnelian"

7:11 "aged men"—"elders"

Some of these translations are not only peculiar but also misleading and wrong. Byington has also introduced certain words not usually found in the Bible such as "jubilate" (Rom. 15:10), "chaplain" (Rom. 15:16), "serving-man" (Matt. 20:26), "twitting" (Matt. 27:44), "lugubrious" (Matt. 6:16), "gormandizer" (Matt. 11:19), "gratis" (Matt. 10:8), "hectoring" (Isa. 3:5), besides those also included above. Awkward renderings were also found in Matthew 9:34; John 4:9; Romans 8:28;

14:1, 5, 20, 21, 23; 15:1; Hebrews 5:11; 11:29; and Revelation 21:1.

It is interesting that in Matthew 16:18 after "Peter" these words are placed: "[in English, 'you are a Rock']." "Every text is inspired by God" (2 Tim. 3:16) is surprising for a literal translation.

This translation has some interesting renderings, but there are too many peculiarities and awkward translations for it to be acceptable, especially since there are so many more excellent versions today. No doubt it will have a wide circulation through the diligent and indefatigable efforts of the Witnesses.

7

The New Jewish Version

The Jewish translation of the Hebrew Scriptures into English began with the version of Abraham Benisch, published in England in 1851. In 1884 *A Jewish Family Bible,* edited by Michael Friedländer, was published for Anglo-Jewry. The first complete Jewish translation for American Jewry was produced in 1853 by Rabbi Isaac Leeser of Philadelphia. Although Leeser was not an expert in Hebrew philology, he did make use of various scholarly German translations by Jews of the nineteenth century. His version became the standard Bible for English-speaking Jews in America, and was also reproduced in England.

With the influx of Jews from western Europe to the American continent in the late nineteenth century, the need for an improved version in English for use in synagogue, school, and home was felt. In 1892, four years after its organization, the Jewish Publication Society of America took steps to prepare such a version. The original plan was to have Jewish scholars in Britain and America work independently on the several books, using Leeser's translation as a base. The resulting translation of each book was then to be submitted to the critical revision of an Editorial Committee under the chairmanship of Dr. Marcus Jastrow. Discussion regarding the translation was to be carried on by correspondence. By 1901 it became evident that this procedure was too slow. In 1903 Dr. Jastrow died, and a few years later a new plan was formulated. A Board of Editors, six in number, was created to work with the new Editor-in-Chief, Max L. Margolis of Dropsie College. Margolis prepared a draft of the version, which was then revised by the Board of Editors.

The version was published in 1917 under the title, *The Holy Scriptures According to the Masoretic Text, A New Translation*. According to the preface,

> It aims to combine the spirit of Jewish tradition with the results of biblical scholarship, ancient, medieval, and modern. It gives to the Jewish world a translation of the Scriptures done by men imbued with the Jewish consciousness, while the non-Jewish world, it is hoped, will welcome a translation that presents many passages from the Jewish traditional point of view.

Behind it, as behind other efforts by Jews at biblical translation, was the sentiment that "the Jew cannot afford to have his translation prepared for him by others. He cannot have it as a gift, even as he cannot borrow his soul from others."

Nevertheless, the 1917 version owed much to the non-Jewish English versions that preceded it. It was modeled after the classic style of the KJV, and was, in reality, only a mild revision of the RV of 1885. While it satisfied the needs of English-speaking Jewry for several decades, it became apparent that the time demanded a new version—one that would speak in a twentieth-century idiom to modern man and embody the latest discoveries in understanding the Bible. Protestants and Catholics had already begun producing new versions.

In 1955 the Jewish Publication Society appointed a committee of seven scholars to prepare a new Jewish translation, beginning with the Torah. Three eminent Hebraists were selected to act as editors: Harry M. Orlinsky (editor-in-chief), H. L. Ginsberg, and Ephraim A. Speiser. Three learned rabbis—Max Arzt, Bernard J. Bamberger, and Harry Freedman—representing, respectively, the Conservative, Reform, and Orthodox divisions of Judaism, were appointed as consultants. The representative of the Jewish Publication Society, Solomon Grayzel, served as the secretary of the committee.

The original draft of the translation, prepared by Orlinsky, was circulated among the members of the committee. The resulting comments, criticisms, and suggestions of each member were also sent to all seven. Periodic meetings were then held in which decisions were made regarding the wording of the text by a majority vote. The MS was then sent to the press and was published in 1962. Eleven years later a second edition was published, embodying a substantial number of improvements. Orlinsky also prepared a helpful companion volume based on the text of the second edition, entitled *Notes on the New Translation of the Torah.* This volume, published in 1969, contains a helpful introduction to the history of Jewish versions in English, in addition to the notes which explain significant departures of *The New Jewish Version* from the version of 1917.

The NJV is not a revision of the Jewish version of 1917, nor of any other version, Jewish or Christian, but is a completely fresh translation of the traditional Hebrew text in living, up-to-date, and highly readable English. Although it is not a mechanical, word-by-word translation, as was the 1917 version, it is, on the whole, faithful to the original Hebrew text. The translators strove for the principle of equivalent effect, i.e., their goal was to produce a version that would carry the same message to modern man as the original did to the world of ancient times. They sought to determine as accurately as possible the meaning of the Hebrew and then to state that meaning in good, contemporary English. They broke away from the traditional biblical English of earlier standard versions.

They therefore endeavored to avoid the use of all obsolete words and phrases. The phrase "and it came to pass," familiar in traditional English versions, has disappeared (Gen. 6:1; 7:10; 8:6, 13; 24:52; 25:11, et al.). The use of "thou" and its various case forms has been abandoned, even in language addressed to God. Surprisingly, the somewhat antiquated idiom "to take to wife" is used several times (Gen. 25:20; 29:28; Exod. 6:20, 23, 25; Lev. 21:14; Deut. 21:11). The translators were well aware of the fact that the Hebrew particle *wāw*, usually translated "and" in the traditional English versions, can be used in a number of senses: conjunctive, disjunctive, and adverbial, depending on the context. Consequently, they translated it not only as "and," but also as "but," "however," "when," "then," "so," "thus," "thereupon," and "although." On occasion it was left untranslated (e.g., Gen. 1:3, 6, 9, 14, 20, 24, 29). This has greatly improved the translation's readability. The sentence structure has in some instances been modified over the 1917 version. Occasionally, long sentences have been broken up into smaller units. At other times sentences have been combined into larger units.

The new version is a model of typographical art. Printed

on excellent paper in large easy-to-read type, with a single column to the page, the text is arranged in paragraphs, though the verse numbers are given in small type.

The version is supplied with useful footnotes. These are of various kinds. Some call attention to significant variants in the ancient MSS and versions (e.g., Gen. 4:8; Exod. 5:5; 19:18; Num. 21:1; Deut. 31:1). Others give the Hebrew word, or indicate that there is a play on a Hebrew word. Others indicate that the Hebrew text is obscure and the translation is uncertain. Where a translation is somewhat free or an idiom is involved, a note calls attention to the literal meaning of the Hebrew (e.g., Gen. 29:1; 31:10). Alternate translations are suggested by the rubric "Or." The rubric "Others" introduces renderings given by previous versions or perhaps preferred by scholars outside the committee. There are also interpretive or explanatory notes (Lev. 13:13; Deut. 26:14).

There are a few instances in which the NJV has departed from the Masoretic Hebrew text. One is in Genesis 49:10 where Shiloh is understood as *shoi lo*, "tribute to him," with the resulting translation being "So that the tribute shall come to him." In Genesis 22:13 instead of "behind him a ram" the NJV with the RSV and others reads "a ram." In Genesis 10:5 the clause "These are the descendants of Japheth" is inserted in brackets (cf. RSV). Conjectural emendations are also made in Numbers 21:24; 25:1. But in comparison with most modern versions, the handling of the Hebrew text is very conservative indeed.

In its handling of the sacred ineffable name, YHWH, the NJV has followed the long-established synagogue custom of rendering it as LORD. In Exodus 6:3, however, this tetragrammaton is printed in Hebrew letters and a footnote explains, "This divine name is traditionally not pronounced; instead Adonai '(the) LORD,' is regularly substituted for it." Deuteronomy 6:4 in this version reads, "The LORD is our God, the LORD alone." In Exodus 3:14, in answer to Moses' request for God's name, the answer is simply transliterated "Eyeh-Asher-Eyeh," for which a footnote provides various suggested translations. The divine name *El-Shaddai*, traditionally translated as "God Almighty," is transliterated (Gen. 17:1; 28:3; 35:11; 43:14; 48:3; Exodus 6:3, et al.). The same is true of *El-Roi*

(Gen. 16:13). *El-Elyon*, however, is translated "God Most High" (Gen. 14:18-20, 22), and *El 'Olam* "The Everlasting God" (Gen. 21:33).

The NJV represents an honest, unbiased attempt by world-renowned Hebrew scholars to put into current English what they believe the Hebrew text says. Nevertheless, it is not to be expected that all of its renderings will find favorable acceptance even among Jews. The translation begins:

> When God began to create the heavens and the earth—the earth being unformed and void, with darkness over the surface of the deep and a wind from God sweeping over the water—God said, "Let there be light"; and there was light.

A complicated sentence of three verses has displaced the three simple sentences of the traditional version. The temporal clause with which the account begins is a possible rendering, but not the only possible one. Though found in other modern versions, such as the NEB, and advocated by competent scholars, it is still debatable. Even more debatable is the rendering "a wind from God sweeping over the water," rather than that of 1917: "the Spirit of God hovered over the face of the waters."

At this point, Christians, who will find this version of inestimable value, may be tempted to accuse the translators of religious bias, though *An American Translation* reads "a tempestuous wind raging over the surface of the waters." It must be granted that *ruach* can mean "wind" or "breath" as well as "spirit." It is so used, e.g., in Genesis 3:8, which the NJV renders "at the breezy time of day," literally "at the wind of the day." But it is doubtful that *ruach elohim* elsewhere in the Pentateuch means "a wind from God." Rather, the phrase means "spirit of God" (Gen. 41:38; Exod. 31:3; 35:31; Num. 24:2). Furthermore, the verb *rachaph* means to "hover" or "flutter" and is used in Deuteronomy 32:11 of an eagle that "hovereth over her young." The medieval Jewish commentator Rashi likened the Spirit of God in Genesis 1:2 to a dove.

In the first edition of the NJV Genesis 1:26 read, "And God said, 'I will make man in My image, after My likeness....'" However, the second edition has returned to the rendering "Let us make man in our image, after our likeness" (cf. Gen. 3:22: "And the Lord said, 'Now that the man has become like one of us...'"). Likewise, the first edition's "Let me, then, go

down and confound their speech there..." (Gen. 11:7) has
been changed to "Let us..." in the second edition.

There is no note to explain why the singulars of the Hebrew
are translated as plurals in Genesis 3:15b: "They shall strike
at your head, and you shall strike at their heels." In Genesis
4:7 where the first edition read, "Sin is the demon at the door,"
the second has "Sin couches at the door." The traditional rendering "the sons of God" in Genesis 6:2 has become "the divine
beings." In vs. 3 the first edition's "My spirit shall not shield
man forever" has been changed in the second edition to "My
breath shall not abide in man forever." In Genesis 16:5 the
NJV renders the Hebrew *tsedeq* (righteousness) as "merit."
Thus the statement regarding Abraham's righteousness by faith,
quoted by Paul in Romans 4:3, is translated, "And because he
put his trust in the Lord, He reclaimed it to his merit."

Leviticus 24:10ff. contains the account of a quarrel between
one of the "mixed multiude" (Exod. 12:38) and a full-blooded
Israelite. During the quarrel the former, a son of an Egyptian
father and a Hebrew mother, uttered a curse in which he
desecrated the name of God. The NJV translates, "The son of
the Israelite woman pronounced the Name in blasphemy" (vs.
11). "The Name" evidently refers to the sacred, ineffable tetragrammaton (YHWH). The blasphemer was placed in custody
until it was determined that the Law against desecrating God's
name applied to the half-breed as well as to the full-blooded
Israelite. The general principle, as translated in the first edition
of the NJV, was: "Anyone who blasphemes his God shall bear
his guilt; but if he pronounces the name Lord (i.e., YHWH)
he shall be put to death" (vss. 15, 16). This rendering apparently reflects the rabbinic concept that it was wrong for the
ordinary man to pronounce the sacred, ineffable name, but the
meaning must be to say the name in blasphemy. The second
clause is somewhat modified in the second edition: "If he also
pronounces the name Lord; he shall be put to death."

With the exception of passages in Deuteronomy in which
"heart and soul" are used in juxtaposition (4:29; 6:5; 10:12;
11:13; 26:16; 30:2, 6, 10), the NJV Torah has correctly
abandoned "soul" as a translation for the Hebrew *nephesh*.
In Genesis 2:7 it is rendered "being": "The Lord God formed
man from the dust of the earth. He blew into his nostrils the

breath of life, and man became a living being." *Nephesh* has also been rendered "creature" (Gen. 1:20), "person" (Gen. 46: 15), "desire" (Exod. 15:9), "feeling" (Exod. 23:9), and even "corpse" (Num. 19:11). Sometimes it is also rendered by a form of the personal pronoun (Gen. 12:13; Deut. 4:9; 12:15, et al.).

In the first edition the term *mishpat*, particularly when used in conjunction with such legal terms as "statute" and "law," was frequently translated as "norm." In the second edition this was changed to "rule" (Deut. 4:1, 8, 14, 44, et al.). It is difficult to find a distinctive word for each Hebrew legal term, but certainly "rule" is better than "norm." In Numbers 12:6 the second edition reads, "When a prophet of the Lord arises among you." This is an improvement over the first edition's "When the Lord speaks through one of you." One could also wish that "spokesman" in Exodus 4:16 would have been rendered "prophet" (cf. Exod. 7:1).

The reader will need to adjust to a number of new religious terms, particularly some connected with the sanctuary and the sacrificial system. The Hebrew *'eduth* is regarded as a synonym with *berith,* "covenant," as a designation for the Decalogue, and, as such, is translated "pact." In Exodus 31:18 and 32:15 the tables of stone inscribed with the Decalogue are called "the two tables of the Pact." Moses was instructed to deposit them in the ark (Exod. 25:16), which was called "the ark of the Pact" (Exod. 25:22), and the entire Tabernacle is designated "the Tabernacle of the Pact" (Exod. 38:21). The "mercy-seat" in the NJV is "the cover." "Show-bread" has become "bread of display" (Exod. 25:30, et al.). Instead of "peace offerings," it has "sacrifice of well-being" (Lev. 3:1, 3, 6, 9). "Afflict your soul" has become "practice self-denial" (Lev. 16:29, 31; 23:27, 32). On the "Day of Atonement" (Lev. 16:30; 23:27) expiation is made on behalf of Israel (Lev. 16:6, 10, 17; 23:28). Should it not, then, rather be called the "Day of Expiation"?

There are other interesting renderings, such as "goat demons" for "satyrs" in Leviticus 17:7; *"seraph* serpents" for "fiery serpents" in Numbers 21:6, 7; and "expanse" for "firmament" (Gen. 1:6f.). Not everyone will be happy with the substitution of "Sea of Reeds" for "Red Sea" (Exod. 10:19; 13:18, et al.). Granted that *Yam Suph* means "sea of reeds," the body of water the name describes evidently refers to what is now called the Red Sea. At any rate, the *Yam Suph* mentioned in connection with the later wilderness wanderings of the Hebrews must refer to the Gulf of Aqabah, for the Israelites touched at Ezion-Geber and Elath (Deut. 1:40; 2:8; Num. 21:4) on their way to Canaan.

The same committee, with the exception of E. A. Speiser who died in 1965, proceeded with the translation of *The Five Megilloth and Jonah,* published in 1969. H. L. Ginsberg acted as the editor-in-chief. This volume has the Hebrew text and the NJV in parallel columns and is designed for both public and private reading. These six documents—Song of Songs, Ruth, Lamentations, Ecclesiastes, Esther, and Jonah—are all associated with commemorative festivals in the Jewish religious calendar.

The volume includes a brief introduction to the five Megilloth as well as introductory essays (by Ginsberg) to each of the documents included. Again, the translation makes use of the latest available resources for the meaning of the text. The translation is well done in good, contemporary English.

In 1973 the translation of the Book of Isaiah was published. Again, H. L. Ginsberg was the editor-in-chief and wrote a rather extensive introductory essay. The same general principles and methods were used as in the translation of the Torah.

A separate committee of translators for the remainder of the *Kethubim* ("the Writings") was set up in 1966. It consists of Moshe Greenberg, Jonas C. Greenfield, and Nahum M. Sarna, world-renowned scholars, together with the learned Rabbis Saul Leeman, Martin Rozenberg, and David Shapiro. Chaim Potok, editor of the Jewish Publication Society, is the secretary. The first product of this committee is *The Book of Psalms,* published in 1972. This is again based on the traditional Masoretic text. No emendations of it were proposed, but occasionally, as the preface indicates, "the traditional accentuation has been disregarded in favor of an alternative construction of a verse that appeared to yield a better sense." The translators used every resource available, Jewish and non-Jewish, from ancient to modern times. They also availed themselves of the results of modern Near Eastern studies in languages and culture, whenever applicable. While using modern literary English, they sought at the same time to retain the imagery of the Hebrew.

The NJV is a monument to careful scholarship, particularly in dealing with the traditional Hebrew text. Its fidelity to this text is unquestionable. Combined with it is a concern to break away from the traditional English translations and produce a version that is clothed in contemporary idiomatic English. In both of these attempts the version is successful. When completed, it will be one of the best versions of the OT available.

8

The Amplified Bible

The Amplified NT was published in 1958 by the Lockman Foundation and Zondervan Publishing House. Four years earlier, in 1954, *The Amplified Gospel of John* had been published. The *Amplified OT* came out in two parts, Part Two in 1962 and Part One in 1964. In 1965 all of these parts appeared in one volume, *The Amplified Bible* (AB), published by Zondervan. The leading figure in the preparation of this translation was Frances E. Siewert, a research secretary, who also wrote the introductions to the earlier publications.

The desire to make the Bible understandable is admirable and translators of the Bible have used different methods to accomplish this common aim. AB does this by amplification. "Its purpose is to reveal, together with the single-word English equivalent to each key Hebrew and Greek word, any other clarifying shades of meaning that may be concealed by the traditional word-for-word method of translation." Its justification is that "amplification merely helps the English reader comprehend what the Hebrew and Greek listener understood as a matter of course." Whether it has succeeded will be determined after careful investigation.

The symbols used in the translation for the various types of amplification are explained at the beginning. There are four types:

Parentheses () and dashes — : signify additional phases of meaning included in the original word, phrase, or clause of the original language.

Commas are used to set off titles of Deity.

Brackets [ ] : contain justified clarifying words or comments not actually expressed in the immediate original text.

Italics: point out certain familiar passages now recognized as not adequately supported by the original manuscripts. Also, "and," "or," and other connectives in italics indicate that the word itself is not in the original text, but it is used to connect additional English words indicated in the same original word.

The format is unfortunate. The verses are arranged as in the KJV: each verse is set off as a separate paragraph in two columns in the one-volume edition. This format militates against understanding the verses in context and leads to reading each verse as a separate, isolated oracle. It would have been better to arrange the verses in normal paragraphs, with the verse numbers less pronounced in smaller type. Also by the present arrangement poetic sections of the Bible cannot be indicated. Unfortunately, no quotation marks are used. There are no headings of any kind. Cross references, found in brackets after the verse, sometimes refer to certain parts of the verse and this method does not allow the specific indication needed. It would be much better to place these in the margin or at the bottom of the page.

Most of the notes in the NT provide the source for the translation or for the expansion. Apparently, the translators relied most heavily on Vincent, Thayer, and Cremer. Most of the notes in the OT are explanatory comments and are much longer than the NT notes. Many of the notes are apologetic in tone, showing how archaeology has "proved" the Bible, how the ark was built to prevent the animals from multiplying, how Noah had many years in which to interest travelers in securing animals for him. There are more notes in Genesis than any other book. On the one hand, one gets the feeling from reading these notes that the translators were pious, and on the other hand, one detects some insecurity on their part in not letting the Bible stand on its own feet.

The books of the Bible are listed not only in canonical but also in alphabetical order. Perhaps it is anticipated that people who are not informed readers of the Bible will turn to this translation.

We give a few sample passages to illustrate the kind of amplification found in this translation:

Gen. 1:1-6

1 In the beginning God (prepared, formed, fashioned,) *and* created the heavens and the earth. [Heb. 11:3.]

2 The earth was without form and an empty waste, and darkness was upon the face of the very great deep. The Spirit of God was moving, (hovering, brooding) over the face of the waters.

3 And God said, Let there be light; and there was light.

4 And God saw the light, that it was good—suitable, pleasing—*and* He approved it; and God separated the light from the darkness. [2 Cor. 4:6.]

5 And God called the light Day, and the darkness He called Night. And there was evening and there was morning, one day.

6 And God said, Let there be a firmament [the expanse of the sky] in the midst of the waters; and let it separate the waters [below] from the water [above].

Ps. 23:1-3

1 The Lord is my shepherd [to feed, guide and shield me]; I shall not lack.

2 He makes me lie down in (fresh, tender) green pastures; He leads me beside the still *and* restful waters. [Rev. 7:17.]

3 He refreshes *and* restores my life—my self; He leads me in the paths of righteousness—uprightness and right standing with Him—[not for my earning it, but] for His name's sake.

Matt. 5:16-22

16 Let your light so shine before men that they may see your moral excellence *and* your praiseworthy, noble *and* good deeds, and recognize *and* honor *and* praise *and* glorify your Father Who is in heaven.

17 Do you think that I have come to do away with *or* undo the Law and the prophets; I have come not to do away with *or* undo but to complete *and* fulfill them.

18 For truly, I tell you, until the sky and earth pass away *and* perish not one smallest letter nor one little hook [identifying certain Hebrew letters] will pass from the Law until all things [it foreshadows] have been accomplished.

19 Whoever then breaks *or* does away with *or* relaxes one of the least important of these commandments and teaches men so, shall be called least important in the kingdom of

heaven; but he who practices them and teaches others to do so shall be called great in the kingdom of heaven.

20 For I tell you, unless your righteousness (your uprightness and your right standing with God) is more than that of the scribes and Pharisees, you will never enter the kingdom of heaven.

21 You have heard that it was said to the men of old, You shall not kill; and whoever kills shall be liable *so* that he cannot escape the punishment imposed by the court. [Exod. 20:13; Deut. 5:17; 16:18.]

22 But I say to you that every one who continues to be angry with his brother *or* harbors malice [enmity of heart] against him shall be liable to *and* unable to escape the punishment imposed by the court; and whoever speaks contemptuously *and* insultingly to his brother shall be liable to *and* unable to escape the punishment imposed by the Sanhedrin, and whoever says, You cursed fool!—You empty-headed idiot! shall be liable to *and* unable to escape the hell (Gehenna) of fire.

An analysis of the above examples indicates that some amplifications are unnecessary such as the words in brackets in Psalm 23. They have not added anything; the meaning is clear without them. Throughout the Bible there are many such examples. A few further examples from Matthew are: 1:11, removal (deportation); 1:17, Exile (deportation); 2:6, Ruler (Leader); 4:23, good news (Gospel); 7:17, healthy (sound); 7:23, openly (publicly); 10:8, freely (without pay); freely (without charge). See also Mark 1:3: "A voice of one crying in the wilderness—shouting in the desert—Prepare the way of the Lord, make His beaten-tracks straight (level and passable)!"

At times there are unjustifiable amplifications that are not derived from the Greek text, such as in Matthew 2:13: "Get up! [Tenderly] take ... the young Child" and 7:7, "keep on knocking [reverently]." Not only are such explanations not derived from the Greek text but they are clearly unnecessary. The Greek text does not need them; neither does the English text. For another striking example of a translation that gives a meaning not found in the Greek, see Mark 8:35: "For whoever wants to save his [higher, spiritual, eternal] life, will lose [the lower, natural, temporal which is lived (only) in earth]; and whoever gives up his life [which is lived (only) on earth], for My sake and the Gospel's, will save [his higher, spiritual life in the eternal kingdom of God]."

There are also additions that are completely redundant since in those instances the one English word is sufficient, as in Matthew 6:19, "gather *and* heap up *and* store"; Matthew 10:37, "loves *and* takes more pleasure"; and Mark 2:19, "Can the wedding guests fast (abstain from food and drink)...?"

When a repeated word is given the same or similar amplification, the style becomes very tedious. Such is the case in Matthew 5:3-11 with the beatitudes. Notice the monotonous repetition: "Blessed—happy, to be envied and spiritually prosperous [that is, with life-joy and satisfaction in God's favor and salvation, regardless of their outward conditions].... Blessed *and* enviably happy, [with a happiness produced by experience of God's favor and especially conditioned by the revelation of His matchless grace].... Blessed—happy, blithesome, joyous, spiritually prosperous [that is, with life-joy and satisfaction in God's favor and salvation, regardless of their outward conditions].... Blessed *and* fortunate *and* happy *and* spiritually prosperous [that is, in that state in which the born-again child of God enjoys His favor and salvation].... Blessed—happy, to be envied, and spiritually prosperous [that is, with life-joy and satisfaction in God's favor and salvation, regardless of their outward conditions].... Blessed—happy, enviably fortunate, and spiritually prosperous [that is, possessing the happiness produced by experience of God's favor and especially conditioned by the revelation of His grace, regardless of their outward conditions]. ... Blessed—enjoying enviable happiness, spiritually prosperous [that is, with life-joy and satisfaction in God's favor and salvation, regardless of their outward conditions].... Blessed *and* happy *and* enviably fortunate and spiritually prosperous [that is, in the state in which one enjoys and finds satisfaction in God's favor and salvation, regardless of his outward conditions]. ... Blessed—happy, to be envied, and spiritually prosperous [that is, with life-joy and satisfaction in God's favor and salvation, regardless of your outward conditions]...." Thus it goes unremittingly from the first "Blessed" to the last. And it may be seriously questioned whether the simple Greek word *makarios* means all this. Another similar repetition within one verse is found in Matthew 12:33: "Either make the tree sound (healthy and good), and its fruit sound (healthy and good), or make the tree rotten (diseased and bad) and its fruit rotten (diseased and bad); for the tree is known and recognized and judged by its fruit." In Genesis 1 the word "good" is amplified seven times with a combination of "suitable," "pleasing," "admirable," "fitting," or "pleasant."

On the other hand, there are some noticeable lacks in amplification. The word "daily" in Matthew 6:11 and "Cananaean" in 10:4 could have been given some explanation. This is the only translation that has "I AM" instead of "I am he" in Matthew 14:27. It has surely gone too far here. It is not suitable to the context. The "piety" of the translators is seen also in capitalization of all pronouns or nouns referring to Jesus even in those instances where such an intention is not present (see for example Matthew 12:24): "But the Pharisees hearing it said, This Man drives out demons only by *and* with the help of Beelzebub, the prince of demons." The footnote gives this explanation: "Capitalized because of what He is, the spotless Son of God, not what the speakers may have thought He was." (See John 5:11f. for another example.) This method is at best confusing.

The translation is in reality a mini-commentary. Some would laud this; others will be critical of it. A person's translation theory will determine how he will react. Inevitably, however, interpretive elements will be included in such a translation. While clarity of meaning is the goal of this type of translation, one wonders if it sacrifices too much in literary beauty and objective accuracy. In her introduction to the NT, Frances Siewert wrote, "One does not expect literary beauty and finesse in a work which must give the plain, unchanged words of various authorities without embellishment." Perhaps this version has its place in individual study but those who do not know the original languages should check it with other translations and a good commentary. Otherwise their choice of a rendering is purely subjective.

In the NT, according to the preface, "the Greek text of Westcott and Hort was pursued with meticulous care." If "pursued" means "followed," the assertion is highly misleading, for their are numerous departures from the text of Westcott and Hort in the direction of the traditional text. These departures are printed in italics, to indicate that these words are "not adequately supported by the original manuscripts." The inclusion of such readings is no doubt due to the piety of the translators and their concern for the readers who have become accustomed to them. These include Matthew 6:13; 17:21; 18:11; 21:44; Luke 4:18, et al. Mark 16:9-20 is included as part of the regular text with no differentiation. Other endings of Mark are not indicated. A short note is found in the footnotes, stating: "Verses 9 to 20 not in the two earliest manuscripts." For a modern Bible this is hardly acceptable. At John 5:3, 4 we find a strange thing. The last part of vs. 3 is included in italics but vs. 4 is omitted altogether, yet these two parts generally go together in the MSS. John 7:53-8:11 is found in the traditional position without any differentiation. The note does not indicate that it is found in different places in the MSS; it only indicates that it "is not found in the older manuscripts, but it sounds so like Christ that we accept it as authentic, and feel that to omit it would be most unfortunate." Even 1 John 5:7, 8 is included in the text with italics. It is strange, however, to find that Revelation 22:14 has "who cleanse their garments" instead of the KJV reading "that do his commandments." For other examples of departure from the Westcott and Hort text, see Matthew 6:4, 6, 8; Colossians 1:14; Acts 8:37; 9:5f.

The OT, according to the introduction, "is based primarily on the accepted Hebrew text." The traditional Hebrew text, however, is sometimes modified by additions and changes derived from the Septuagint and other ancient versions or the Qumran scrolls (see Gen. 4:8; 44:4; Ps. 37:23, 24; Prov. 7:22; 10:10; 11:16; 18:9, 19, et al.). The most striking example in the 1962 edition is the insertion in italics of a substantial passage from the Septuagint between Job 2:9 and 10.

The AB purports to be "free from private interpretation" and "independent of denominational prejudice." But there are, nevertheless, passages that appear to reflect a theological bias. Isaiah 7:14 reads, "Therefore the Lord Himself shall give you a sign, Behold, the young woman *who* is unmarried *and* a virgin shall conceive and bear a Son, and shall call his name Immanuel —God with us." Note also 1 Peter 3:19, 20: "In which He went and preached to the spirits in prison, [the souls of those] who long before in the days of Noah had been disobedient...."

Another example is Matthew 16:18: "And I tell you, you are Peter [Petros, masculine, a large piece of rock], and on this rock [petra, feminine, a huge rock like Gibraltar] I will build My church, and the gates of Hades (the powers of the infernal region) shall not overpower it—or be strong to its detriment, or hold out against it." Unfortunately, in spite of brackets, parentheses, or other signs, most readers will consider that what is in the text, including the explanations or interpretations, is part of Scripture.

The Greek word *thumiaterion* in Hebrews 9:4 is wrongly translated "altar of incense," since the note seems to be referring to the golden censer when it refers to the fact that it was not permanently kept in the Holy of Holies, but taken in on the Day of Atonement.

In checking 1 Corinthians 1:1-9 closely with the Greek we find the following amplifications:

1:1 will *and* purpose
     apostle (special messenger)
1:2 church (assembly)
     consecrated *and* purified *and* made holy
     [who are] selected *and* called
     saints (God's people)
     "any place" instead of "every place"
     call upon *and* give honor
1:3 Grace (favor and spiritual blessing)
     (heart) peace
1:4 grace (the favor and spiritual blessing)
1:5 [So]
     in full power *and* readiness of speech (to speak of your faith)
     complete knowledge *and* illumination (to give your full insight into its meaning)
1:6 [our]
     confirmed *and* established *and* made sure
1:7 not (consciously) falling behind *or* lacking
     spiritual endowment *or* Christian grace (the reception of which is due to the power of divine grace operating in your souls by the Holy Spirit)
     wait *and* watch (constantly living in hope)
     coming ... *and* [His] being made visible to all
1:8 establish ... —keep you steadfast, give you strength, and guarantee your vindication, that is, be your warrant

against all accusation or indictment—[so that you will be]

1:9 faithful—reliable, trustworthy and [therefore] ever true to His promise, and He can be depended on companionship *and* participation

The translation apart from the amplification has no great merit. It is characterized by "a determined effort to keep, as far as possible, the familiar wording of the earlier versions." The value is supposed to reside in the amplification. However, as we study the amplification, the great majority of the additions do not really add much. At times, as we have seen, they constitute a private interpretation. It would be much better to take a faithful translation such as the *American Standard Version* and use a good commentary as needed. It is contended that a particular Greek word cannot be translated by one English word. There is no doubt that this is true at times. However, the English words that are used to translate have overtones and if we were to carry out this purpose consistently, we would have to use several English words to explain and make precise the preceding English word, *ad infinitum*. Thus, although a single English word seldom says all that the author intended, a multiplication of words says more than he wished to convey (e.g., see 1 Cor. 10:13). The criticism directed toward Barclay's NT is more applicable here: There is all too much danger of the ordinary man assuming that the interpretations and amplifications are part of God's revelation. Scripture is quite capable of being understood, and the Holy Spirit is still present.

9

The Jerusalem Bible

The Jerusalem Bible (JB) has the distinction of being the first complete Catholic Bible to be translated into English from the original languages (1966). The Confraternity OT (now part of the complete Bible in the NAB), Spencer's NT, and other portions of the Bible had already been translated from the original before this time. Since the JB was published, the NAB has also been translated completely from the original languages. Previously all Catholic Bibles were translated from the Latin Vulgate, which was a translation itself. Such an excellent version as that of Monsignor Knox was perceptibly affected by this limitation.

One needs to keep in mind the double objective of the translators of the JB. It aims to bring the Bible into contemporary language and to deepen one's understanding of it with explanatory notes. The notes are a substantial part of this translation and serve a very important function. Unfortunately, the small print will discourage a full use of them. In an earlier day, much objection would have been raised against notes being placed in the Bible because they were usually so decidedly sectarian and even inflammatory, especially in the sixteenth and seventeenth centuries. However, helpful notes that lead to a better understanding of Scripture will be welcomed. As a whole, the notes in JB are of this sort.

The notes are a translation from the one-volume French edition of *La Bible de Jerusalem,* published by the scholars of the Dominican Biblical School of Jerusalem. The first edition of this came out in 1956. The biblical text, however, is based on the original, although checked closely with the French where questions of interpretation and text arose. The translators worked under the general editorship of Fr. Alexander Jones of Christ's College, Liverpool.

Because it has such a substantial amount of notes, this Bible is a hefty one with 2,062 pages and weighing just under five pounds. A smaller abbreviated paperback edition is now available. The price for the large edition, $16.95, will limit its purchase to a few. Besides the notes for the text itself, there are introductory notes for sections of the Bible, such as the Pentateuch, and for certain individual books. At the end there are helpful supplements, including a chronological table, a genealogical table of the Hasmonean and Herodian dynasties, an explanation of the biblical calendar, a table of weights and measures, an index of biblical themes in the notes, and maps of different periods and subjects. Cross references for texts are provided in the outside margin. Headings introduce portions of Scripture. The text itself is printed in one column, with the verse numerals in the inside margins.

In general, JB is considerably freer than the RSV but not as free as *Phillips*. It has more of the Bible in poetic form than any previous Bible, especially in the Gospel of John. Personal names are in the form found in the RSV. This removes the strangeness that the Protestant reader formerly found in reading Catholic Bibles.

This is a Catholic Bible, therefore what the Catholic calls the deutero-canonical books and the Protestant the Apocrypha are included. They are not segregated but are scattered throughout—the historical, wisdom, and prophetic books in their appropriate sections. Moreover, the additions to Esther are scattered throughout the book but are distinguished from the rest of the text by being printed in italics. In Daniel Susanna is chapter 13 and Bel and the Dragon is chapter 14. These are not in italics.

The archaic forms of the second person singular are completely eliminated even in prayer. The name of God is given as *Yahweh* as in the original. The ASV had used "Jehovah" but both the RSV and the NEB went back to the KJV practice of using LORD or GOD, the former when the word *Yahweh* stood alone or with the word for God, *Elohim*, and the latter when it stood with the Hebrew word for Lord, *Adonai*. Yah-

weh is the correct form of the name, but Christians no doubt will have difficulty getting accustomed to saying: "Yahweh is my shepherd, I lack nothing."

To get the flavor of the JB we will compare a section from the Gospels and the Epistles from the RSV, JB, and Phillips:

> Matt. 6:1-4
>
> Beware of practicing your piety before men in order to be seen by them; for then you will have no reward from your Father who is in heaven.
>
> Thus, when you give alms, sound no trumpet before you, as the hypocrites do in the synagogues and in the streets, that they may be praised by men. Truly, I say to you, they have their reward. (RSV)
>
> Be careful not to parade your good deeds before men to attract their notice; by doing this you will lose all reward from your Father in heaven. So when you give alms, do not have it trumpeted before you; this is what the hypocrites do in the synagogues and in the streets to win men's admiration. I tell you solemnly, they have had their reward. But when you give alms, your left hand must not know what your right is doing; your almsgiving must be secret, and your Father who sees all that is done in secret will reward you. (JB)
>
> Beware of doing your good deeds conspicuously to catch men's eyes or you will miss the reward of your Heavenly Father.
>
> So, when you do good to other people, don't hire a trumpeter to go in front of you—like those play actors in the synagogues and streets who make sure that men admire them. Believe me, they have had all the reward they are going to get! No, when you give to charity, don't even let your left hand know what your right hand is doing, so that your giving may be secret. Your Father who knows all secrets will reward you. (Phillips, 1st ed.)
>
> Rom. 12:1, 3
>
> I appeal to you therefore, brethren, by the mercies of God, to present your bodies as a living sacrifice, holy and acceptable to God, which is your spiritual worship. Do not be conformed to this world but be transformed by the renewal of your mind, that you may prove what is the will of God, what is good and acceptable and perfect. (RSV)
>
> Think of God's mercy, my brothers, and worship him, I beg you, in a way that is worthy of thinking beings, by offering your living bodies as a holy sacrifice, truly pleasing to God. Do not model yourselves on the behavior of the world around

you, but let your behaviour change, modelled by your new mind. This is the only way to discover the will of God and know what is good, what it is that God wants, what is the perfect thing to do. (JB)

With eyes wide open to the mercies of God, I beg you, my brothers, as an act of intelligent worship, to give him your bodies, as a living sacrifice, consecrated to him and acceptable by him. Don't let the world around you squeeze you into its own mold, but let God remold your minds from within, so that you may prove in practice that the plan of God for you is good, meets all his demands and moves toward the goal of true maturity. (Phillips, 1st ed.)

Although it is a problem to translate weight, measure, money, and time expressions into modern equivalents, it is preferable to do this so that the reader may better understand the context. It may not be important to know the amount of money involved in the parable of the talents, but it is crucial in the parable of the unmerciful servant (Matt. 18:23-35). JB has translated or transliterated the expressions but not with their modern equivalents. Thus talents, pounds, denarius, cubit, hour, etc., are kept in the translation. To compensate for this, however, JB makes these explanations in its notes. Hopefully, people will go to the trouble of reading them.

The translation of the NT especially seems much freer than it needs to be. Many times this freedom does not enhance the meaning of the text, but more often it leads to a slight change in the meaning. Sometimes words are omitted or added unnecessarily. The following examples will illustrate what we mean:

JB translates 1 Corinthians 7:1, 2 in this manner: "Now for the questions about which you wrote. Yes, it is a good thing for a man not to touch a woman; but since sex is always a danger, let each man have his own wife and each woman her own husband." The expression "since sex is always a danger" does not do justice to the Greek, which is best translated as by the NEB as "because there is so much immorality." The implication in the JB translation is that Paul is giving this counsel as something due to the normal dangers existing in society, whereas Paul is giving this counsel because of an extraordinary situation. Corinth was no ordinary city. Immorality was rampant and the church was being infected by its surroundings (note 1 Corinthians 5 and 6:12-20). JB translates Matthew 6:2 in the following way: "So when you give alms, do not have it trumpeted before you." The Greek only says, "Do not sound the trumpet before you." JB follows Phillips in reading more into the text than it actually says. Phillips expresses it more directly: "Don't hire a trumpeter to go in front of you." In 1 Corinthians 12:13 the words "into one body" have been inexplicably omitted. "Will" is omitted and "send greetings" is added unnecessarily in 1 Corinthians 1:1. In 1 Corinthians 1:4 "grace" has become "graces" and "of God" has been omitted after it. In the next verse "in him" has been omitted. These examples are sufficient to indicate the inaccuracy of a translation that is meant for serious study of the Word as the notes attest.

The text of JB is interesting to study because of its tendency to include what Protestants exclude. Take, for instance, Mark 16:9-20. Modern Protestant Bibles do not include this passage in the text, or at least not in the same type as the text. JB includes this portion with no differentiation. In the note, explanation is given for this: It is "included in the canonically accepted body of inspired scripture." The note goes on to explain that "this does not necessarily imply Marcan authorship which, indeed, is open to question." It further explains the different endings that various MSS give to Mark. Several questions come to mind regarding the principle of accepting later additions as being also canonical. When was the Scripture canonically accepted? What MS or MSS were canonically accepted? If this principle is followed, it would seem that most of the late readings would be accepted into the text and the early readings rejected. But there is no consistency in the application of the principle. Such poorly accepted readings as those found in Luke 24:6, 12, 36, 40, 51; John 1:13; 5:3, 4; Hebrews 9:11, are included. A note added to John 5:3, 4 indicates that the best witnesses omit this reading. John 7:53-8:11 is not only included, it is also found at this place in the text, even though the note states that the author of this passage is not John. And, on the other hand, certain readings that one would expect to be included on the same basis are omitted, such as Matthew 6:13; 18:11; 12:47; Luke 9:56; Acts 8:37, to name only a few. The tendency is definitely on the side of including more questionable readings than either the RSV or the NEB. In Acts JB has selected some interesting Western readings that few other English translations have accepted. These are: "Hades" instead of "death" in 2:24; the addition of "and by no other" in 4:10; "three days afterwards" instead of "on the third day" in 10:40; "in the first psalm" instead of "in the second psalm" in 13:33; and "seek the deity" instead of "seek God" in 17:27.

Both NEB and Phillips translate Matthew 16:18, "You are Peter the rock," but JB translates it straightforwardly, "You are Peter," although the note brings out the above interpretation. Following NEB, JB translates John 1:3, 4: "All that came to be had life in him," connecting the last part of vs. 3 with vs. 4. This is allowable on the basis of the Greek text. Another ambiguous text is Romans 9:5. It can be translated as the RSV and NEB have done it, "To them ... according to the flesh, is the Christ. God who is over all be blessed for ever." JB has instead: "Christ who is above all, God for ever blessed!" JB equates Christ with God, whereas the former translations make a distinction. On 1 Corinthians 7:36 JB follows the traditional father-daughter view. 1 Timothy 3:2 is translated, "He must not have been married more than once."

We have already mentioned the notes in this Bible. They are a significant part of the translation. As a whole, they are judicious and helpful. The reader will gain much and will profit in his understanding of the Bible through a reading of the notes. In the past, notes in Catholic Bibles were objectionable to Protestants. No one can say that about the notes in this Bible, though some of the notes have a distinctly Catholic flavor to them. For example, the note on Matthew 1:25 states, "The text is not concerned with the period that followed and, taken by itself, does not assert Mary's perpetual virginity which, however, the gospels elsewhere suppose and which the Tradition of the Church affirms." Compare this with the note in the Douai-Rheims version: *"Till she brought forth her firstborn son.* From these words Helvidius and other heretics most impiously inferred that the blessed Virgin Mary had other children besides Christ: but St. Jerome shews, by divers examples, that this expression of the Evangelist was a manner of speaking usual among the Hebrews, to denote the word *until,* only what is done, without regard to the future." On Matthew 12:46, where Jesus' brothers are mentioned, the note reads, "Not Mary's children but near relations, cousins perhaps, which both Hebr. and Aramaic style 'brothers.'"

First Corinthians 3:15 has been used by Catholics to support the doctrine of purgatory. The note reads, "This is not a direct reference to purgatory but several Doctors of the Church have taken it as a basis for that doctrine." RSV, NEB, and Phillips all have "wife" or "Christian wife" in 1 Corinthians 9:5, but JB translates, "Christian woman." The note on this verse says, "Lit. 'a sister, a woman (wife?).'" The question at issue here is whether the apostles were married or not. Catholics who believe in clerical celibacy naturally presuppose the apostles to have been unmarried.

The note for Genesis 3:15, after explaining the version with reference to the Messiah, reads, "The Latin version has a feminine pronoun ('she' will crush . . .) and since, in the messianic interpretation of our text, the Messiah and his mother appear together, the pronoun has been taken to refer to Mary; this application has become current in the Church." Another passage applied to Mary is Revelation 12:1. Here the note reads, "It does not seem probable that John had Mary in mind or intended any allusion to the physical birth of the Messiah in the incarnation." However, it is instructive to see that these notes are generally nondogmatic, especially when they are compared with notes in earlier Bibles.

A very explicit note is found on Matthew 16:19: "Catholic exegetes maintain that these enduring promises hold good not only for Peter himself but also for Peter's successors. This inference, not explicitly drawn in the text, is considered legitimate because Jesus plainly intends to provide for his Church's future by establishing a regime that will not collapse with Peter's death. Two other texts, Luke 22:31f. and John 21:15f., on Peter's primacy emphasise that its operation is to be in the domain of faith; they also indicate that this makes him head not only of the Church after the death of Christ but of the apostolic group then and there." Other Catholic notes are found in Matthew 5:3; 6:11; 16:18. The note appended to Matthew 19:11, 12 reads, "Christ invites to perpetual continence those who would consecrate themselves entirely to the kingdom of God."

A very definite asset, at least from the Protestant reader's point of view, is that the names of biblical characters are given in the form found in Protestant Bibles, such as the RSV and NEB. However, there is one word representing Catholic terminology that a Protestant will have to translate, the word "holocaust" for "burnt offering."

The translation is not homogeneous throughout. The translation of Matthew does not seem as free as that of Mark. In fact, the translation seems to become freer as it goes along, being freest in the Epistles. The same is true in the OT. Genesis does not seem as free as Exodus. On the whole, the translation is good, though not distinctive. There are not many striking translations. There are still some awkward spots and some bad translations in what we judge to be a generally good translation.

The feature that makes this translation valuable is the copious informative and instructive notes.

10

Barclay's New Testament

William Barclay, long known for his popularization of scholarly research in readable prose, has now produced a two-volume translation of the NT for the average reader. One of the aims listed in the foreword "was to try to make the New Testament intelligible to the man who is not a technical scholar" (I, 5). The first volume, containing the Gospels and Acts, appeared in 1968. The second, including the rest of the NT, was released in 1969. Both were published by Collins.

A short introduction precedes each book or groups of books (such as 1 and 2 Thessalonians). The arrangement of the books in each section of the NT is in chronological sequence. Thus the order for the first section is Mark, Matthew, Luke, Acts, John. The first Epistle of Paul is Galatians, followed by 1 Thessalonians, etc.

There are few notes. When they do appear, they are usually textual-critical notes indicating a different reading in some MSS for the verse indicated. There are no headings or titles. There is a short foreword in both volumes, a chapter entitled "On Translating the New Testament" at the end of Volume I, and at the end of Volume II two appendices. The first of these in sixty-two pages treats various NT words in alphabetical sequence. These words are taken from the KJV and are followed by the Greek original. Each is explained by the author. The second appendix, "Notes on Passages," lists those passages the translator has expanded in the text and gives an explanation of their meaning. Throughout, the pronoun "you" is used for the second person singular.

In the foreword Barclay gives as his second aim "to make

a translation which did not need a commentary to explain it" (I, 5). As he admits, this is an impossibility. But in trying to do this he has at times moved away from a legitimate translation to a paraphrase or commentary. Barclay will accept this criticism, for he contends that translation is to some extent interpretation and that "the aim of the translator must be to produce a translation which can stand by itself, and which needs no commentary to make it intelligible" (I, 317). He also maintains that translation "will necessarily involve what is known as paraphrase" (I, 317). We can expect, then, a bit of freedom in this translation. How we judge it will depend on where we stand on the spectrum of translation theory.

Barclay illustrates his method by his translation of certain words. The word "adulterous" in "an evil and adulterous generation" (Matt. 16:4) was translated "apostate generation," since the meaning is not that it is a generation characterized by sexual sin but one that has fallen away from God. "Can ye be baptized with the baptism that I am baptized with?" (Mark 10:38) is modified into "Can you be submerged in the sea of troubles in which I must be submerged?" The word "cup" in "Are ye able to drink of the cup that I shall drink of . . . ?" (Matt. 20:22) is translated, "Can you pass through the bitter experience through which I must pass?"

Illustrations of Barclay's use of expansion are found in Matthew 9:17 and 11:7 (the italicized words indicate the expanded portions): "No more do people pour new *fermenting* wine into old wineskins *that have lost* their elasticity"; and " 'What did you go out to the desert to see?' he said, '*Was it to see what you can see any day there*—the long grass swaying in the wind?' "

There are two expressions in the Greek that Barclay feels may be omitted in the translation without any loss of meaning. One of these is the word or words usually translated "lo" or "behold." The other is the phrase "it came to pass."

Barclay feels also that manners and customs have to be taken into consideration in translation. The translation should explain the custom or at least make clear its meaning. E.g., Barclay says that Matthew 3:12 in the KJV—"Whose fan is in his hand, and he will thoroughly purge his floor. . ."—is not intelligible to Westerners. Thus, he translates it, "He is going to winnow the chaff from the corn, and he will clear every speck of rubbish from his threshing-floor." The "fan" was a broad-bladed tool that was used to toss the grain into the air; the chaff was blown away by the wind and the heavy grain fell to the floor. Barclay simply translates, "He is going to winnow the chaff from the corn." The American needs to translate "corn" into "grain."

Another example of expansion to explain the local custom is found in Matthew 10:14: "And whosoever shall not receive you, nor hear your words, when ye depart out of that house or city, shake off the dust of your feet," which Barclay translates, "If anyone refuses you a welcome or a hearing, as you leave that house or town, shake the last speck of its dust from your feet, as if you were leaving a heathen town." According to Barclay, it was a custom that whenever a Jew left a Gentile city, he would shake the dust off his feet to remove the pollution of that city. Mark 7:11 reads, "It is Corban, that is to say, a gift, by whatsoever thou mightest be profited by me." Barclay translates it like this: " 'This money that I might have contributed to your support is Korban' (that is, a gift dedicated to the service of God and usable for no other purpose)." The explanation is included in the translation.

Barclay has also reshaped certain Greek sentences to put them into idiomatic English. This includes the use of subordination where Greek does not use it, and vice versa; changing the imperative, which is used more freely in Greek, to a form with "must"; changing the vocatives, which are hardly ever used in English, into another form; changing clauses that begin with "he that," "whoever," "everyone," etc., to an infinitive clause; and the inversion of certain Greek sentences when translated into English.

The Greek text from which Barclay translates is that of the United Bible Societies (UBS). However, he has deviated from that text in some instances. In Matthew 27:16, 17 the prisoner is called Jesus Barabbas, but in the UBS text "Barabbas" is enclosed in single brackets, indicating that it is of dubious textual validity. Barclay has given no indication of this but includes it as though it were part of the original text. The passage concerning the adulterous woman, John 7:53-8:11, is included at the end of the Gospel of John in the UBS text, but Barclay has placed it in the traditional position in the same size type as the rest of the text. He distinguishes it from the preceding and following texts by indentation and a note indicating that the best and most ancient MSS do not contain the story.

It is interesting to check a few ambiguous passages to see which meanings Barclay selects. In Matthew 16:18 he clearly makes Peter the rock on which the church is built, as in NEB: "I tell you, you are Peter—the man whose name means a rock —and on this rock I will erect my Church. . . ." In Mark 15:39 the Roman centurion ("company commander" according to Barclay) confesses, "This man was indeed a son of God!" contrary to RSV (2nd edition) and AV but in agreement with Phillips and NEB. In John 1:4 he connects part of vs. 3 with vs. 4 to read, "As for the whole creation, the Word was the life principle in it. . . ," as in NEB. In Romans 9:5 he agrees with NEB and RSV in opposition to Phillips and KJV in not explicitly identifying Christ with God: "Theirs are the fathers, and in human descent it is from them that the Messiah comes. God who is over all be blessed for ever and ever! Amen." In 2 Timothy 3:16 he agrees with the NEB and KJV, RSV, and Phillips in reading, "Every divinely inspired scripture is . . ." instead of "All Scripture is inspired of God."

Something of the freedom in Barclay's translation may be seen as it is compared carefully with the original in 1 Corinthians 1:1-10. The left column gives the original in translation and the right Barclay's translation.

1:1	Paul	This is a letter from Paul
	the brother	our colleague
1:2	church	congregation
	sanctified in Christ Jesus	those whose union with Christ has consecrated their lives to God
	called *to be* saints	those whom God has called to be his own
1:3	peace	every blessing
1:4	for the grace	I thank him for his grace
	in him	through your union with him
	with all speech and all knowledge	with the result that you are equipped with every kind of knowledge and with complete ability to communicate
1:6	as the testimony of Christ	You are in fact the proof that

	Barclay	RSV
	was confirmed among you	what Christ promised has happened
1:7	the revelation of our Lord Jesus Christ	the time when our Lord Jesus Christ will again burst upon the stage of history
1:8	in the day of our Lord Jesus Christ	on the day when our Lord Jesus comes
	blameless	no one will be able to level any charge against you
1:9	God is faithful	You can rely on God
	Fellowship of his son	share the life of his Son

Some interesting translations of Barclay from Matthew follow, compared with RSV:

	Barclay	RSV

Barclay — **RSV**

3:15
'For the present,' Jesus answered 'let it be so, for the right thing for us to do is to do everything a good man ought to do!'

But Jesus answered him, "Let it be so now; for thus it is fitting for us to fulfil all righteousness."

3:17
This is my Son, the Beloved and Only One.

This is my beloved Son.

4:17
Kingdom of Heaven is almost here

kingdom of heaven is at hand

5:16
lovely things

good works

6:24
God of heaven and of the god of this world's wealth

God and mammon

6:33
Make the Kingdom of God, and life in loyalty to him, the object of all your endeavour

But seek first his kingdom and his righteousness

10:4
Simon, the Nationalist

Simon the Cananaean

12:42
there is a greater event than Solomon here

something greater than Solomon is here

16:1
some visible divine action

a sign from heaven

19:8
if it had not been that your hearts are quite impervious to the real commandment of God

for your hardness of heart

21:33

a pit in which the juice could be extracted from the grapes	a winepress

22:18

Jesus was well aware of their malicious motives. 'You are not out for information,' he said to them, 'you are out to make trouble in your two-faced maliciousness. . . .'	But Jesus, aware of their malice, said "Why put me to the test, you hypocrites?"

26:28

This means my lifeblood, through which the new relationship between man and God is made possible	for this is my blood of the covenant

26:41, 42

Sleeplessly watch and pray, for you may well all have to face your ordeal of temptation. I know that you mean well and that you want to do the right thing, but human nature is frail.' . . . 'if there is no escape from this situation unless I go through it to the bitter end . . .'	Watch and pray that you may not enter into temptation; the spirit indeed is willing but the flesh is weak.". . . . "if this cannot pass unless I drink it. . . ."

28:1

Late on the Sabbath	Now after the Sabbath

The following longer passages from the Gospels and one from the Epistles, give more of the flavor of this translation:

Matt. 23:5-15

'Their every action is designed for self-display. They wear outsize prayer-boxes, and exaggerate the size of the tassels of their robes. They like the top places at banquets and the front seats in the synagogues. They like to be deferentially greeted as they move through the market-places, and to be called Rabbi by ordinary people. You must not let anyone call you Rabbi. There is One who is your teacher, and you are all brothers. You must not call any man on earth father. There is One who is your Father, and he is in heaven. You must not let anyone call you leaders. There is One who is your leader, I mean the Messiah. Your top-ranking man must be your servant. If a man exalts himself, he will be humbled; and, if he humbles himself, he will be exalted.'

'Tragic will be the fate of you experts in the Law and you Pharisees with your façade of ostentatious piety! You shut the door of the Kingdom of Heaven in men's faces. You will not go in yourselves, and you will not allow those who are trying to get in to go in.

'Tragic will be the fate of you experts in the Law and you Pharisees with your façade of ostentatious piety! You roam sea and land
to make one convert, and, when he has become a convert, you make
him twice as much hell-begotten as yourselves.'

John 1:1-3
When the world began, the Word was already there. The Word was
with God, and the nature of the Word was the same as the nature
of God. The Word was there in the beginning with God. It was
through the agency of the Word that everything else came into
being. Without the Word not one single thing came into being.

Rom. 8:1-6
We can therefore say that there is now no condemnation for those
whose life is one with the life of Christ. For, when through union
with Christ Jesus I came under the law of the life-giving Spirit, I
was emancipated from the law of death-bringing sin. For what the
law was unable to do—that is to say, to effect this emancipation from
sin—because human nature rendered it impotent and ineffective, God
did. He did it by sending his own Son with a human nature like our
sinful nature. He sent him to deal with sin, and to deal with it as
a human person. He thus left sin without a case, and, because he
won the victory over sin, the legitimate demand of the law is satisfied in us too, in us whose lives too are no longer directed by our
lower nature, but by the Spirit. Those who have allowed their lower
nature to become the rule of their lives have an attitude to life which
is dominated by their lower nature; those who have taken the Spirit
as the rule of their lives have an attitude to life which is dominated
by the Spirit. To have a mind dominated by our lower human nature is to turn life into death; to have a mind dominated by the
Spirit is to have real life and every blessing.

Notable is the fact that Barclay has set more of the NT in
poetry than previous versions, especially in the Sermon on the
Mount (Matt. 5-7) and in the Book of Revelation. It is also
evident that he has sought to bring out the force of the Greek
tenses, especially in the imperative. Thus we have the following
constructions: Matthew 6:25, "Stop worrying"; Matthew 7:1,
"Don't make a habit of judging others"; and Matthew 7:7,
"Keep on asking."

Several criticisms have been made against this version. The
expensive and cumbersome format will militate against its sales.
Two separate volumes for the NT make it inconvenient to
carry. A. D. Harvey's observation is accurate when he says
that "the total impression is a perplexing mixture of the new
with the traditional, the technical with the non-technical....

The style, too, is a curious mixture. Sometimes it is frankly colloquial ('That's your look-out,' Matt. 27:4), sometimes strangely archaic ('When the devil had exercised his every tempting wile,' Luke 4:13; 'Share my vigil,' Matt. 26:38)" (*Theology* LXXII [1969], 368).

The most serious criticism against Barclay's translation is his interpretative comments added in the translation, which Harvey calls "this highly personal and sometimes even idiosyncratic translation" and which the editor of the *Churchman* calls "academic arrogance." Referring to the "Notes on Passages," the latter says:

> Here a number of brief passages are singled out for expansion and short comment. Dr. Barclay concedes that this strays over into interpretation, but thinks it has to be done for the nontechnical reader. No doubt the intention is good, but is there not an (unintentional, of course) academic arrogance about this? Have modern scholars ceased to believe in the perspicuity of Scripture, and is twentieth-century man so devoid of spiritual perception that he must now exchange reliance on an infallible teaching church for Scripture mediated by scholars? It is our conviction that a high doctrine of Scripture must mean that translation and interpretation are to be kept rigidly separate. There is all too much danger, as Charles Cranfield has recently pointed out in our columns, of the *ordinary* man whom Dr. Barclay seeks to help assuming that Dr. Barclay's interpretations are part of God's revelation. Scripture is quite capable of speaking for itself, and the Holy Spirit has not departed. It is probably a sign of the inadequacy of so much modern systematic theology (even in Reformed Scotland) that scholars imagine ordinary readers *must* have their aids. What such a situation reveals is the inadequate doctrine of Scripture and the Spirit held by those who so imagine. (*Churchman* LXXXIII [1969], 253, 54)

Interpretive translations are unavoidable to a certain extent. However, the danger of personal, subjective, and idiosyncratic translations arising in a one-man effort is so much greater than it is in a group translation where one is checked by others.

11
Today's English Version

On September 15, 1966, the American Bible Society published a new modern speech translation of the NT with the title, *Good News for Modern Man: The New Testament in Today's English Version* (TEV). The TEV soon outstripped in popularity even the NT of the NEB. A second edition was published on October 1, 1967, "incorporating," the translator tells us, "many changes both in style and substance, aimed at making the translation more faithful and accurate, more natural, and easier to understand." A third edition, embodying further improvement, was published in 1971. During the first six years of its existence some thirty-five million copies of the TEV have been sold world-wide. This phenomenal record may be due, in part, both to its reasonable price and its promotion by the Bible society. But it is obvious it has an inherent worth that has given it a wide appeal to English-speaking people everywhere.

The translation was prepared by Robert G. Bratcher, Research Associate of the Translations Department of the American Bible Society. He had previously produced a new translation of the Gospel of Mark, entitled "The Right Time," and was requested by the American Bible Society to translate the entire NT. The Bible societies customarily sponsor versions in the world's major languages to meet the needs of the people who have little formal education or who, regardless of education, are not familiar with the archaic language of the traditional church versions. Bratcher's basic text was submitted for suggestions and approval to translation consultants of the American Bible Society, and to the Translation Department of the British and Foreign Bible Society.

"The text from which this translation was made," according to the preface, "is the Greek New Testament prepared by an international committee of New Testament scholars, sponsored by several members of the United Bible Societies [UBS] and published in 1966" (p. iv). There are several respects, however, in which TEV fails to do justice to the critical judgment of the editors of the Bible societies' Greek New Testament (second edition) in the matter of text. For one thing, the UBS Greek text contains certain words and even whole verses (e.g., Matt. 16:2b, 3; Luke 23:34; 24:12, 40) enclosed in single brackets to indicate that they have "dubious textual validity." But when they are rendered into English, the TEV gives no indication of any doubt about their textual validity. Thus, in Matthew 27:16, 17 we get the reading "Jesus Barabbas," with no way of knowing that because of the comparatively meager external evidence, the editors of the Greek text had at least some doubt whether the double name was the true reading. Likewise, in Luke 10:1, 17 we get the reading "seventy-two," with no indication that the Greek editors had a certain doubt about the addition of "two."

More serious is the TEV's handling of passages with double brackets. Passages that were so marked by the editors of the Greek NT were "regarded as later additions to the text, but . . . are of evident antiquity and importance." These passages were translated into English by the TEV with no note in the first edition to indicate doubtful authenticity; however, they are enclosed in single brackets. A notable exception is the ending of Mark. The TEV includes the longer ending of Mark (Mark 16:9-20) in single brackets under the title "An Old Ending to the Gospel," as well as the shorter ending under the title "Another Old Ending," also in single brackets and numbered as verses 9 and 10.

But most serious of all is the introduction in single brackets of seventeen passages not found in the UBS Greek text, but cited as variants in the critical apparatus (see Matt. 17:21; 18:11; 23:14; Mark 7:16; 9:44, 46; 11:26; 15:28; Luke 17:36; 22:43-44; 23:17; John 5:3b-4; Acts 8:37; 15:34; 24:6b-8a; 28:29; Rom. 16:24). The brackets are used to indicate that these passages "are not in the oldest and best manuscripts of the New Testament" (p. iv). But if a translation is to include secondary material because of its age, one wonders why the doxology of the Lord's Prayer (after Matt. 6:13) was left out, and why these additional words to Luke 9:55 were omitted: "and he said 'You do not know what manner of spirit you are of; for the Son of man came not to destroy men's lives but to save them.' " There are other ancient "Western" additions that could have been included, especially in Acts, and the addition to Matthew 27:49, which has the support of several of the better uncials. It appears that only such additions as had found their way into the traditional Erasmus-Stephanus-Beza Greek text received consideration. The inclusion of these passages represents a retrogression in the direction of the Received Text. While there are textual critics who would argue for the genuineness of some of these additions, there is little that can be said for the inclusion of John 5:3b, 4. The superstitious belief expressed in this attempted explanation of the moving of the water (vs. 7) has little to commend it as a genuine part of the story of the healing of the lame man at the pool. To the credit of the translator of the TEV, the *Comma Johanneum* has not been interpolated as 1 John 5:7, 8. Antiquity cannot be claimed for this Trinitarian passage.

We can only mention other departures from the UBS Greek text. One concerns the position of the story of the woman taken in adultery, which the UBS text has in double brackets at the end of the Gospel of John, but which the TEV places in single brackets in its traditional place as John 7:53-8:11. In a number of passages the TEV follows different MS readings from those preferred by the editors of the UBS edition (see Mark 6:20, 22; Luke 21:19; Acts 7:46; 10:19; 12:25; Rom. 8:28; 1 Cor. 13:3; 2 Cor. 8:7; Heb. 4:2; 2 Peter 3:2; Jude 5; Rev. 21:3). Three of these are worthy of note. The TEV follows those MSS that insert "God" as the subject of the first clause in Romans 8:28 and translates, "We know that in all things God works for good with those who love him, those whom he has called according to his purpose." In 1 Corinthians 13:3 the TEV has reverted to the more traditional reading "to be burned," rather than accepting the UBS reading "that I may boast." In 2 Peter 3:10 the TEV translates a difficult reading as "On that Day the heavens will disappear with a shrill noise...." At the back of the NT volume there is included a list of "Other Readings and Renderings" for the general reader.

The TEV is based on a concept of translation known as "dynamic equivalence." Eugene Nida of the American Bible Society describes it thus: "To translate is to try to stimulate in the new reader in the new language the same reaction to the text the original author wished to stimulate in his first and immediate readers." This is, to be sure, an unattainable goal that can be only approximately achieved. But in striving toward it, the translator is less concerned with a literal word-by-word rendering and more concerned with the meaning of the original and the way that meaning can best be stated in natural English. "This means," Bratcher says, "that no attempt is made to translate a given Greek word by the same word in English, but always to use the English word or expression that most faithfully and naturally represents this meaning of the Greek word in the context in which it is used." The translator is primarily concerned with faithfulness to the message of the original. Having determined what that message is, he asks himself, "How would the author have said this if he were writing in English?" This principle has been used not only in the TEV, but also in the NEB and other recent translations.

But one of the hallmarks of the TEV is its use of common language English. By this is meant that part of the English language understood by people from all walks of life and all levels of education who read and write English. Although no arbitrary limit is set on the vocabulary, a studious effort is made to keep the language simple and direct. The Bible must be made understandable not only to Christians with little formal education, but also to non-Christians who are unfamiliar with technical religious vocabulary. Not only must the language of the elite be avoided, but also slang. Regional and provincial expressions, as well as idioms, are kept to a minimum.

To make it more intelligible to the common man, expressions are modernized wherever practicable. "Caesar" becomes "Emperor" or "Roman Emperor" (Luke 2:1; 3:1; 20:22ff.; Acts 25:10f.; 26:32, et al.). "Centurion" is given as "army officer" (Matt. 27:54 et al.), "Roman officer" (Matt. 8:5), "captain in the Roman army" (Acts 10:1), "officer in the Roman army" (Acts 27:1), or simply "commander" (Acts 23:17, 23), or "officer" (Acts 22:25, 26). "Publicans" are "tax collectors" (Matt. 5:46 et al.), not a flattering comparison for modern collectors of internal revenue. The "captain of the temple" is the "officer in charge of the temple guards" (Acts 4:1; 5:24, 26). The "Sanhedrin" is the "Council" (Matt. 26:59; John 11:47), defined in the "Word List" in the back of the NT as "the supreme religious court of the Jews," but the authority of that body went beyond religious matters, and included legislative as well as judicial powers.

The modern equivalents are given for expressions of time (Matt. 14:25; 20:3, 5, 9; 27:46; John 1:39; 4:52), distances (John 21:8; Rev. 21:17; Acts 1:12; 27:28), capacity (Matt. 13:33; Luke 16:6, 7; John 2:6; Rev. 6:6), and money. Monetary equivalents are especially difficult and often only a rough approximation is attempted as in the parable of the unforgiving servant who owed "millions of dollars" but would not be patient with a fellow who owed him "a few dollars" (Matt. 18:24, 28). In what is usually designated the Parable of the Talents, "one servant received $5000, another $2000, and another $1000" (Matt. 25:15).

Wherever practicable, the TEV avoids the use of the technical religious terms of the standard versions, "Antichrist," for example, is given as the "enemy of Christ" (1 John 2:18, 22); "bishops" are "church leaders" (Phil. 1:1; 1 Tim. 3:2; Titus 1:7); "deacons" are "church helpers" (Phil. 1:1; 1 Tim. 3:8, 12); "raca" is translated as "you good-for-nothing" (Matt. 5:22) and "mammon" as "money" (Matt. 6:24). Where such modernizations did not seem feasible, the old terms are retained and briefly explained in the word list at the back of the NT. This word list explains the proper names of places and persons, but it also includes in its 171 items such terms as altar, amen, apostle, blasphemy, demon, dill, elders, hyssop, myrrh, nard, parable, prophet, Sabbath, Scriptures, vow, winnowing shovel, etc.

The translator has also sought to clothe the great gospel ideas of the NT in words the common man, unused to theological language, can understand and appreciate. Thus, "repent" of the standard versions usually becomes "turn away from your sins" (e.g., Matt. 3:2; 4:17; Mark 1:15; Acts 2:38, et al.), though "repent" is retained in a number of passages (e.g., Luke 15:7, 10; Acts 3:19; Rev. 2:22, et al.). The noun "repentance" is similarly treated. To the Pharisees and Sadducees who came to be baptized, John said, "Do the things that will show that you have turned away from your sins" (Matt. 3:8). The Lord "does not want anyone to be destroyed, but wants all to turn away from their sins" (2 Peter 3:9). The great Pauline word "justify" is usually translated as "put right with God" (Rom. 2:13; 3:20, 24, 26; 5:1, 9; Gal. 2:16, et al.). The "foreknew," "predestined," "called," "justified," and "glorified" of Romans 8:29, 30 became respectively "already chosen," "set apart," "called," "put right with himself," and "shared his glory." The gospel truth contained in the words "reconcile" and "reconciliation" is beautifully expressed by the metaphor of "changing us from God's enemies into his friends" (2 Cor. 5:18-20). "We were God's enemies, but he made us his friends through the death of his Son" (Rom. 5:10f.). For "adoption" it reads "made God's sons" (Rom. 8:15, 23; 9:4; cf. Eph. 1:5). "It is through Christ that all of us, Jews and Gentiles, are able to come in the one Spirit into the presence of the Father" (Eph. 2:18). "Advocate" is given as the One "who pleads for us" (1 John 2:1), and "propitiation" is given as "the means by which our sins are forgiven" (1 John 2:2; cf. Rom. 3:25).

Usually the noun "resurrection" is rendered "rise from death" (Matt. 22:23; Mark 12:18; Luke 14:14; 20:35) or "rise to life" (Matt. 23:30; Mark 12:23; Luke 20:33) or similar expressions, though "resurrection" is retained in John 11:25. In addition to translating "Gehenna" (Matt. 5:22, 29, 30 et al.) and "Hades" (Matt. 11:23 Luke 10:15) as "hell," and the verb using "Tartarus" as "threw them into hell" (2 Peter 2:4), the noun "destruction" is also so given in four passages. According to the TEV, Jesus declared that "the gate is wide and the road is easy that leads to hell, and there are many who travel it" (Matt. 7:13). Peter tells Simon Magus, "May you and your money go to hell" (Acts 8:20). And according to Paul, those who make their bodily desires their god "are going to end up in hell" (Phil. 3:19). And the "Wicked One" who comes at the "final Rebellion" "is destined for hell" (2 Thess. 2:3). Although the Greek noun for "destruction" and its corresponding verb may refer to total and definitive destruction (especially when contrasted with being saved), these words are not an equivalent to the present-day notions of "hell." The latter has overtones (and temperature) not implied by the Greek.

The objective of keeping the language of the TEV direct and simple has resulted in other translational procedures. Long and involved sentences are broken up into smaller units. Romans 1:1-7 is one sentence in the Greek but is translated as six sentences. The still longer Greek sentence of Ephesians 1:3-14 is broken up into fourteen English sentences. Rhetorical questions are sometimes translated as simple statements. Thus in Matthew 5:46, "Do not even the tax collectors do that?" is rendered, "Even the tax collectors do that!" Likewise, in vs. 47, "Do not even the pagans do that?" becomes "Even the pagans do that!" Instead of the question "Is there anything a man can give to regain his life?" is the statement "There is nothing a man can give to regain his life" (Mark 8:37).

At times metaphors are changed to similes. In Luke 11:34, instead of saying as the RSV does, "Your eye is the lamp of the body," the TEV reads, "Your eyes are like a lamp for the body." Other examples are the following: "Their mouths are like an open grave; wicked lies roll off their tongues, and deadly words, like snake's poison, from their lips" (Rom. 3:13). "But thanks be to God! For in union with Christ we are always led by God as prisoners in Christ's victory procession. God uses us to make the knowledge about Christ spread everywhere like a sweet smell. For we are like a sweet-smelling incense offered by Christ to God..." (2 Cor. 2:14f.). The simile of the mother hen is used in Matthew 23:37 to express Jesus' love for the people of Jerusalem: "Jerusalem, Jerusalem!... How many times have I wanted to put my arms around all your people, just as a hen gathers her chicks under her wings, but you would not let me!" At other times metaphors are changed into nonmetaphors. "The finger of God" becomes "God's power" (Luke 11:20). "Cut to the heart" (RSV) is changed to "deeply troubled" (Acts 2:37). "He does not bear the sword in vain" becomes "his power to punish is real" (Rom. 13:4). "Have put on Christ" is converted to "have taken upon yourselves the qualities of Christ" (Gal. 3:27).

The translation is attractively printed with large easy-to-read type in the third edition. The text is arranged in paragraphs, rather than being chopped up into separate verses as in the

KJV. The verse numbers, however, are given in small type at the beginning of each verse. There are topical headings printed in boldface in the various sections of the documents. These lend themselves well to the Gospel pericopes but are less satisfactory in the Epistles, and at times they break up a continuous argument. There are no footnotes or marginal references. Italics are used for transliterations of Aramaic expressions (e.g., Mark 5:41; 15:34), and occasionally for emphasis (1 Cor. 15:27; 16:21; Philem. 19). Quotation marks are freely used for direct address of speakers, OT passages quoted, explanations of names (e.g., Matt. 1:23). Exclamation points are used generously.

Some of the passages are printed in poetic form. Among these in the Gospels are the Beatitudes (Matt. 5:3-10), the Lord's Prayer (Matt. 6:9-13), the Magnificat (Luke 1:46-55), the Benedictus (Luke 1:67-79), and the Nunc Dimittis (Luke 2:29-32). In the Pauline Letters such passages as Philippians 2:6-11; 1 Timothy 3:16; and 2 Timothy 2:11-13 are also in poetic form. Passages quoted from the Psalms and OT prophets are similarly treated.

An outstanding feature of the NT is its 191 imaginative and artistic line drawings that reinforce aspects of the printed text. These simple but effective drawings were done by Mlle. Annie Vallotton, a Swiss-born artist living in Paris. They add much to the appeal of this translation and help to make it speak to modern man.

At the back of the volume following the "Word List" and the four pages of "Other Readings and Renderings" already mentioned, there is an index, "which locates, by page numbers, some of the more important subjects, persons, places, and events in the New Testament" (Preface, p. vi). Finally, there are maps of the NT World, NT Palestine, and Jerusalem with its surrounding areas and the plan of Herod's Temple.

The American Bible Society is also sponsoring a TEV of the OT. The target date for publication of the entire OT is 1975 or 1976. The translation is the work of a committee of six. Three of these—Dr. Robert G. Bratcher who is the chairman, Dr. Keith R. Crim, and Dr. Herbert G. Gretter—are working full-time on the project. The other three are Dr. Roger Bullard, Dr. Heber Peacock, and Dr. Barclay Newman. Besides these, Brynmar Price of the staff of the British and Foreign Bible Society serves as a consultant. Parts of the translation have been published as separate booklets. *The Psalms for Modern Man* appeared in 1970. *Job for Modern Man* was published in 1971 with the subtitle *Tried and True. Wisdom for Modern Man,* the translation of Proverbs and Ecclesiastes, came from the press in 1972.

As with the NT, the committee strives for "common language translation" and "dynamic equivalent translation." The translators used free verse in translating the Psalms and they tried, as the preface states, to put them "in easy-flowing, rhythmical lines that can be effective in public worship as well as in private devotion." Simplicity has a beauty all its own. The first three verses of Psalm 1 will serve to illustrate the TEV OT:

> Happy is the man
>   who refuses the advice of evil men,
> Who does not follow the example of
>   sinners,
> or join those who make fun of
>   God.
> Instead, he enjoys reading the law of the
>   Lord,
> and studying it day and night.
> He is like a tree that grows beside a
>   stream;
> it gives fruit at the right time,
>   and its leaves do not dry up.
> He succeeds in everything he does.

In conclusion, although one might wish that a word here and there, or certain verses, had been translated differently, the TEV effectively meets the objectives the American Bible Society set for it. Most of the criticisms levelled against it do not take into consideration the principles of dynamic equivalence and common language translation that constantly guided the translators. The TEV is an honest attempt by skilled translators to clothe the message of the Bible in language that is simple, plain, and meaningful to modern man. Through it the Word of God has come alive to many a person who never has read, and never would read, a version in sixteenth-century English. Anyone who reads English can comprehend this version. It truly carries "good news for modern man."

12
The New English Bible

In 1946, the year in which the *Revised Standard Version* of the NT was published in the United States, plans were laid in the British Isles for the production of the *New English Bible* (NEB). As the result of the initiative taken by the annual General Assembly of the Church of Scotland in approaching other churches regarding a new version, delegates from the Church of England, the Church of Scotland, and the Methodist, Baptist, and Congregational churches met in conference in October. It was decided to undertake the production of a completely new translation.

In the following year representatives of these churches were appointed to form a "Joint Committee on the New Translation of the Bible," which met in July, 1947. At its third meeting in January, 1948, the committee invited also the Presbyterian Church of England, the Society of Friends, the Churches in Wales, the Churches in Ireland, the British and Foreign Bible Society, and the National Bible Society of Scotland to appoint representatives.

At a later time representatives of the Roman Catholic Church in England and Scotland also attended as observers.

Three panels were assigned to translate respectively the OT, the Apocrypha, and the NT. The work of each panel was submitted for scrutiny to a group of literary advisors to make recommendations regarding the English style.

The first edition of the NT was published in 1961. The complete Bible was published in March, 1970, in two editions: a Library Edition of three volumes, OT, Apocrypha, and NT (second edition); and the Standard Edition in one volume, with or without the Apocrypha. The new Bible is an "authorized" version in the sense that it was produced under the official auspices of the leading Protestant churches of the British Isles. It therefore has a status and an authority no private translation could have.

The NEB differs from the RSV in three chief respects. In the first place, it purports to be a completely new rendering of the original Hebrew, Aramaic, and Greek, and not just a revision of older English versions. As its name implies, the RSV is a revision of the *American Standard Version,* which was the American edition of a revision of the *King James Version.* The KJV was itself a revision of older English revisions of the work of William Tyndale, the real father of all these English Bibles. The *New English Bible* has abandoned the Tyndale–King James tradition, and attempted an entirely fresh translation into clear and contemporary English.

The second difference, closely related to the first, concerns the method of translation. The translators of the Tyndale tradition sought to present a literal word-for-word rendering, as far as they were able to do so consistent with English idiom. In fact, from *The Geneva Bible* on down to the KJV, English words that were not actually representative of corresponding words in the original but were regarded as necessary to make sense in our language were put in italics.

The method of translation used in the NEB is much freer. Instead of being a word-for-word translation, it is a "meaning-for-meaning" rendering. Prof. C. H. Dodd, in his "Introduction to the New Testament," describes it thus:

> We have conceived our task to be that of understanding the original as precisely as we could (using all available aids), and then saying again in our own native idiom what we believed the author to be saying in his. . . . In doing our work, we have constantly striven to follow our instructions and render the Greek, as we understand it, into the English of the present day, that is into the natural vocabulary, constructions, and rhythms of contemporary speech (p. vii).

In the third place, the NEB NT differs from the RSV in many passages in its underlying Greek text. The Greek MSS and early versions of the NT confront the translator with a variety of readings, and he must in a given verse choose either to follow one of the standard Greek editions or assume the role of textual critic and decide on his own which reading to follow. The latter course was followed by the NEB translators. C. H. Dodd states this point as follows:

> There is not at the present time any critical text which would command the same degree of general acceptance as the Revisers' text did in its day. Nor has the time come, in the judgement of competent scholars to construct such a text, since new material constantly comes to light and the debate continues. The present translators therefore could do no other than consider variant readings on their merits, and having weighed the evidence for themselves, select for translation in each passage the reading which to the best of their judgement seemed most likely to represent what the author wrote... (p. v).

On the basis of this eclectic principle, the translators reconstructed the Greek text as they went along. In the vast majority of cases they accepted readings that have been adopted by the major critical Greek texts of our time. But frequently they daringly adopted Greek readings that are supported by a very small group of MSS of the so-called "Western" type, of which Codex Bezae (D) and the Old Latin version are representative. Their Greek text, edited with introduction, textual notes, and appendix by R. V. G. Tasker, was published in 1964 under the title *The Greek New Testament*. A few important differences between it and the critical editions of Westcott-Hort, Nestle-Aland, and the United Bible Societies, as well as the Received Text lying behind the KJV, will serve to illustrate its occasional daring acceptance of "Western" readings.

No known Greek MS omits the name "Jesus" from Matthew 1:18, but the NEB follows the Old Latin, the Old Syriac, and the Vulgate versions in leaving it out; hence the rendering, "This is the story of the birth of the Messiah." Matthew 5:11 in the NEB reads, "How blest you are, when you suffer insults and persecution and every kind of calumny for my sake." The last part of the verse in the RSV reads, "and utter all kinds of evil against you falsely on my account." In the Greek text used by the NEB the word "falsely" is omitted on the basis of D, six MSS of the Old Latin, the Old Syriac and the Georgian versions, plus a few early Fathers. Nevertheless, the translation "calumny" implies false accusations maliciously reported. The

NEB omits all of Matthew 9:34 following D, three Old Latin MSS, and the Sinaitic Syriac, on the assumption that this verse is an assimilation to Matthew 12:24. "Lebbaeus" is substituted for "Thaddaeus" in the list of the twelve apostles in Matthew 10:3 on the basis of D and a couple of Old Latin MSS.

In place of "moved with pity" in Mark 1:41, the NEB follows the reading "being angry" of D and a few Old Latin MSS, which it translates weakly as "in warm indignation." Among the variety of forms in which MSS give the charge of Jesus to the blind man healed at Bethsaida in Mark 8:26, the NEB has adopted the simple one found in no currently known Greek MS, but in one important Old Latin document: "Do not tell anyone in the village."

In Luke 5:17 the NEB substitutes "and there were come together" for "who had come," on the basis of D and one Old Latin MS. The verse is then translated as two sentences: "One day he was teaching, and Pharisees and teachers of the law were sitting around. People had come from every village of Galilee and from Judaea and Jerusalem. . . ." Instead of "Consider the lilies, how they grow; they neither toil nor spin" in Luke 12:27, the NEB with D, the Old Syriac, and two Old Latin MSS have "Think of the lilies: they neither spin nor weave."

In Acts 1:26 the reading of D and its Latin counterpart,. "the twelve apostles" is read instead of "the eleven apostles." "By his holy prophets" is read in Acts 3:21, with D and a couple of Old Latin MSS, instead of "by his holy prophets from of old." In Acts 4:25 the phrase "by the Holy Spirit" is inserted, with D, before "by the mouth of," resulting in the translation "who by the Holy Spirit, through the mouth of David thy servant, didst say."

There are other interesting readings in the NEB Greek text that are not peculiarly Western. In Mark 8:38, as in its parallel of Luke 9:26a, "words" is omitted with the resulting translation, "If anyone is ashamed of me and mine [i.e., my followers] in this wicked and godless age, the Son of Man will be ashamed of him, when he comes in the glory of his Father and of the holy angels." The striking reading found in some "Caesarean" type MSS that give the name of the notorious prisoner released in place of our Lord as "Jesus Bar-Abbas" is adopted in Matthew 27:16f. In Luke 10:1, 17 the NEB has the interesting reading "seventy-two" rather than "seventy," and in this is supported by Codex Vaticanus as well as Western and other MSS. John 13:10 reads, "A man who has bathed needs no further washing." But the omission here of "needs only to wash his feet" rests on weak MS evidence.

The textual basis for the OT of the NEB is the traditional Masoretic Hebrew (and Aramaic) text as printed in Rudolf Kittel's *Biblia Hebraica* (third edition). Originally this traditional text was written in consonants only, and the vowels were supplied by the reader. In later times, however, the rabbis added the vowel signs to preserve what they regarded as the true pronunciation. Through the centuries this traditional text has suffered from copyists' errors and scribal emendations and consequently does not always represent what was originally written. Where errors in the text were apparent, the translators tried to recover the original by consulting the portions extant in the *Dead Sea Scrolls* and, for the first five books, the Samaritan Pentateuch, which differs considerably from the Hebrew, mostly in minor and unimportant ways, but which occasionally has cogent readings. Use was also made of such ancient versions as the Septuagint, the Syriac, the Vulgate, and the Aramaic Targums in the endeavor to recover pre-Masoretic readings. In instances where such research failed to provide satisfactory solutions, the translators resorted to emendation of the text, first by substituting other vowels, and then, if they regarded it as necessary, by changing the consonants as well. Emendations in the consonantal text are designated in the footnotes as "*Prob. rdg.*" (i.e., probable reading). It is to be expected that some exegetes of the Bible will regard this or that surgical operation on the sacred text as too hasty and unnecessary.

The translators have also occasionally changed the order of materials in the text. For example, in Genesis 26, vs. 18 is placed between vss. 15 and 16. Verses 6 and 7 of Isaiah 41 are inserted between vss. 20 and 21 of Isaiah 40. In Jeremiah 12 part of vs. 14 and all of vs. 15 are given after vs. 17. Verses 13 and 14 of Jeremiah 15 are removed from the text and put in a footnote. Amos 5:7 is transposed to follow vs. 9. In several places in Joel 3:9-12 the order of the lines has been rearranged. Zechariah 2:13 is followed by chapter 4:1-3 and vss. 11-13. The remaining verses (4-10) of chapter 4 are left in their normal place after chapter 3:10. In Zechariah 13, vss. 7-9 are transposed to follow 11:17. A legitimate question may well be raised at this point: Is such a rearranging of the materials in harmony with modern concepts of sequential thought the proper function of translators, or should translators confine their activity to rendering the text in the order in which it has been handed down?

Another deviation from custom has been the complete omission of the superscriptions from the Psalms. These ancient editorial titles were part of the traditional text and are found in the oldest Hebrew MSS known. Their great antiquity is shown by the fact that as early as the time of the translation of the Greek OT, the significance of some of the technical musical terms was already unknown as their rendering in the LXX reveals. Many Bible students will regard the omission of these ancient titles as unfortunate. The translators of the NEB have no antipathy to headings as such, for they have inserted many of them in the text of other parts of the Bible.

The NEB, like the RSV, has returned to the practice of the KJV in normally translating the sacred, covenant name YHWH as "Lord." This sacred name, called the tetragrammaton and occurring some 6,800 times in the OT, came to be regarded as too sacred to be pronounced. Hence, the practice arose of substituting the Hebrew word *Adonai,* meaning "Lord," for it when reading the sacred text. When the vowel signs were added to the consonantal text, the Masoretes pointed the tetragrammaton with the vowels used to pronounce *Adonai.* The late medieval form "Jehovah" is an artificial form combining these vowels with the consonants of the tetragrammaton. Scholars today are generally agreed that the correct form is "Yahweh." Nevertheless, the customary form "Jehovah," which had already been used four times in the KJV (Exod. 6:3; Ps. 83:18; Isa. 12:2; 26:4) was retained in the NEB in a few passages where the name is explained (Exod. 3:15; 6:3; 33:18f.; 34:5, 6), with a footnote explaining its pronunciation. It is also used in such place names as Jehovah-jireh (Gen. 22:14), Jehovah-nissi (Exod. 17:15, 16), Jehovah-shalom (Judg. 6:23, 24), and Jehovah-shammah (Ezek. 48:35).

The NEB rendering of the first two verses of the Bible is,

to say the least, debatable: "In the beginning of creation, when God made heaven and earth, the earth was without form and void, with darkness over the face of the abyss, and a mighty wind that swept over the surface of the waters." A footnote gives the traditional rendering, "In the beginning God created heaven and earth." Another footnote gives "and the spirit of God hovering," for "a mighty wind that swept." These footnotes indicate that the translators were not in complete agreement on the new renderings. The arguments pro and con for the new or the traditional translation are too technical to be dealt with here, but suffice it to say that a comparison with other modern versions and recent commentaries indicates that Bible scholars of equal repute can be cited for either interpretation.

At the conclusion of the creating activity of each day of creation week is the statement appropriately translated, "Evening came, and morning came, a second day" (vs. 8), "a third day" (vs. 13), "a fourth day," (vs. 18), "a fifth day," (vs. 23), and "a sixth day" (vs. 31). "Thus the heavens and the earth were completed with all their mighty throng" (Gen. 2:1). In the following sentence the NEB follows the Samaritan Pentateuch and the LXX in reading "the sixth day," rather than the Hebrew, which has "the seventh day." "On the sixth day God completed all the work he had been doing, and on the seventh day he ceased from all his work" (Gen. 2:2). It is doubtful that this change is justifiable. The activities of the sixth day have already been described. Also, if we follow the well-known principle of textual critics that the more difficult reading is to be preferred, we would retain the Hebrew "the seventh day." God completed His work on the seventh day by inaugurating the Sabbath. This He did by desisting from His creative work and by blessing and sanctifying the seventh day.

For the most part, the NEB translators have done an outstanding piece of work in conveying the thought of both Testaments into modern English. They have been aware of modern trends in understanding and interpreting the text. Showing a sensitivity to the meaning of the various Greek tenses, they have tried, where practicable, to put the meaning into English.

It may be helpful at this juncture to give a few samples of their translations.

Micah 6:6-8

What shall I bring when I approach the LORD?
How shall I stoop before God on high?
Am I to approach him with whole-offerings or yearling calves?
Will the LORD accept thousands of rams
or ten thousand rivers of oil?
Shall I offer my eldest son for my own wrongdoing,
my children for my own sin?

God has told you what is good;
and what is it that the LORD asks of you?
Only to act justly, to love loyalty,
to walk wisely before your God.

Luke 10:41, 42

But the Lord answered, 'Martha, Martha, you are fretting and fussing about so many things; but one thing is necessary. The part that Mary has chosen is best; and it shall not be taken away from her.'

Luke 3:14

'Exact no more than the assessment.' Soldiers on service also asked him, 'And what of us?' To them he said, 'No bullying; no blackmail; make do with your pay!'

Matthew 5:3

'How blest are those who know their need of God; the kingdom of Heaven is theirs.'

Matthew 6:7, 8

'In your prayers do not go babbling on like the heathen, who imagine that the more they say the more likely they are to be heard. Do not imitate them. Your Father knows what your needs are before you ask him.'

Matthew 22:15-18

Then the Pharisees went away and agreed on a plan to trap him in his own words. Some of their followers were sent to him in company with men of Herod's party. They said, 'Master, you are an honest man, we know; you teach in all honesty the way of life that God requires, truckling to no man, whoever he may be. Give us your ruling on this: are we or are we not permitted to pay taxes to the Roman Emperor?' Jesus was aware of their malicious intention and said to them, 'You hypocrites! Why are you trying to catch me out?'

2 Corinthians 2:14, 15

But thanks be to God, who continually leads us about, captives in Christ's triumphal procession, and everywhere uses us to reveal and spread abroad the fragrance of the knowledge of himself! We are indeed the incense offered by Christ to God, both for those who are on the way to salvation, and for those who are on the way to perdition.

The language of the NEB is, of course, English. But what kind of English? According to the "Introduction to the New Testament," the object of the translators was to give "a faithful rendering of the best available Greek text into the current speech of our time" (p. v). They were commissioned "to make the attempt to use consistently the idiom of contemporary English" (p. vi). Similarly, in the "Introduction to the Old Testament" (p. xviii) we are told, "They have tried to keep their language as close to current usage as possible, while avoiding words and phrases likely soon to become obsolete."

How well have the translators succeeded in carrying out these objectives? This is a difficult question to answer, since current English in the United Kingdom may differ in many respects from current speech in America. It is to be expected that the NEB will use the "Queen's English," and therefore some words and expressions employed may sound unusual to American ears. The British character of the language will frequently challenge the American reader, and he may at times wonder if "current" and "contemporary" English means twentieth-century English or includes nineteenth-century English as well. At any rate, he will note a number of differences between his own language and that of the "Queen's English."

Although differences in spelling have little significance, the alert American reader will note a large number of words ending in -our instead of -or, such as armour, colour, clamour, favour, honour, labour, and neighbour. He will also note that some words that he prefers to end with -er end in -re, such as sceptre (Gen. 49:10, et al.), theatre (Acts 19:29, 31), and reconnoitre (Josh. 2:1). Some words that he spells with an "s" are spelled with a "c," such as offence (2 Cor. 6:3; 11:7), defence (Acts 19:3), and pretence (Phil. 1:18). "Mouldy" (Josh. 9:5, 12) he spells without the "u." "Plough" (Deut. 22:10), "ploughing" (Luke 17:7), and "ploughman" (1 Cor.

9:10) he spells with "ow" rather than "ough." He notes both "jailer" (Acts 16:23, 27) and "gaoler" (Isa. 10:4). "Caldron" is spelled "cauldron" (Job 41:20; 1 Sam. 2:14).

British usage is reflected also in the vocabulary. Amounts of money are sometimes given in British terms: "Are not sparrows five for twopence?" (Luke 12:6). "Presently there came a poor widow who dropped in two tiny coins, together worth a farthing" (Mark 12:42). "Are we to go and spend twenty pounds on bread to give them a meal?" (Mark 6:37). "Why this waste? The perfume might have been sold for thirty pounds and the money given to the poor" (Mark 14:5). "He met a fellow-servant who owed him a few pounds" (Matt. 18:28). Likewise some expressions of time reflect British life: "I stayed with him for a fortnight" (Gal. 1:18). "But I shall remain at Ephesus until Whitsuntide" (1 Cor. 16:8).

One of the most common differences between British and American English is in the use of the word "corn." "Corn" in Britain means grain, particularly wheat, whereas in the United States and Canada (also Australia) it refers to Indian corn or maize. The latter was, of course, unknown in the Middle East in Bible times and the NEB naturally follows the British usage, as did the KJV. Americans should think of wheat when they read, "Once about that time Jesus went through the cornfields on the Sabbath; and his disciples, feeling hungry, began to pluck some ears of corn and eat them" (Matt. 12:1). "A sower went out to sow. . . . Some seed fell on rocky ground, where it had little soil, and it sprouted quickly because it had no depth of earth; but when the sun rose the young corn was scorched, and as it had no root it withered away" (Matt. 13:4-6). "A man sowed his field with good seed; but while everyone was asleep his enemy came, sowed darnel among the wheat, and made off. When the corn sprouted and began to fill out, the darnel could be seen among it" (Matt. 13:25f.). "But Samson said, 'This time I will settle my score with the Philistines; I will do them some real harm.' So he went and caught three hundred jackals and got some torches; he tied the jackals tail to tail and fastened a torch between each pair of tails. He then set the torches alight and turned the jackals loose in the standing corn of the Philistines. He burnt up standing corn and stooks as well, vineyards and olive groves" (Judg. 15:3-5).

A number of other words appear in the NEB that are evidently in use in Britain but quite unknown to most Americans. One is "stooks," meaning "shocks," in the above Samson story. Another is the use of "weeds" for mourning garments in the expression "widow's weeds" (Gen. 38:14, 19; Isa. 47:8; Rev. 18:7). As a term for a heap of stones piled up as a memorial, the Scottish word "cairn" occurs six times in the story of Laban and Jacob's meeting that resulted in making a covenant (Gen. 31:46ff.). "In spate," meaning "in flood," is also chiefly Scottish (Job 6:17; 40:23; cf. 11:2). One wonders if the following represents a Scotticism: "Do not be haughty, but go about with humble folk" (Rom. 12:16). The word "hind" means "female deer" (Ps. 42:1; Hab. 3:19), for which Americans use "doe."

When the translators speak of using current speech and contemporary English, one is tempted to ask, contemporary for whom? One has the feeling that at times terms are used that would be known only to the educated. And perhaps "contemporary" includes also the nineteenth century. Note the italicized words in the following quotations:

Now his sons used to *foregather* (Job 1:4)
the stronger man seizes it from the *panniers* (Job 5:5)
they reach them only to be *balked* (Job 6:20)
Of myself I *reck* nothing (Job 9:21)
not for him to *swill down* rivers of cream (Job 20:17)
I do not *descry* him (Job 23:9)
I broke the fangs of the *miscreant* (Job 29:17)
tormented by a ceaseless *ague* in his bones (Job 33:19)
and its lair in the *saltings* (Job 39:6)
Can you pull out the whale with a *gaff* (Job 41:1)
strangers will *batten* on your wealth (Prov. 5:10; cf. Rev. 17:16)
he will get nothing but blows and *contumely* (Prov. 6:33)
and give them to his *lackeys* (1 Sam. 8:14, 15)
your *runnels* of water pour into the street (Prov. 5:16)
he and the king of the south will make *feints* at one another (Dan. 11:40)
does that mean that Christ is an *abettor* of sin? (Gal. 2:17)
What are they all but *ministrant* spirits? (Heb. 1:14)
Moses, then, was faithful as a *servitor* (Heb. 3:5)
to fetch cedar-wood from the Lebanon to the *roadstead* at Joppa (Ezra 3:7)
And there shall be a *causeway* there (Isa. 35:8)
Alas, alas for the great city ... *bedizened* with gold and jewels and pearls (Rev. 18:17)

Do you bring in the lamp to put it under the *meal-tub* ...? (Mark 4:21)

You strain off a *midge*, yet gulp down a camel! (Matt. 23:24)

On the other hand, the English of the NEB is often brisk, tangy, and arrestingly good:

The men in charge of them took to their heels (Mark 5:14)

This touched them on the raw and they ground their teeth with fury (Acts 7:54)

So they fell foul of him (Mark 6:4)

You are the people who impress your fellow-men with your righteousness; but God sees through you (Luke 16:15)

He saw how crafty their question was, and said, 'Why are you trying to catch me out?' (Mark 12:15)

while I was with you, if I ran short, I sponged on no one (2 Cor. 11:9)

Out! Pester me no more! (Exod. 10:27)

Up with you! Be off, and leave my people, you and your Israelites (Exod. 12:31)

But if you go on fighting one another, tooth and nail, all you can expect is mutual destruction (Gal. 5:15)

the long-winded ramblings of an old man (Job 8:2)

and begins to bully the other servants (Matt. 24:49)

he began to feel the pinch (Luke 15:14)

I count it so much garbage (Phil. 3:8)

Some readers may regard some expressions as a bit too familiar for the sacred Scriptures:

Your calf-gods stink, O Samaria (Hos. 8:5)

Do you think you can hoodwink men like us? (Num. 16:14)

and answer with a bellyful of wind (Job 15:2)

This is more than we can stomach (John 6:60)

Not indulging in double talk, given neither to excessive drinking nor to money-grubbing (1 Tim. 3:8)

they got wind of it (Acts 14:6)

that I may not be left picking lice (S. of Sol. 1:7)

On the other hand, in the story of Paul the prisoner once notes the use of technical legal language:

and they laid an information against Paul before the Governor (Acts 24:1)

When the prisoner was called, Tertullus opened the case (vs. 2)

and when I was in Jerusalem the chief priests and elders of the Jews laid an information against him, demanding his condemnation (Acts 25:15)

> But Paul appealed to be remanded in custody, for His Imperial Majesty's decision (vs. 21)
>
> I stand in the dock today (Acts 26:6; cf. Phil. 1:7)

Occasionally the language has a pedantic flavor:

> at parricides and matricides...in his eternal felicity (1 Tim. 1:9-11)
>
> inculcate abstinence from certain foods (1 Tim. 4:3)
>
> I call him a pompous ignoramus. He is morbidly keen on mere verbal questions and quibbles...all typical of men who have let their reasoning powers become atrophied (1 Tim. 6:4)
>
> It is an intractable evil, charged with deadly venom (James 3:9)
>
> the smoke of her conflagration (Rev. 18:18)

In relation to the original, the English rendering is sometimes quite paraphrastic and interpretive. What is literally "to those who have believed on his name" is given as "to those who have yielded him their allegiance" (John 1:12). The literal "If you abide in my word" is made to read, "If you dwell within the revelation I have brought" (John 8:31). The literal rendering "that the works of God might be displayed in curing him" becomes "so that God's power might be displayed in curing him" (John 9:3). The translation of Exodus 11:1 is certainly paraphrastic: "After that he will let you go; he will send you packing, as a man dismisses a rejected bride." Note also vs. 7: "Not a dog's tongue shall be so much as scratched." The insertion of the word "phylactery" into Exodus 13:16 is unquestionably in the nature of an interpretation and most probably an incorrect one: "You shall have the record of it as a sign upon your hand, and upon your forehead as a phylactery...." The literal phrase "by [or, in] his blood" becomes "by his sacrificial death" (Rom. 3:25), or "by Christ's sacrificial death" (Rom. 5:9). The Greek word rendered "propitiation" in the KJV becomes in 1 John 2:2 and 4:10 "the remedy for the defilement of our sins" and in Romans 3:25 "the means of expiating sin."

The version is printed in an attractive form with one column to the page. The verse numbers are given in the left-hand margin. Subject headings are given in large type. The poetic portions of Scripture such as the Psalms, Proverbs, and a large part of the prophets, are printed in poetic form. Quotation marks are used throughout.

Before the complete Bible was printed, the translators took the opportunity of reviewing the renderings given in the 1961 edition of the NT, particularly in the light of criticisms that had been made. Although the basic translation remains the same, some four hundred revisions were made. This means that when the NEB NT is quoted, one should state which edition is being used.

By and large, the NEB gives a valid reproduction of the thought of the sacred Scriptures. The reader must bear in mind, however, that the intention of the translators was to give a thought-by-thought and not a word-by-word translation. This often results in paraphrastic and interpretative renderings. The reader who knows his Greek New Testament will also note that the application of the eclectic principle followed in dealing with MSS frequently led to the adoption of readings with very little MS support. The strongest point of the NEB is its vigorous and colorful English style, though the American reader will find it necessary to refer occasionally to his dictionary of the English language.

13
The New American Bible

Just as it was inevitable that the NEB should be published as the English Protestant counterpart of the American RSV, so also it was inevitable that the NAB should be published as a counterpart of the English Catholic JB. However, this NAB has been in process for over three decades, being originally known as *The Confraternity Version*. In fact, the NT, a revision of Rheims-Challoner based on the Latin Vulgate, was published in 1941. When in 1943 the famous encyclical on Scripture studies was issued by Pope Pius XII recommending translation from the original text, work on the OT was begun, based on the original text. By 1969 the OT was complete, including the Apocrypha. Of course, the NT had to be retranslated, this time from the Greek text. With the publication of the NAB in 1970, there exists for the first time a complete American Catholic Bible translated from the original languages. The translation team included fifty-nine Catholic and five Protestant scholars.

The OT is based on the Hebrew and Aramaic (the Masoretic text), but no critical modern translation slavishly follows the Masoretic text in every instance. In 1 Samuel the RSV deviates fifty-eight times and the NEB one hundred and forty-four times, but the NAB departs from the Masoretic text two hundred and fifty-one times, choosing to follow the Qumran Scroll and/or the LXX (Keith Crim, Review of NAB, *Interpretation*, XXVI [1972], 78).

The Greek text used in the NT is Nestle-Aland's *Novum Testamentum Graece* (25th ed., 1963), with some assistance from the United Bible Societies' Greek NT. Here again it has not followed this text in every instance. Unfortunate is its use of brackets to indicate what are called "doubtful readings of some merit." Such readings are found, for example, in Matthew 5:5; 17:21; 21:44; 24:36; John 5:3; Ephesians 1:1. Some readings not found in the Nestle-Aland text have been included in the translation. These include Luke 24:12; 24:40; 24:51. At the end of Mark it has followed the Nestle-Aland text by including both longer and shorter endings within the text section. There is a line, however, between these endings and no line between Mark 16:8 and the longer ending. Besides these two endings it has also included, separated by a line from the shorter ending, the ending found in the Freer Logion. According to the note at this place, the longer ending "has traditionally been accepted as an inspired part of the gospel" although "vocabulary and style argue strongly that it was written by someone other than Mark." The story of the woman taken in adultery is found in brackets at its traditional position in John even though the explanation in the footnote indicates it is out of place there. This passage is found in different places in different MSS but is missing in the best early MSS.

The NAB has short introductions to the different parts of the OT—the Pentateuch, the Historical Books, the Wisdom Books, and the Prophetic Books. It also has an introduction to each book of the Bible. These are moderately liberal in tone. The text is set in two columns in very readable type. It is in paragraph form with verse numbers in very light, small type, perhaps a bit too light. The names of biblical personages and places (except for "Gethsemane") are those customarily found in Protestant Bibles. At the end of the Bible are included the "Dogmatic Constitution on Divine Revelation," a "Glossary of Biblical Theology Terms," "A Survey of Biblical Geography," and some maps.

NAB has fewer footnotes than JB and at times they are even less Catholic in flavor. For example, in Genesis 3:15 no mention is made of Mary. This is true also in Revelation 12:1. No mention of purgatory is made in 1 Corinthians 3:13. In Matthew 13:55 and Mark 6:3 the Greek words *adelphos* and *adelphē* are translated "brother" and "sister" respectively. No note concerning this is appended to the former passage, but in Mark 6:3 we find the following: "The question about the brothers of Jesus and his sisters (v. 3) cannot easily be decided on linguistic grounds. Greek-speaking Semites used the terms *adelphos* and *adelphē*, not only in the ordinary sense of blood brother and sister, but also for nephew, niece, half-brother, half-sister, and cousin." Then follows clearly where the writer stands: "The question of meaning here would not have arisen but for the faith of the church in Mary's perpetual virginity." It is a bit more apologetic regarding the perpetual virginity of Mary as the note on Matthew 1:25 indicates: "The evangelist emphasizes the virginity of the mother of Jesus from the moment of his conception to his birth. He does not concern himself here with the period that followed the birth of Jesus, but merely wishes to show that Joseph fully respected the legal character of the paternity imposed on him by the divine will. Moreover the New Testament makes no mention anywhere of children of Joseph and Mary."

The use of "thou," "thee," "thine," and related verb forms has been dropped. "You" is used for both singular and plural forms. Unlike the JB with its use of "Yahweh," the NAB has gone back to the more acceptable "Lord."

There is some rearrangement of verses in the NAB. In Jeremiah, for instance, 11:19-23 is placed between 12:6 and 12:7. More drastic is the rearrangement in Ezekiel. The order, beginning with 8:3, is 8:5-18; 9:1-11; 11:24, 25; 8:1, 2, 4; 10:20-22, 14, 15, 9-13, 16, 17, 8, 18, 19; 11:22, 23, 1-21. More such changes are made in Hosea. The JB also did some rearranging, especially in Hosea. Previously the translation known for this was that of Moffatt.

The translation itself is simple, clear, and straightforward and reads very smoothly. It is good American English, not as pungent and colorful as the NEB. Its translations are not striking but neither are they clumsy. They seem to be more conservative in the sense that they tend not to stray from the original. That is not to say that this is a literal translation, but it is more faithful. It does not make daring transcultural translations such as Phillips' "Shake hands with everyone" for "Greet one another with a holy kiss." The following passages illustrate these characteristics:

Psalm 91:1-3

You who dwell in the shelter of the Most High,
    who abide in the shadow of the Almighty,
Say to the LORD, "My refuge and my fortress,
    my God, in whom I trust."
For he will rescue you from the snare of the fowler,
    from the destroying pestilence.

Isaiah 40:1, 2

Comfort, give comfort to my people,
    says your God.
Speak tenderly to Jerusalem, and proclaim to her
    that her service is at an end,
    her guilt is expiated;
Indeed, she has received from the hand of the LORD
    double for all her sins.

Matthew 5:31, 32

"It was also said, 'Whenever a man divorces his wife, he must
give her a decree of divorce.' What I say to you is: everyone
who divorces his wife—lewd conduct is a separate case—forces
her to commit adultery. The man who marries a divorced
woman likewise commits adultery."

Romans 12:1, 2

And now, brothers, I beg you through the mercy of God to
offer your bodies as a living sacrifice holy and acceptable to
God, your spiritual worship. Do not conform yourselves to
this age but be transformed by the renewal of your mind, so
that you may judge what is God's will, what is good, pleasing
and perfect.

Some striking translations of this version are:

In the beginning, when God created the heavens and the
earth, the earth was a formless wasteland, and darkness cov-
ered the abyss, while a mighty wind swept over the waters
(Gen. 1:1, 2).

"Dome" for "firmament" in Genesis 1:6

"sky" for "heaven" in Genesis 1:8

When they heard the sound of the LORD God moving about
in the garden at the breezy time of the day...(Gen. 3:8).

Reform your lives! The reign of God is at hand (Matt. 3:2).

When he saw that many...were stepping forward for this
bath (Matt. 3:7).

The mouth speaks whatever fills the mind (Matt. 12:34).

You...leave the inside filled with loot and lust! (Matt. 23:25).

To the presiding spirit of the church in Ephesus...(Rev. 2:1).

He shall rule them with a rod of iron and shatter them like crockery (Rev. 2:27).

In certain ambiguous passages, interesting translations appear. Matthew 16:18 reads, "I for my part declare to you, you are 'Rock,' and on this rock I will build my church." This is not altogether surprising, since Protestant Bibles already had moved in this direction. In John 1:4 NAB has followed NEB in joining vs. 3 and vs. 4 so that it reads, "Whatever came to be in him, found life, life for the light of men." NAB is the only translation we know that chooses to translate 1 Corinthians 7:21 in the following way: "Even supposing you could go free, you would be better off making the most of your slavery." It has chosen to keep the word "virgin" in 1 Corinthians 7:36, but the word obviously means "betrothed" as in RSV instead of "daughter" as in KJV. Unlike the ambiguous form of the translation of 1 Corinthians 9:5 in the JB "to take a Christian woman round with us," with the note "Lit. 'a sister, a woman (wife?).' To look after the apostle's needs," the NAB translates it more unambiguously than even Protestant translations: "Do we not have the right to marry a believing woman like the rest of the apostles and the brothers of the Lord and Cephas?" Catholic translators have sought to avoid admitting that the apostles were married because of their teaching on celibacy. First Timothy 3:2, as expected, has the phrase "married only once." "Little while" is included in Hebrews 2:7: "You made him for a little while lower than the angels," thus clearly indicating that this passage from Psalms is understood messianically by the writer. The translators chose not to identify Christ with God in their rendering of Romans 9:5, since they isolated the benediction from what precedes. Thus it reads, "Blessed forever be God who is over all! Amen."

In a comparison of NAB with JB, note the following differences:

NAB	JB
Ps. 23:1-3	
The LORD is my shepherd; I shall not want.	Yahweh is my shepherd, I lack nothing.

In verdant pastures he gives
  me repose;
Beside restful waters he leads me;
  he refreshes my soul.
He guides me in right paths
  for his name's sake.

In meadows of green grass he
  lets me lie.
To the waters of repose he leads
  me;
  there he revives my soul.
He guides me by paths of virtue
  for the sake of his name.

Rom. 7:7, 8

What follows from what I have said? That the law is the same as sin? Certainly not! Yet it was only through the law that I came to know sin. I should never have known what evil desire was unless the law had said, "You shall not covet." Sin seized that opportunity; it used the commandment to rouse in me every kind of evil desire. Without law sin is dead. . . .

Does it follow that the Law itself is sin? Of course not. What I mean is that I should not have known what sin was except for the Law. I should not for instance have known what it means to covet if the Law had not said *You shall not covet*. But it was this commandment that sin took advantage of to produce all kinds of covetousness in me, for when there is no Law, sin is dead.

Matt. 6:1, 2

Be on guard against performing religious acts for the people to see. Otherwise expect no recompense for your heavenly Father. When you give alms, for example, do not blow a horn before you in synagogues and streets like hypocrites looking for applause. You can be sure of this much, they are already repaid.

Be careful not to parade your good deeds before men to attract their notice; by doing this you will lose all reward from your Father in heaven. So when you give alms, do not have it trumpeted before you; this is what the hypocrites do in the synagogues and in the streets to win men's admiration. I tell you solemnly, they have had their reward.

One immediate observation we make is the overall brevity and the directness of the American translation. In the first passage the JB favors the prepositional phrase, whereas the NAB prefers the shorter adjectival modifier. In the second passage the directness of the NAB shows through. It is not only shorter, it has a sentence in the positive form that the JB had in the negative. In the last passage, the American version is plain and straightforward, whereas the British version is more colorful and spicy. These are typical differences between the two translations.

A close check of the translation of 1 Corinthians 1:1-10

with the Greek indicates that it is a faithful translation. Where it is not following the Greek literally, usually the translation is derivable from the context or makes explicit that which is implicit in the original; for example, the addition of "send greetings" and "you" in vs. 2, the omission of "of God" after "favor" in vs. 4 and "concerning you" after "informed" in vs. 11.

Besides some of the observations we have made above concerning the text and footnotes, the translators have been criticized for a lack of consistency and for not having an adequate plan for the work as a whole.

Regarding the question of consistency, Bruce Metzger (*Princeton Seminary Bulletin,* LXIV [1971], 92) mentions the translation of the word *makarios* (blessed) and the word *basileia* (kingdom). It is not necessary or even desirable that a certain Greek or Hebrew word be always translated by the same English word. Words do change meanings as they are used in different texts. However, certain technical words or words used in the same contexts should not be translated with different English words. In the Beatitudes in Matthew 5 and Luke 6, *makarios* is translated "blest," but in the seven times it is found in Revelation it is translated "happy." Other translations of this word are "go well with" (Luke 12:37, 38), "fortunate" (Luke 12:43), "pleased" (Luke 14:14). This last verse is followed by the translation of the same word with "happy" in the next verse (Luke 14:15). In the OT the Hebrew word for "blessed" is translated "happy" in most cases, but "blessed" is found in Ecclesiastes 10:17, Isaiah 30:18, and Daniel 12:12.

The same inconsistency is found in the translation of the Greek word for "kingdom." Matthew 3:2 reads, "Reform your lives! The reign of God is at hand," but Matthew 4:17 reads, "Reform your lives! The kingdom of heaven is at hand." Again Matthew 4:23 refers to the proclamation of "the good news of the kingdom," while Matthew 9:35 refers to the proclamation of "the good news of God's reign." In Matthew 13 it is "the reign of God" that is always likened to something, except in vs. 45 where it is "the kingdom of heaven." Not only is the word *basileia* translated in two different ways, but "God" is substituted for "heaven" in an arbitrary manner. The translation "reign" is not a good one in Matthew 26:29: "I tell you,

I will not drink this fruit of the vine from now until the day when I drink it new with you in my Father's reign." Other words used to translate *basileia* are "kingship," "dominion," and "nation." For "burnt offering" NAB has used the unfortunate translation "holocaust," which today signifies something quite different from the sacrifice of burnt offering. Only in Mark 12:33 is the word translated "burnt offering."

The translation of the word *dikaiosunē*, usually translated "righteousness," has always been a problem for translators. The cognate Greek verb appears to be translated "to justify," but the noun is translated in various ways, depending on the context. In Matthew 3:15 it is translated "God's demands," but in the rest of Matthew as "holiness." "All that is right" and "uprightness" are some other translations. In Romans, however, it seems to be consistently translated "justice." This does not seem to be the best translation in certain cases such as Romans 4:5, 6, "But when a man does nothing, yet believes in him who justifies the sinful, his faith is credited as justice. Thus David congratulates the man to whom God credits justice without requiring deeds"; Romans 4:9, "For we say that Abraham's faith was 'credited as justice' "; and Romans 6:13, "Rather, offer yourselves to God as men who have come back from the dead to life, and your bodies to God as weapons for justice." This is also true in Romans 5:17 and 6:16.

Another point Dr. Metzger makes is the reference to pronouncements of Councils in the footnotes. He refers to John 3:5; 20:22, 23; 20:28; James 5:15. Of most interest to readers will be that found in connection with John 21:15ff., where this annotation is found: "The First Vatican Council cited this verse in defining that the risen Jesus gave Peter the jurisdiction of supreme shepherd and ruler over the whole flock."

Keith Crim's criticism (*Interpretation*, XXVI [1972], 77), it seems, is well founded. It would be interesting to note the changes that will be made when the entire work is reviewed for revision. He writes:

> The beginning of the work is usually dated to the issuance of the Encyclical *Divino afflante Spiritu* in 1943, so that the project was spread over almost three decades. Those years have seen so many changes in the life of the church, so much

advance in biblical studies, so great an increase in our knowledge of linguistics and translation procedures that a total reworking would have been required to make the earlier books consistent with those translated later. Some books were revised or even retranslated, but this only increases the feeling that there was no adequate plan for the work as a whole.

Nevertheless, this translation is a remarkable achievement. As we have mentioned before, this is the first complete American Catholic Bible translated from the original languages.

14

The New American
Standard Bible

The Lockman Foundation is a nonprofit Christian corporation formed in 1942 in La Habra, California, to promote Christian Education, Christian Evangelism, and above all, Bible translation in several languages. In English it has produced two
noteworthy translations: *The Amplified New Testament* and the
New American Standard Bible.

The publication of the latter began with the Gospel of John
in 1960, followed by the four Gospels in 1962, the NT in 1963,
and the entire Bible in 1971. The "Preface to the New American Standard Bible A.D. 1963" briefly sets forth the principles
and objectives on which the revision was made. It begins, "The
producers of this translation were imbued with the conviction
that interest in the American Standard Version should be renewed and increased." Certainly the ASV was a monument to
the best British and American scholarship and biblical learning
of the latter half of the nineteenth century. The Lockman
Foundation was disturbingly aware that this "monumental
product of applied scholarship, assiduous labor and thorough
procedure . . . was fast disappearng from the scene." The recognized value of that version, it was felt, "deserves and demands perpetuation. . . . Recognizing a responsibility to posteri-
ty, the Lockman Foundation felt an urgency to rescue this
noble achievement from an inevitable demise, to preserve it, as a
heritage for coming generations, and to do so in such a form
as the demands of passing time dictate."

To achieve this objective the revision must be put "in clear
and contemporary language." The twofold purpose of the
editorial board was "to adhere to the original languages of the

Holy Scriptures as closely as possible and at the same time to obtain a fluent and readable style according to current English usage." Accordingly, a group of sixteen men worked on each Testament. The goal of using contemporary English in the revision often required a departure from the word-for-word literalness of the ASV, one of its chief faults.

With regard to the NT, which was published first, we are told that "consideration was given to the latest available manuscripts with a view to determining the best Greek text." In most instances the twenty-third edition of the Nestle Greek NT was followed. Thus, the underlying Greek text differs in a number of passages from that on which the ASV was based. Furthermore, in Matthew the doxology of the Lord's Prayer (6:13) and two whole verses (18:11; 23:14) are printed in brackets, though they are found only in the footnotes of both the ASV and the Nestle Greek Text. Contrary to Nestle, but like the ASV, Luke 24:12 is printed in the text, but also in brackets. The NASB also follows the ASV, contrary to Nestle, in printing the "Long Ending" of Mark in the text (16:9-20) in brackets, as well as the "Shorter Ending" in italics with the title "Addition." It also has in brackets the story of the woman discovered in the act of adultery (John 7:53-8:11). John 1:18 follows Nestle in reading "the only begotten God" rather than "the only begotten Son" as in the ASV. For other differences from the text of the ASV, see Mark 1:29; 2:4, 16; 6:14; 7:4, 24; 12:33; Luke 9:2, 59; 10:42; 24:36, 40, 51; John 8:16; 10:18; 13:32; 15:8; etc.

Several features of the general format of the version are worthy of note. For one thing, there is only one column of text on each page. Unfortunately, however, it does not follow the ASV in arranging the text in sense paragraphs. Rather, each verse, like the KJV, is printed as a separate unit. Such an arrangement tends to blind the reader to the connection of verses with one another, and gives the false impression that each verse is a unit by itself. It is true that paragraphs are designated by bold-face numbers, but some readers may tend to overlook them.

Except in language addressed to Deity, the use of "thou," "thee," and "thy" has been replaced by "you" and "your." To avoid ambiguity, this pronoun in the 1963 edition of the NT was designated "you^s" or you^{pl}" when it could not be determined from the context whether a singular or plural was meant. Thus, the 1963 edition of the NT of Matthew 5:21f. reads: "You^{pl} have heard that the ancients were told, 'You^s shall not commit murder;'... but I say to you^{pl}... If therefore you^s are presenting your offering..." and so on through the chapter. This distinction is sometimes important for a correct exegesis (e.g., the plural in 1 Cor. 3:16), but the practice was evidently found to be too clumsy to be retained when the whole Bible was published in 1971. Personal pronouns referring to God the Father, Jesus Christ, and the Holy Spirit begin with a capital letter. This is true when they refer to Jesus Christ, irrespective of the speaker's attitude toward our Lord (e.g., the mob, Matt. 26:68; 27:22; Herod, Matt. 2:8; the high priest, Matt. 26:63; Pilate, Matt. 27:11-14; et al.).

The translators of the NASB NT gave careful attention to the rendering of Greek tenses. Often in the Greek text of the Gospels the present tense is used to describe a past event with the vividness of a present happening. There are 151 uses of this "historical present" in the Gospel of Mark alone. The usage of the present is translated by an English past tense marked with an asterisk.

In translating the Greek past tenses, the NASB translators sought to distinguish between the undefined action of the aorist and the continuous action of the imperfect. As in other translations, the aorist tense was translated by the English past, or, in some instances, by the perfect, or even by the past perfect. At times, when the aorist emphasizes the entrance into an act or state (ingressive aorist), they tried to reproduce this idea in English; e.g., "He became afraid" (Matt. 14:30), "they all got drowsy" (Matt. 25:5), "they became silent" (Luke 20:26), "for this brother of yours was dead and has begun to live" (Luke 15:32) (compare these passages in the RSV).

The imperfect tense is used to indicate continuous action in past time. It is often rendered in the NASB by the English past progressive (or past continuous); e.g., "he was doing." However, the repeated use of the past progressive results in a very stilted and unidiomatic English style. No English writer today would say: "And He was teaching them many things in parables, and was saying to them in His teaching, 'Listen *to this!'*" (Mark 4:2, 3); "And with many such parables He was speaking the word to them as they were able to hear it; and He was not speaking to them without parables; but He was explaining everything privately to His own disciples" (Mark 4:33, 34); "... and many of the Corinthians when they heard were believing and being baptized" (Acts 18:8).

The translators did much better with the customary imperfect: "All who were owners of lands or houses would sell them and bring the proceeds of the sales, and lay them at the apostles' feet; and they would be distributed to each, as any had need" (Acts 4:34, 35). "And a certain man who had been lame from his mother's womb, ... whom they used to set down every day at the gate of the temple..." (Acts 3:2; see also Mark 15:6; Luke 2:41; 21:37).

But apparently the prevailing use of the imperfect in the NT in the minds of the translators was the inceptive which signifies the beginning of an action. Usually they translated this as, e.g., *"began* to do." "Began" is italicized, according to the preface, to distinguish it from the Greek verb meaning "begin." Inadvertently, however, "began" is not in italics in Matthew 16:7; Mark 1:31; and Luke 12:17. Matthew 15:36 is translated, "He broke *them* [the seven loaves] and started [no italics] giving *them* to the disciples." But in Luke 7:6, "Now Jesus *started* on His way with them," "started" is italicized. The number of imperfects interpreted as having an inceptive meaning is far greater than most grammarians could accept. A quick check indicates that there are some 170 in the Gospels and Acts, with about 100 in Luke-Acts.

Several imperfects are translated in a tendential (or conative) sense; e.g., "And they tried to give Him wine" (Mark 15:23), "John tried to prevent Him" (Matt. 3:14), "they were going to call him Zacharias" (Luke 1:59; see also Mark 9:38; Luke 9:49; Acts 7:26; 18:4; 26:11). But in such cases, "tried" and "were going" are not in italics.

The future perfects in Matthew 16:19; 18:18 are rendered, "Whatever you shall bind on earth shall have been bound in heaven, and whatever you shall loose on earth shall have been loosed in heaven." Similarly the perfects in John 20:23 are translated, "If you forgive the sins of any, *their sins* have been forgiven them [marginal note: "I.e., have previously been forgiven"]; if you retain the *sins* of any, they have been retained."

In their treatment of questions, the translators have tried to reproduce the nuances of the Greek. Questions introduced by the Greek particle *ou (ouk, ouchi)* expect an affirmative answer and are generally so worded (see Matt. 7:22; 13:27, 55; Luke 12:6; 17:17; Acts 13:10; Rom. 2:26; 1 Cor. 9:1; 14:23; for exceptions, see Mark 14:60; Acts 21:38). Questions introduced by the particle *me (meti)* expect a negative answer. These are translated by a double clause—one a negative statement, the other a question: "Grapes are not gathered from thornbushes, nor figs from thistles, are they?" (Matt. 7:16); "You do not want to go away also, do you?" (John 6:67); "When the Christ shall come, He will not perform more signs than those which this man has, will He?" (John 7:31; see also Matt. 16:25; John 7:47, 51; 21:5; Rom. 11:1; 1 Cor. 6:3; 12: 28-30, et al.).

For the OT, which was published in 1971 after about ten years of labor, the revisers used as their basic text the latest edition of Kittel's *Biblia Hebraica*. In general, they stuck closely to this Hebrew text, though occasionally correcting it by the use of Hebrew MSS and ancient versions. In Judges 16:13, 14, for example, to the words " 'If you weave the seven locks of my hair with the web' " they added in square brackets these words from the Greek: " 'and fasten it with a pin, then I shall become weak and be like any other man.' So while he slept Delilah took the seven locks of his hair and wove them into the web."

The OT book in which the most changes in the traditional Hebrew text were made is Isaiah, where some thirty changes occur. Like the RSV, for example, the NASB has "you" in 1:29 rather than "they." It also agrees with the RSV in reading, "deep as Sheol or high as heaven," rather than the traditional "either in the depth or in the height above" (ASV) in 7:11. In 14:4 the "golden city" (ASV) becomes "the fury" (by changing *madhebah* to *marhebah*). In several instances, the readings of the copy of Isaiah in the *Dead Sea Scrolls* were followed (e.g., 37:20, 27; 56:5, 10). In 49:17 the translators followed the ancient versions and the *Dead Sea Scrolls* in reading, "Your builders hurry" rather than, "Your sons hurry."

A major departure of the NASB from the ASV is in abandoning the use of "Jehovah" to designate the personal covenant God, the God of revelation. It is now known that "Jehovah" is an incorrect transliteration of the tetragrammaton YHWH. Like the RSV, the NASB has gone back to the ancient practice of translating it as Lord or sometimes as God (see the marginal notes on Exod. 3:14; 6:3). Such place-names as "Jehovah-jireh" (Gen. 22:14), "Jehovah-nissi" (Exod. 17:15), and "Jehovah-shalom" (Judg. 6:24) in the ASV are translated respectively, "The Lord Will Provide," "The Lord is My Banner," and "The Lord is Peace" (see marginal notes for each).

The Semitic idiom translated in the ASV "and it came to pass" has been retained in the NASB, but slightly modernized as "and it came about" or "and it happened." The RSV committee, on the other hand, regarded this Hebrew idiom as "meaningless" in English, and "in the interest of simplicity and directness" left it untranslated.

The NASB has followed the ASV in transliterating the Hebrew word for the place of the dead as "Sheol." The corresponding term in the NT, "Hades," is likewise transliterated. "Gehenna," however, is translated as "hell" (Matt. 5:22, 29, 30; 10:28, et al.) or "the eternal fire" (Matt. 18:9).

The NASB has retained the practice, begun in the Geneva Bible and continued through the KJV and ASV, of printing in italics words for which there are no exact equivalents in the original but which have been added to make the translation conform to English idiom. Neither the KJV nor the ASV were successful in achieving complete accuracy or consistency in this use of italics, nor has the NASB achieved this well-nigh impossible goal. For example, when there is an ellipsis of the Greek word for "day," should it be italicized in English? In Matthew 28:1 and John 20:1, 19, the NASB reads "the first *day* of the week"; but in Mark 16:2, 9; Acts 20:7; and 1 Corinthians 16:2, "the first day of the week." In Luke 13:32 it has "the third *day*"; but in Acts 27:19, "the third day"; while in Hebrews 4:4, "the seventh *day*." Day is italicized in the expression "the next *day*" in Luke 13:33, but it is not in a number of similar constructions in Acts (20:15; 21:1, 8, 18; 23:32; 25:17; 27:3, 18, 19). There is an ellipsis of the word for "water" in both Matthew 10:42 and James 3:11. The former is given as "a cup of cold water" and the latter as "both fresh and bitter *water.*" The verb "to be" is often not expressed in the original. In a translation should it, therefore, be in italics? In Galatians 1:5 we have "to whom *be* the glory," but 1 Corinthians 15:57 et al., "thanks be to God." The Greek of John 5:12 has simply "take up and walk." By italicizing *your* in the rendering, "Take up *your* pallet, and walk," the NASB gives the impression that "pallet" is in the original but "your" is not, whereas both are lacking.

A prominent feature of the NASB is its marginalia and cross references placed in a column more than an inch wide on the outer edge of each page. Superscript numbers in the text refer to the marginalia, which are arranged by verses. Several kinds of marginal notes are included. Some are textual, i.e., they call attention to readings in MSS that vary from the text followed in the translation (e.g., Matt. 6:13; 19:9; Mark 1:1, 29; 9:44, 46; Luke 22:19; 24:36). Such textual notes are less numerous than in the ASV. Translational notes are far more frequent, particularly those that give the literal meaning of the original language when a freer rendering was preferred (see Matt. 7:28; 9:15; 18:6; Luke 19:22, et al.). Other translational notes suggest an alternative rendering for a word or phrase (Matt. 5:45; Luke 7:25; Rom. 4:1; 1 Cor. 2:13; 2 Tim. 3:16; Rev. 22:1, et al.). There are also explanatory notes on the meaning of geographical and personal names (Gen. 4:24; 12:9; 14:18-20; 16:14; 17:1, 5; 24:10; 25:26; 28:19; 29:32, 34, 35; 30:8, 11, 13, 18; 31:47, 49; 32:2, 28; Exod. 2:10, et al.).

Notes are included explaining the value of such coins as the talent (Matt. 18:24), denarius (Matt. 18:28; 20:9; Luke 10:35; John 6:7; 12:5; Rev. 6:6), drachma (Luke 15:8), didrachma (Matt. 17:24), stater (Matt. 17:27), mina (Luke 19:13), assarion (Matt. 10:29; Luke 12:6), and lepton (Luke 12:59). Others define measures and weights, as cubit (Gen. 6:15), log (Lev. 14:10), span (Isa. 40:12), bath (Isa. 5:10), ephah and hin (Lev. 19:36), homer (Num. 11:32), and kab (2 Kings 6:25). Still others explain such obscure terms as raca (Matt. 5:22), Mammon (Matt. 6:24; Luke 16:9, 11, 13), magi (Matt. 2:1), tax-gatherers (Matt. 5:46; 9:10; Luke 19:2), and Twin Brothers (Acts 28:11). A note to Titus 1:12 suggests the author of the quotation "Cretans are always liars, evil beasts, lazy gluttons." The paranomasia of Jeremiah 1:11, 12, between the "almond tree" *(shaked)* and "watching" *(shoked)* is also explained. A note defines the sinners of Luke 15:1 as "irreligious or non-practicing Jews," and "the Fast" of Acts 27:9 as "the Day of Atonement in October."

Finally, there are interpretive notes such as the explanation of "hate" in Luke 14:26 as meaning "by comparison with his love" for Christ, and "through the Spirit" in Acts 21:4 as signifying "because of impressions made by the Spirit." The "signs" Jesus did are explained in John's Gospel as *"attesting miracles,* i.e., one which points to the supernatural power of God in redeeming grace" (John 2:11). In the ASV all marginalia are given as footnotes on each page.

Small superscript letters in the text refer to the cross references, also arranged by verses. A sample check here and there indicates these have been taken over from the ASV. Some are printed in italics to indicate they are parallel passages. These carefully selected cross references are of great value to the serious Bible student. The wide column containing them, along with the marginal notes, make the page less attractive to the general reader.

In conclusion, one may say that the NASB represents a conservative and literal approach to the translation of the Scriptures. In the OT, the traditional Hebrew text is only occasionally modified by readings from Hebrew MSS and ancient versions. In the NT, while the twenty-third edition of the Nestle Greek NT forms the basic text, that text has been considerably modified in the direction of the "Received Text" of which the KJV is a translation. A number of verses resting on doubtful MS authority have been reintroduced into the text from the margin. There is a hesitancy to follow a modern critical Greek text. But the version does represent an honest attempt to be faithful to the Hebrew text and to the Greek readings adopted. It seeks to give an accurate literal rendering of the Hebrew and Greek. Unfortunately, however, it has failed to reach its stated goal of putting the Scriptures in "a fluent and readable style according to current English usage." Its stilted and nonidiomatic English will never give it a wide popular appeal. It does, however, have great value as a study Bible, and this is perhaps its significant place as a translation.

15

The Living Bible

For a number of years the need for putting the thoughts of the Bible writers into modern understandable English had been growing on the mind of a Wheaton, Illinois, businessman, Kenneth Nathaniel Taylor. He first became acutely aware of the need for a modern speech Bible when he was a speaker for Inter-Varsity on various college campuses in the United States and Canada. Later in his own growing family he noted the puzzled expressions on the faces of his children, now ten in number, as he read to them from the classic KJV. When he questioned them regarding their understanding of what he had read, he found they had failed to get the message. So he began to explain the passages in simple, everyday English they could understand. Thus, each day he gained experience in rewording the Bible in a simple, conversational style.

This led to his first systematic attempt, in 1956, to produce a written paraphrase of a book of Scripture. Riding a commuter train each day from his home in Wheaton to his work in Chicago, where he was the director of the Moody Literature Mission of the Moody Press, he conceived the idea of using commuter time, which most people wasted, in the production of a new modern speech rendering of the Scriptures. He began with the Book of Romans, using as his basis the extremely literal ASV.

Taylor has his roots in conservative evangelical Christianity. He received his Bachelor of Arts degree from Wheaton College in 1938, studied at Dallas Theological Seminary from 1940 to 1943, and received the Master of Theology degree from Northern Baptist Theological Seminary in 1944. He was with the Moody Literature Mission of the Moody Press from 1947 to

1962. Then he decided to form his own publishing company to promote the paraphrases he was producing. He called his new firm Tyndale House after William Tyndale, the father of the English Bible.

Taylor gives this adequate definition of what he understands by paraphrasing the Scriptures: "To paraphrase is to say something in different words than the author used. It is a restatement of an author's thoughts, using different words than he did." His diligence in carrying on this task is shown by the publication of portions of his paraphrase in the years that followed his first efforts in 1956. In 1962 he published a rendering of the NT letters with the title, *Living Letters*. This was followed by *Living Prophecies* in 1965, *Living Gospels* in 1966, and the *Living New Testament* in 1967. It is obvious that he hoped to make the Bible a living book with a vibrant message for today's world. In 1967 he also put out *Living Psalms*, followed by *Living Lessons of Life and Love* in 1968, *Living Books of Moses* in 1969, and *Living History of Israel* in 1970. The complete *Living Bible* (LB) came from the press in 1971.

Because of its readability, this new rendering into modern idiomatic English has been well received and widely acclaimed. Its circulation has been enhanced by the Billy Graham Evangelistic Association, which has publicized it on television and has given away hundreds of thousands of copies. Taylor has succeeded in making the Bible come alive for vast numbers of people, particularly for the young. In 1965 Wheaton College conferred on him the honorary degree of Doctor of Literature.

According to the preface of the *Living New Testament*, the basic text for this new rendering was the ASV of 1901. The Greek text used for the NT of the ASV, as for its 1881 English counterpart, was a marked improvement over the Received Text used as a basis for the KJV. Even so, in the light of MS discoveries and textual studies since 1881, it is clear that further improvements in the Greek text are needed. It is therefore disappointing to note that the LB does not even fully accept the critical text used for the ASV. A few of the passages in the NT that are of doubtful authenticity and were therefore removed from the ASV text and placed in footnotes are restored to the text by the LB (see Matt. 17:21; 18:11; Mark 15:28; John 5:3b-5; Acts 8:37; 24:6b-8a; Rom. 16:24). In most of these cases the LB has a footnote calling the reader's attention to the fact that many ancient MSS omit the passage. It is difficult to understand why Taylor restored John 5:3b-4; however, he did place it in parentheses.

In the OT there is also at least one departure from the basic text. In Genesis 4:8 the LB reads, "One day Cain suggested to his brother, 'Let's go out into the fields.' " The ASV has simply, "And Cain told Abel his brother." The Hebrew does not contain the words "Let us go into the fields," but they are found in the Samaritan Pentateuch, the LXX, and the Syriac versions. The LB, however, has no footnote revealing this fact.

For the most part, the LB is a simplified, easy-to-follow rendering in effective and idiomatic, present-day English. Colossians 1:16, 17 will serve as an example: "Christ himself is the Creator who made everything in heaven and earth, the things we can see and the things we can't; the spirit world with its kings and kingdoms, its rulers and authorities; all were made by Christ for his own use and glory. He was before all else began and it is his power that holds everything together."

At times the text is greatly expanded by imaginative details for which there is no warrant in the original. A clear example is in Amos 1:1, 2. Here the ASV gives a literal word-for-word translation of the Hebrew. It gives the title as "The words of Amos who was among the herdsmen of Tekoa. . . ." In the LB this becomes two full sentences: "Amos was a herdsman living in the village of Tekoa. All day long he sat on the hillsides watching the sheep, keeping them from straying." The ASV continues, ". . . which he saw concerning Israel." In the LB this becomes: "One day in a vision, God told him some of the things that were going to happen to his nation, Israel. . . . This is his report of what he saw and heard."

On the other hand, the paraphrase at times does less than justice to what the original says. Psalm 19:7-9, which extols the wonders of God's law in a beautifully structured piece of literary art, will serve as an example. The original has six different names for the written revelation and ascribes six different characteristics and functions to it. In the LB the literary beauty of the poem has given way to simple assertions: "God's laws are perfect. They protect us, make us wise, and give us joy and light. God's laws are pure, eternal, just."

One of the literary masterpieces of the OT is Isaiah 40. On the whole, the thought of the chapter is quite adequately represented in the LB. But after the appeal in vs. 26, "Look up into the heavens! Who created all these stars?" an analogy completely untrue to the original is given: "As a shepherd leads his sheep, calling each by its pet name, and counts them to see that none are lost or strayed, so God does with stars and planets!" A footnote to the word "shepherd" says, "Implied," but there is nothing in the Hebrew implying this figure of speech. Rather, the actual analogy is far more majestic, designed to display, as the prophet declares, the greatness of God's might and the force of His power. Unfortunately, this intent of the verse is completely missing in the LB. The analogy is not that of a shepherd, but of a great general reviewing his army, for that is what the word "host" used in the ASV means. God as the Lord of hosts leads forth the stars as a general summons his forces. He is a supreme general who knows by name every star in infinite space, and not one in that vast multitude fails to respond to its master.

Taylor cannot be faulted for his simple, direct rewording of the ASV into everyday English. But when he assumes the role of a commentator, and freely interprets or reinterprets a passage, his fidelity to the original is often subject to question. Above everything else, a translation must be faithful to the text of the original. It should be seriously questioned whether a translator has the right to read his own interpretation into the text. Was the forbidden tree in the Garden of Eden, for example, a "Tree of Conscience"?

Taylor interprets "the sons of God" in Genesis 6 as "evil beings from the spirit world." He holds that they were God's "created, supernatural beings, but no longer godly in character" (footnote), who fell in love with women on earth, "the daughters of men." Hence he translates:

> Now a population explosion took place upon the earth. It was at this time that beings from the spirit world looked upon the beautiful earth women and took any they desired to be their wives. . . . In those days, and even afterwards, when the evil beings from the spirit world were sexually involved with human women, their children became giants, of whom so many legends are told (Gen. 6:1, 2, 4).

He does, however, admit in the footnote: "Some commentators believe that the expression 'sons of God' refers to the 'godly line' of Seth, and 'daughters of men' to the men of the line of Cain."

Christians of various persuasions have long debated the correct translation of the Hebrew word *'almah* in Isaiah 7:14. Taylor translates, "A child shall be born to a virgin." But then in a footnote he writes:

> The controversial Hebrew word used here sometimes means "virgin" and sometimes "young woman." Its immediate use here refers to Isaiah's young wife and her new-born son (Isaiah 8:1-4). This, of course, was not a virgin birth. God's sign was that before this child was old enough to talk (verse 4) the two invading kings would be destroyed. However, the Gospel of Matthew (1:23) tells us that there was a further fulfillment of this prophecy, in that a virgin (Mary) conceived and bore a son, Immanuel, the Christ. We have therefore properly used this higher meaning, "virgin," in verse 14, as otherwise the Matthew account loses its significance.

The interpretation given of the opening words of the last book of the Bible is questionable: "This book unveils some of the future activities soon to occur in the life of Jesus Christ" (Rev. 1:1). From the viewpoint of grammar, it is true that the title as given in the ASV, "The Revelation of Jesus Christ," could theoretically mean either "a revelation given by Jesus Christ" or "a revelation about Jesus Christ." But the rest of the verse makes it obvious that the first of these is intended, not the second. And even if we were to take the second interpretation, it would still be far from referring to "some of the future activities soon to occur in the life of Jesus Christ." The last clause of vs. 1 also is not true to the original: ". . . and then an angel was sent from heaven to explain the vision's meaning."

Verse 10 in the ASV begins, "I was in the Spirit on the Lord's day." In the LB this becomes, "It was the Lord's Day and I was worshiping." Certainly this is an unusual interpretation of being "in the Spirit." It occurs again in 4:2; 17:3; and 21:10 and means the Spirit took control of him, i.e., he was given a vision.

The LB rendering of the first beatitude does less than justice to Jesus' words: " 'Humble men are very fortunate!' he told

them, 'for the Kingdom of Heaven is given to them' " (Matt.
5:3). While humility is a Christian virtue, there is something
deeper implied here. The "poor in spirit" are those who have a
deep sense of spiritual poverty (see Isa. 66:2). They are not
only humble but have a feeling of spiritual destitution, and
recognize their need of God, in contrast to those who feel rich
in spiritual achievement and religious understanding.

The careful student of the Gospels also feels compelled to
protest the distorted picture of Jesus' messianic claims as set
forth in the LB. It is a well-known fact that Jesus was very
reticent about referring to Himself as the Messiah. When others
designated Him as such, He did not refuse to accept it, but
He evidently preferred not to be thus addressed. There can be
little doubt that this was because of the political overtones
associated with the word "Messiah." That term did not give the
people an adequate picture of His mission. Hence, Jesus preferred to be known as the "son of man" (see Mark 9:29-31;
Matt. 26:63, 64, ASV). This was His own characteristic self-
designation, used more than eighty times in the Gospels. Since
the title never appears on the lips of Jesus' followers, its usage
must go back to Jesus Himself. In all probability it stems
from the designation of the heavenly figure in Daniel 7:13.
Unfortunately, in the LB this characteristic self-designation
has disappeared from the text of the Gospels. In its place one
finds "the Messiah" (Mark 9:13; Luke 21:27; 24:6), "I, the
Messiah" (Matt. 8:20; 9:5; 11:19; 12:8, et al.), or simply "I"
(Matt. 10:23; 13:42; 16:13, et al.). Thus, according to this
paraphrase, our Lord freely and repeatedly claimed to be the
Messiah.

In his preface, Taylor frankly admits there are dangers in
paraphrases:

> For whenever the author's exact words are not translated from
> the original languages, there is a possibility that the trans-
> lator, however honest, may be giving the English reader some-
> thing that the original writer did not mean to say. This is be-
> cause a paraphrase is guided not only by the translator's skill
> in simplifying but also by the clarity of his understanding of
> what the author meant and by his theology. For when the
> Greek or Hebrew is not clear, then the theology of the transla-
> tor is his guide along with his sense of logic.... The theo-

logical lodestar in this book has been a rigid evangelical position.

It may be seriously questioned whether a translator should be guided by his theology in translating the Word of God. Should he not rather submit his theology to the Word? The function of a translator is to determine as accurately as possible what the original writer said, and then to state this as precisely as possible in effective English. Taylor, however, did not work directly from the original Hebrew, Aramaic, and Greek documents, but from a standard English translation of the late nineteenth and early twentieth centuries. The LB, therefore, suffers from the limitation of being a secondary translation, i.e., it is a translation of a translation. It is further limited by the fact that the translator frankly states he was guided by his theology. It would no doubt be helpful for the reader to know what Taylor means by "a rigid evangelical position." But this is not spelled out.

One can, perhaps, guess at some aspects of it by noting certain renderings in the LB along with footnotes that are given. The ASV gives a literal translation of Psalm 115:17, "The dead praise not Jehovah, neither any that go down into silence." But in the LB this becomes "The dead cannot sing praises to Jehovah here on earth." The ASV rendering of Psalm 6:5 reads, "For in death there is no remembrance of thee: In Sheol who shall give thee thanks?" The LB translates, "For if I die I cannot give you glory by praising you before my friends," apparently implying that he could praise God in heaven. In the LB, Ecclesiastes 9:5 is "For the living at least know that they will die! But the dead know nothing; they don't even have their memories." But a footnote declares, "These statements are Solomon's discouraged opinion, and do not reflect a knowledge of God's truth on these points!" Psalm 73:24 in the ASV reads, "Thou wilt guide me with thy counsel, and afterward receive me to glory" (possibly meaning "honor"). The last clause in the LB is "and afterwards receive me into the glories of heaven."

In the NT Paul's famous saying "For I am already being offered, and the time of my departure has come" (2 Tim. 4:6, ASV) is translated, "My time has almost run out. Very soon now I will be on my way to heaven." First Thessalonians 4:14 in the LB reads, "For since we believe that Jesus died and then came back to life again, we can also believe that when Jesus returns, God will bring with him all the Christians who have died." The ambiguous wording of this paraphrase makes it doubtful as to what Taylor had in mind. In the light of other passages, such as those quoted above, this translation is probably intended to convey the idea that God will bring these departed ones back from heaven with Jesus when He returns. While some commentators follow this interpretation, a more probable one is that God will bring back to life those Christians who have died. Faith in the resurrection of Christ thus calls for faith also in the resurrection of those who have fallen asleep in death as Christians.

The Hebrew word for the place of the dead, *Sheol*, is consistently transliterated in the ASV. The LB, however, frequently translates it as "hell," as though it were a place of punishment—contrary to Hebrew thought. "The wicked shall be sent away to hell" (Ps. 9:17). "Hell is licking its chops in anticipation of this delicious morsel, Jerusalem" (Isa. 5:14). "But they don't realize that her former guests are now citizens of hell" (Prov. 9:18). "The denizens of hell crowd to meet you as you enter their domain" (Isa. 14:9).

In other places *Sheol* is translated "grave." Psalm 16:10 is adequately rendered, "For you will not leave me among the dead; you will not allow your beloved one to rot in the grave." However, when this passage is quoted in Acts 2:27, the meaning is distorted by inserting the word "body" in contrast to "soul": "You will not leave my soul in hell or let the body of your Holy Son decay." Thus a false dichotomy, foreign to OT thinking, is introduced into the quotation. This is made abundantly clear in vs. 31 where the word "soul" is inserted and "flesh" is rendered "body": "The Messiah's soul would not be left in hell and his body would not decay."

In arguing for the resurrection, Jesus asked the Sadducees, "Have you not read in the book of Moses . . . how God spake unto him saying, I am the God of Abraham, and the God of Isaac, and the God of Jacob?" (Mark 12:26, ASV, quoting Exod. 3:6). Then He added, "He is not the God of the dead, but of the living" (vs. 27). This comment of Jesus is given in the LB as follows: "God was telling Moses that these men, though dead for hundreds of years, were still very much alive; for he would not have said, 'I *am* the God' of those who don't exist! You have made a serious error." In the parallel in Luke 20:38 the LB has, "To say that the Lord *is* some person's God means that person is *alive,* not dead! So from God's point of view, all men are living." In Matthew 22:32, the other Gospel parallel, the LB reads, "So God is not the God of the dead, but of the living." But a footnote explains: "I.e., if Abraham, Isaac, and Jacob, long dead, were not alive in the presence of God, then God would have said, 'I *was* the God of Abraham, etc.'" Thus in all three passages Taylor interprets Jesus' comment as meaning that Abraham, Isaac, and Jacob are alive in the presence of God.

While this interpretation is given by several commentaries, it cannot be the correct one, and it points out the danger in a translator's trying to interpret Scripture for the reader rather than letting the Word speak for itself. Clearly in this context the subject under discussion is the resurrection of the dead, which the Sadducees denied (Matt. 22:23, 31; Mark 12:18, 26; Luke 20:27, 37). Jesus is quoting from Exodus 3:6, not to argue for the immortality of the soul, but to show that the Sadducees were wrong in denying a resurrection. And we may well ask, How would the continuous existence of the ancient patriarchs prove the resurrection? A note in the *Oxford Annotated Bible* (p. 1201) gives a better explanation: "The idea here is that men who are related to God in faith have life even though physically dead. Resurrection is the divine act by which men will achieve the fulness of life intended in creation and lost through sin and death."

In Luke 20:34ff. Jesus sets forth the common NT theme of two antithetical ages: the present age and the age to come. In the present age there is marriage, the production of children, and ultimately death. "But those who are accounted worthy to attain to that age and to the resurrection from the dead neither marry nor are given in marriage, for they cannot die any more, because they are equal to angels, and are sons of God, being sons of the resurrection" (Luke 20:35, 36, RSV). By the fact of "physical birth men are a part of this age, which continues until the parousia of Christ" (Matt. 24:3; 13:49f.). They be-come a part of the age to come by the resurrection, and it is "those who are accounted worthy" who attain to that age. It was in anticipation of this resurrection that Jesus could speak of the God of the patriarchs as the God of the living. He beheld the results of His redemptive work as though it were already existing.

In view of a coming resurrection—in view of the certainty of the fact that there is to be one—they all live unto God. The argument is similar to Paul's explanation that God had made Abraham the father of many nations (Rom. 4:17), the latter part of which the LB appropriately translates, "And this prom-ise is from God himself, who makes the dead live again and speaks of future events with as much certainty as though they were already past."

There are numerous other readings whose fidelity to the original is questionable. "For Moses gave us only the Law with its rigid demands and merciless justice, while Jesus Christ brought us loving forgiveness as well" is the translation given of John 1:17. But this not only reads a great deal into the pas-sage that is not there, but it also gives a distorted view of the Pentateuch. Salvation means more than bringing people to heaven (Rom. 1:16, 17), and the righteousness of God is more than a "way to heaven" (Rom. 3:21, 22). Taylor admits that his translation of Matthew 13:52, "Those experts in Jewish law who are now my disciples have double treasures—from the Old Testament as well as from the New," is "highly ana-chronistic" (footnote). But if it is anachronistic, what defense is there for using it to translate Jesus' words? The rendering of 1 Corinthians 16:2 is also anachronistic: "On every Lord's Day each of you should put aside something from what you have earned during the week...." The Greek has simply "on the first day of the week," and there is no evidence that it was called "the Lord's Day" in the first century. The translation of Acts 20:7 is also questionable: "On Sunday, we gathered for a communion service." Again, the Greek has, "On the first day of the week...." The meeting referred to was obviously a night farewell service. It is not entirely clear whether the days are reckoned on the Jewish basis from sundown to sundown, or on the Roman basis from midnight to midnight. But the former seems most likely, in which case the meeting was held on Saturday night (see NEB, TEV). Moreover, it is not clear that this was a communion service. The original has "to break bread." This expression can mean either an ordinary meal (Acts 2:42, 46) or the Lord's Supper. In any case, it was not called a "communion service" in NT times. Other questionable interpretations are given in Hebrews 5:7; 13:10; 2 Corinthians 7:14; 1 Peter 3:18f.; 5:1; 2 Timothy 2:8; 3:16, et al.

Taylor is to be congratulated for producing an appealing and readable paraphrase that may well arouse a new interest in the Bible. Although his vernacular at times borders on vulgarity (e.g., 1 Sam. 20:30), the language is, in the main, highly readable and effective. For an accurate rendering of the teaching of the sacred Word, however, it often comes far short. It is a secondary version inasmuch as it is a translation of a translation. Furthermore, although the Greek text on which the NT of the ASV is based was a marked improvement on the Received Text of the KJV, there are better Greek texts available. Taylor could therefore have produced a more accurate translation had he chosen a modern critical edition of the Greek text and faithfully followed it. Furthermore, in his paraphrasing Taylor takes many liberties in leaving out or adding materials, and it is, therefore, unsafe to build one's concept of biblical truth on so free a version. He himself suggests, "For study purposes, a paraphrase should be checked against a rigid translation." By a "rigid translation" he perhaps means some literal version like the ASV. Certainly it is unsafe to follow the LB without first checking it against a more faithful translation, or, better yet, against a good critical text of the original Hebrew, Aramaic, and Greek.

16
The New International Version

The most recent of the major modern-speech Bibles is *The New International Version* (NIV), the NT of which was published in September, 1973. It is a completely new translation made directly from the original languages of the Bible. The decision to produce it was formalized by a group of biblical scholars meeting in Chicago in 1965. This was the culmination of several years of exploratory study by Evangelicals from a number of different churches beginning in the 1950s, before the flood of modern translations began. This study was initiated when interested groups from the Christian Reformed Church and the Commission on Education of the National Association of Evangelicals found each other. The project launched in Chicago in 1965 received a new impetus in 1967 when the New York International Bible Society agreed to sponsor it financially.

Though a number of modern-speech versions have appeared since the project was first conceived, there is still a distinctive place for a new translation suitable for private reading as well as public worship. Some of the modern versions have language that is too informal, regional, or colloquial to be suitable for liturgical or church use. In others, the English is not idiomatic, but artificial and wooden. Some are excessively free or paraphrastic and lack fidelity to the sacred original text. Some are one-man productions, which have not been subjected to the checks and balances of a large committee and therefore contain idiosyncrasies.

The NIV is called an "International" version because, in the first place, the committee producing it consists of distinguished

Bible scholars from such English-speaking countries as Canada, England, Australia, and New Zealand, as well as the United States. In the second place, English is today an international language, and the translators have sought to use vocabulary common to the major English-speaking nations of the world. They have sought to avoid the use of Americanisms on the one hand and Anglicisms on the other. Their success in avoiding the former is evident from the fact that, though a British edition was published in 1974, few changes in vocabulary were felt necessary, though British spelling was adopted. The version is also transdenominational in character. The translators come from many denominations, including Baptist, Brethren, Church of Christ, Episcopalian, Lutheran, Mennonite, Methodist, Nazarene, Presbyterian, Christian Reformed, and others. An interchange among such a wide variety of religious persuasions is an effective safeguard against sectarianism.

The governing body of the project consists of fifteen members, most of whom are well-known biblical specialists in the USA. The Executive Secretary of this committee is Dr. Edwin H. Palmer. Among the one hundred translators whose services have been enlisted are a number of world-renowned scholars, including Gleason Archer, Roland K. Harrison, William Hendriksen, E. M. Blaiklock, Elmer B. Smick, William Lane, Leon Morris, Ralph Earle, Donald J. Wiseman, to name but a few.

The initial translation of each book is the work of a small team of scholars. After they have done their best with the text, their work is submitted for restudy and revision, with constant reference to the original, by an Intermediate Editorial Committee. It then goes to the General Editorial Committee for further review and thorough revision. Inasmuch as a sensitive feeling for English style does not always go with scholarship in biblical languages, the work is next submitted to literary consultants and tested for clarity and idiom. The suggestions made are kept in mind by the governing body as the translation is reviewed and further revised. Before being issued in final form, it is again read by literary consultants.

Few translations since the KJV of 1611 have been as carefully done as this one. At each stage of the process there has been a wrestling of various minds with the sacred text and an honest attempt to say in simple, clear English what the Bible writers express in the originals. It is difficult to conceive a plan that could have better checks and balances than the one used. Along with this, attention has been given to the literary quality of the English and an attempt has been made to achieve a version worthy of memorization.

In reading this translation, one will find very few awkward constructions. The translation as a whole is straightforward, clear, and reliable. It is generally written in a dignified manner; only rarely does one find something he might judge to be too colloquial. Before examining the translation more closely, let us examine the Greek text used for this translation.

No specific Greek edition is mentioned as the base for the translation. Instead, an eclectic text was used. This means that one has to examine each of the passages where textual variants appear separately. However, only the key passages will be examined. First of all, most of the harmonizing passages that were added in Matthew and found in the KJV have been omitted (such as those found in Matt. 5:44; 17:21; 18:11; 21:36; Luke 9:54, 55, 56; 23:17; 23:18; 24:6, et al.). Obviously late readings (found in the KJV) have also been omitted, such as the second half of Matthew 6:13, "For thine is the kingdom and the power and the glory forever. Amen"; John 5:3, 4; Acts 8:37; and 1 John 5:7, 8. Unfortunately, however, Matthew 21:44; Luke 24:6a, 12, 36, 40, and 51 are included in the text. The longer passages, such as Mark 16:9-20 and John 7:53-8:11, are also still placed in the text, according to their verse numeration, in the same print. Lines are drawn before and after the passages and notes indicate that early MSS omit these passages. In the case of the passage in Mark, none of the other endings are given either in the same print or in the footnotes. In regard to the passage in John, no explanation is given as to the fact that when it is included it is sometimes found at the end of the Gospel of John or after Luke 21:38. In Romans 8:28 the NIV has "in all things God works for the good of those who love him." There are some passages that are disputed by scholars. In regard to these, the NIV has included Luke 22:19b, 20; Matthew 12:47; Luke 22:44; Matthew 16:2, 3. In John 5:2 NIV has selected "Bethesda" instead of "Bethzatha"; in Ephesians 1:1 it has included "Ephesus"; in Matthew 27:16 it has omitted "Jesus" before "Barabbas"; in Mark

1:41 it has "filled with compassion" instead of NEB's "in warm indignation."

Certain passages are ambiguous in the Greek text and thus have been translated differently by different versions. The NIV translation is given first, followed by the alternative translation or translations:

Mark 15:39

"Surely this man was the Son of God!"

"Truly this man was a son of God." NEB, RSV (1st ed.)

John 1:3, 4

"without him nothing was made that has been made. In him was life, and that life was the light of men."

"No single thing was created without him. All that came to be was alive with his life, and that life was the light of men." NEB

John 1:9

"The true light that gives light to every man was coming into the world."

"That was the true Light, which lighteth every man that cometh into the world." KJV

Romans 9:5

"Theirs are the patriarchs, and from them is traced the human ancestry of Christ, who is God over all, forever praised! Amen."

"to them belong the patriarchs, and of their race, according to the flesh, is the Christ. God who is over all be blessed for ever. Amen." RSV, NEB

1 Corinthians 7:36

"If anyone thinks he is acting improperly toward the virgin he is engaged to, and if she is getting along in years and he feels he ought to marry, he should do as he wants. He is not sinning. They should get married."

In the KJV, it is implied that the "virgin" is the father's daughter. In the RSV, the "virgin" is the man's betrothed and in NEB she is a man's "partner in celibacy."

1 Thessalonians 4:4

"that each of you should learn to control his own body in a way that is holy and honorable."

"That each one of you know how to take a wife for himself in holiness and honor." RSV

1 Timothy 3:2
"the husband of but one wife"
"married only once" RSV; "faithul to his one wife" NEB

A very interesting passage in recent translations has been Matthew 16:18. NIV has "And I tell you that you are Peter, and on this rock...." However, the note reads *"Peter* means *rock."* It is not as explicit as NEB's "You are Peter, the Rock," but is not far from it. This is rather surprising for a conservative version. The traditional conservative position is that "Peter" means a rolling stone.

Reading this version in isolation, one discovers few expressions that are unusual, because of archaic, awkward, or too-colloquial language. In the Gospel of Matthew, the following were noted: In 1:18 "to be with child" does not seem modern enough, though most of the modern versions still use that phrase. Phillips has "to be pregnant," which seems more appropriate for a modern translation. In 1:25 "he had no union with her" is not the idiom of today. It is better than "knew her not" of the RSV, but Phillips, NEB, and JB read, ". . . had no intercourse with her," which is a much better reading. Putting a lamp "under a bowl" sounded a bit strange. There are differences here in the translations, to be sure, such as "meal-tub" (NEB), "bushel" (RSV), "tub" (JB), and "bucket" (Phillips), but somehow "bowl" does not seem to be right. Without a qualifying adjective, it implies something too small. "Do not murder," found earlier in NEB, is the modern way of expressing "Thou shalt not kill," but somehow it does not seem to be strong enough. JB has "You must not kill." "Put up with you" in 17:17 and "he grabbed him" in 18:28 seem a bit colloquial to us, although other earlier versions have used these expressions. "Capstone" in 21:42 is not the same as "corner-stone." "Spices" in 23:23 is an unnecessary addition. "Yes, it is you" in 26:25 seems a bit too direct for what is intended and fails to capture the Oriental manner of expressing statements in an indirect way. "Gave up his spirit" in 27:50 is not modern idiom.

The above is not a long list, indicating that the version generally reads well. It has very few awkward expressions, but on the other hand not many striking ones either.

Some interesting translations of NIV are "the darkness has not understood it" (John 1:5), "lived for a while among us"

(John 1:14), "one and only Son" (John 3:16, 18), "verdict" (John 3:19), "how dare you lecture us" (John 9:34), "this is getting us nowhere" (John 12:19), "Counselor" (John 14:16), "child of hell" (John 17:12), "sacrifice of atonement" (Rom. 3:25), "evil is right there with me" (Rom. 7:21), "the Lord will carry out his sentence on earth with speed and finality" (Rom. 9:28), "eternally condemned" (Gal. 1:8, 9), "Peter" instead of "Cephas" (Gal. 1:18; 2:9, 11, 14), "the whole world is a prisoner of sin" (Gal. 3:22), "who cut in on you" (Gal. 5:7), "basic principles of this world" (Col. 2:8, 20).

In any translation there will be differences of opinion regarding the validity or appropriateness of certain translations. Bruce has questioned the translation of John 1:5 and 14 (*Christianity Today,* Sept. 28, 1973, pp. 25, 26). Questionable also is the translation of "verdict" in John 3:19. What follows it does not read like a verdict. The JB's "on these grounds sentence is pronounced" is an excellent translation of this. "Child of hell" in John 17:12 is an unfortunate translation. It fails to translate correctly the Hebrew idiom, for one thing, and for another it mistranslates the Greek word. Again, the JB has a better translation: "the one who chose to be lost." "Eternally condemned" (Gal. 1:18; 2:9, 11, 14) is probably too strong. The translation "Peter" where the Greek clearly reads "Cephas" is difficult to understand. A note would have been sufficient to explain that "Cephas" is "Peter." Bruce also noted that the same Greek word translated "righteousness" in Romans 3:21, 22 is translated "justice" in 3:26. The same type of thing has happened in Matthew 16:25, 26 where NIV has translated the same Greek word as "life" in vs. 25 but "soul" in v. 26. In Acts 1:10, 11 the same Greek word is translated "sky" in vs. 10 but "heaven" in vs. 11.

To see exactly what differences or similarities it had with several different types of translations, a careful comparison was made between selected passages in this translation and those of the RSV and NEB. The first passage compared was Matthew 5:3-10. Here NIV deviated from the RSV only slightly. "Shall" of the RSV was changed to "will." In 5:6 RSV had "satisfied"; NIV, "filled." In 5:7 RSV had "shall obtain mercy"; NIV, "will be shown mercy." In 5:10 RSV had "for righteousness' sake"; NIV, "because of righteousness." NEB differs so much that it is not possible to make this type of comparison. This indicates the conservative nature of the NIV.

The second passage analyzed was Luke 15:11-32. Here there are many more differences from the RSV than in the previous passage. The NIV has moved away from the literalism of the RSV, especially in regard to the translation of the conjunction "and." Sometimes it has a different conjunction; sometimes it simply drops it. "And he said" of the RSV in 15:11 has been changed radically to "Jesus continued." The NIV has taken liberties here by adding "Jesus," which is not in the Greek and altered "said" to "continued." While some of the changes are not improvements, it is surprising, when one makes a close comparison, to note how NIV modernizes more than RSV. These include NIV's "my share of the estate" for "the share of the property that falls to me," "property" for "living," "set off for a distant country" for "took his journey into a far country," "wild living" for "loose living," "there was a severe famine" for "a great famine arose," "food to spare" for "bread enough and to spare," "here I am starving to death" for "I perish here with hunger," "set out" for "arise," "against you" for "before you," "finger" for "hand," "let's have a feast and celebrate" for "let us eat and make merry," "what was going on" for "what this meant," "fattened" for "fatted," "pleaded with" for "entreated," "so I could celebrate" for "that I may make merry," "squandered" for "devoured," "everything I have" for "all that is mine," "we had to celebrate" for "it was fitting to make merry."

It is interesting to compare the above NIV changes with the NEB readings. For those changes noted above NEB reads, "my share of the property," "the whole of his share," "left home for a distant country," "reckless living," "a severe famine fell," "more food than they can eat," "here am I, starving to death," "set off," "against you," "finger," "let us have a feast to celebrate the day," "what it meant," "fatted," "pleaded with," "for a feast," "running through your money," "everything I have," and "how could we help celebrating." There are a good number of similarities between NIV and NEB.

Besides those above, we note the following (the first reading is that of the NEB): "younger" — "younger one," "flung his arms around him" — "threw his arms around him," "Quick! fetch a robe, my best one" — "Quick! Bring the best robe," and "I have slaved for you" — "I've been slaving for you." The reading of "pigs," "he came to his senses," "still a long way off," and "sandals," is identical in both.

Some NEB influence seems apparent from the above examination. What is worthy of note also is the extremely conservative nature of the RSV translation. In spite of all the criticism leveled at it when it was first published, looking back from our vantage point today, it seems to be a very conservative translation. It is obvious from our examination that it failed to modernize the language adequately. NIV has done this, but NEB had already done so some time before.

The final passage we examine is Romans 7:4-12. The NIV improves on the RSV in 7:4 with "So, my brothers" for "Likewise, brethren," and "sinful nature" for "flesh" in 7:5. However, although there are considerable changes, no significant improvements were observed. Again the NEB is much freer than the NIV.

The NIV has a short preface and relatively few notes. Other than these, it provides no additional helps. There are no maps or indexes or introductions to individual books or groups of books. The notes give cross references, alternative translations or readings, and short explanatory remarks. The material is printed in one column with rather inconspicuous verse numbers. There are short paragraph headings.

The preface mentions that "brackets are occasionally used to indicate words or phrases supplied for clarification." This is not to suggest that the brackets have taken the place of italics as used in the KJV. Nevertheless, the same type of inconsistency arises with the use of brackets and one wonders why brackets were felt to be necessary in the places where they are added and not necessary at other places. For example, Galatians 2:4 reads, "[This matter arose] because some false brothers had infiltrated our ranks." In Galatians 4:17 we have "What they want is to alienate you [from us]." However, Romans 11:11 reads, "Did they stumble so as to fall beyond recovery?" "Beyond recovery" is implied but is not in the Greek text; yet it is not bracketed. It is unfortunate that this policy was followed, because it is difficult to know exactly what should be bracketed and what should not.

The NIV has also been inconsistent in translating expressions of time, money, measure, and distance. In Matthew 18:24 the servant owed the king "ten thousand talents," explained in a note as "several million dollars," and his fellow-servant owed him "a hundred denarrii," explained as "a few dollars." The laborers received "a denarius for the day" (Matt. 20:2), and the "denarius" is the sample for tribute money (Mark 12:15). "Talents" and "minas" are also used in Matthew 25:14-30 and Luke 19:11-27 respectively. But in John 12:5 the perfume was worth "a year's wages" (300 denarii), and in John 6:7 "eight months' wages" (200 denarii) "would not buy enough bread for each one to have a bite!" In John 1:39 "tenth hour" is used and "seventh hour" in John 4:52. Luke 24:13; John 6:19; and 11:18 translate "stadia" into "miles," but this is not done in Revelation 14:20 (1,600 stadia) and 21:16 (12,000 stadia), although in each case the note indicates the approximate number of miles. In John 21:8 "cubits" is translated into "yards" but in Revelation 21:17 "144 cubits" is used. "Tenth hour" (John 1:39) and "seventh hour" (John 4:52) are still used instead of modern equivalents.

The NIV has followed the current practice of replacing the obsolete "thou," "thee," "thy," and "thine" with the forms of "you" even when Jesus or the Father is addressed. By this many problems are avoided where one has to decide whether Jesus is being addressed as merely a man or as a divine person. Also quotation marks are used for direct address. While this is a good practice, it leads inevitably to differences in a few places. Especially is this true in John 3 in Jesus' conversation with Nicodemus. Following NEB, JB, NAB, and Phillips, NIV has ended the quotation of Jesus after vs. 21. RSV ended the quotation after vs. 15.

On the whole, one must say that the NIV translation is accurate and clear. It does not have the color or striking characteristics of Phillips or the NEB but it is dependable and straightforward. It is more modern than the RSV and less free than NEB or Phillips. It will probably be used widely as the Bible for conservative Christians.

17
Guidelines for Selecting a Version

The Bible has been translated more often and into more languages than any other book in the world. It speaks today in over 1,200 languages. More than that, it speaks with multiple voices in many of the world's leading languages. This is especially true in English. No period of history has had such a profusion of English Bibles as the present century, and particularly the last thirty years. It may be seriously questioned whether the present generation has need of additional new English versions. However, no version of the Bible can ever be considered final. Translations must keep pace with the results of scholarly research, particularly as ambiguities and obscurities in the sacred text are removed. There is also the possibility, if not probability, that new discoveries of ancient MSS will yet be made that will throw light on the original wording. Translations must also keep abreast of the slow, subtle changes constantly taking place in the English language to make sure the Scriptures communicate to modern man.

There has never been an age when Bibles were so readily available as today. They can be bought in paperback, cloth, or leather. The great quantity and variety of versions has bewildered many a would-be reader of the sacred pages. The question is frequently asked, "What is the best version?" There is no simple answer to this question, but there are guidelines that may prove helpful.

To the younger generation it is quite clear that the KJV, for all its literary beauty, is hopelessly out of date. It may still speak to the Bible lover of the older generation who has become familiar with its sixteenth-century English, but for the majority of English-speaking people its language has become almost a foreign tongue. There is grave danger that the continued use of this version may give modern man the impression that the Bible belongs to another age, and that it is irrelevant to the twentieth century.

But if the KJV is abandoned, what version is to take its place? Perhaps no one version will be sufficient for today. This may well be an age when multiple versions are needed. If one asks, "Which version is best?" we need to add the questions, "Best for whom?" and "Best for what?" A version suitable for a child just learning to read may not appeal to a college youth. Adults accustomed to church language may not care for a version in which the familiar terms of biblical English are discarded. A version found helpful in private reading at home may not be suitable for pulpit use in public worship. A Bible suited for committed Christians may not speak with the same force to non-Christians.

There are various purposes that different versions are designed to serve. It would be unfair to judge every version on the same basis. Almost every version contains an introduction that, among other things, states the objectives the translator or translators had in mind in producing the work. What are some of the purposes the new versions are designed to serve?

A number of versions are designed for private reading at home. The popular version of J. B. Phillips began as an attempt to make Paul's letters communicate to modern youth, such as those in London. The unanticipated use of this version as an authoritative text for Bible study groups so alarmed the translator that he felt compelled to produce a second edition, published in 1972. He had used a rather poor Greek text as the basis of the first edition. For the second edition he substituted the United Bible Societies' Greek Testament. Furthermore, his high regard for the truth of the sacred Scriptures frightened him when he realized the extent of the freedom he had used in his first edition. He writes, "This passion of mine for communication . . . has led me sometimes into paraphrase and sometimes to interpolate clarifying remarks which are certainly not in the Greek." Hence, in the second edition he seeks to be more loyal to the Greek text.

The Living Bible, as the author of this very free paraphrase,

Kenneth N. Taylor, asserts, has value for "rapid reading" and for acquiring a "sweeping movement" of the story of redemption. But for careful study it is too free in adding, leaving out, and even changing materials to be trusted. Taylor himself has admitted, "For study purposes a paraphrase should be checked against a rigid translation."

There are recent versions particularly suitable for careful study. One of these is the *New American Standard Bible,* which represents a very conservative and literal approach to the text. It reveals an honest attempt to reproduce accurately the nuances of the original languages and has taken over the valuable cross references of the ASV. However, though it has great value as a study Bible, its stilted and nonidiomatic English makes it unsuitable for pulpit use.

The Amplified Bible with its multiple renderings is also not suitable for public reading, but is at times suggestive and stimulating in private study. It is in the nature of a miniature commentary. The introduction to it plainly states, "It is not a substitute for other translations. It is intended to supplement them, authentically, concisely, and in a convenient form."

For use in public worship the RSV is the best successor to the KJV. It seeks to combine the values of the historic Protestant versions with modern vocabulary and the latest in biblical scholarship. The NEB is also designed for pulpit use but is much freer and at times too colloquial. It is too early to tell how the NIV will rate, but the NT appears to be very suitable for use in worship.

Some translations are designed to serve the needs of readers with a limited English background. *The Bible in Basic English,* for example, has a limited vocabulary of 850-1000 words, with an additional 50 special "Bible" words. Charles Kingsley Williams in his translation, *In Plain English,* uses a vocabulary of about 1650 words, 160-170 of which are explained in the glossary. Such translations sacrifice literary beauty for simplicity and ease of understanding. No rigid limit was set for the vocabulary of *Today's English Version.* Nevertheless, it uses "words and forms accepted as standard by people everywhere who employ English as a means of communication."

Some translations indicate special care in bringing out the force of the Greek verbs as well as other elements of the original.

Charles B. Williams' *The New Testament in the Language of the People* concentrates primarily on the translation of the Greek verbs, while Kenneth S. Wuest's *Expanded Translation of the New Testament* extends to other elements of the language as well. The latter especially has been criticized for overtranslation of the Greek. Such translations again sacrifice beauty of style to achieve their goal. This is true also of the NASB.

Inasmuch as different versions serve different purposes, it would not be fair to evaluate them all by the same standards, as we have said. These varying objectives also suggest the desirability of having more than one version available. These versions should not be chosen merely on the basis of personal appeal. It is not safe merely to say, "I like the way this version renders this verse." Obviously, it does not necessarily follow that the rendering is correct. Nevertheless, the element of personal appeal, subjective as it is, is not wholly out of place when used in connection with more basic guidelines. If a version is to be read, it must have appeal; it must speak. But there are more basic criteria. What are they?

The first criterion concerns the underlying text from which the translation is made. The Wycliffe Bible, which was the first complete English Bible, was a translation of the Latin Vulgate. The Vulgate has been the standard Bible of Roman Catholicism for hundreds of years. The Rheims-Douai and the recent Ronald Knox versions are translations of it. This means they are translations of a translation. The NAB, however, is an excellent Catholic translation based on the originals. *The Living Bible* is not directly based on the originals but is a paraphrase of a translation, the ASV. The NT of all of the standard Protestant Bibles from Tyndale through the KJV were based on an inferior Greek text, known as the Received Text or the TR (Textus Receptus). This text goes back to the work of Erasmus, who first published the Greek NT in 1516. His text was made from a handful of Greek MSS dating from the Middle Ages. Between them and the autographs were many copyings, with consequent errors creeping in. Many of these inaccuracies, as Sir Frederic Kenyon said, "now can be corrected with absolute certainty from the vastly wider information which is at our disposal today."

This is not to say that the TR is a bad text or that it is a heretical text. It contains the Gospel of Jesus Christ. But some parts of it are not in the form which the original writers wrote. With regard to the great bulk of the words in the NT there is no dispute. Nevertheless, some important passages are affected. Some of the major differences between the TR and a modern critical text are found in the following areas: (1) the omission or inclusion of substantial passages: Matthew 16:2b, 3; Mark 16:9-20; Luke 22:19b, 20, 43, 44; John 7:53-8:11; 1 John 5:7, 8; (2) the omission or inclusion of shorter passages, such as Matthew 6:13; 17:21; 18:11; 21:44; Mark 9:44, 46; Luke 9:56; Acts 8:37; Romans 16:24; (3) the substitution of an important word or set of words for another, e.g., Acts 20:28; 1 Timothy 3:16; Revelation 22:14; and (4) the omission or inclusion of a significant word or small group of words, e.g., Matthew 6:4, 6; 1 Corinthians 6:20; 11:24; 1 John 3:1.

Most twentieth-century translations of the NT are based on one or another of the following critical Greek texts: Westcott-Hort, Nestle-Aland, and that of the United Bible Societies. The translators of the NEB, however, constructed their own Greek text from the MSS as they went along and often in the Gospels they daringly followed "Western" readings. In some modern versions there is also an occasional use of "conjectural emendations" where it was felt the true original text was not preserved in the MSS. It is in this way that the name "Enoch" came into the text of 1 Peter 3:19 in Moffatt, Goodspeed, and Schonfield's NTs. Several modern versions in John 19:29 conjecturally substitute "spear," "pike," or "javelin" (Gr. *hyssōi* for "hyssop." Though one MS actually reads that way, it must be considered a conjecture (see Moffatt, Goodspeed, Authentic, Rieu, NEB, et al.). Likewise in Philemon 8, a number of recent versions substitute "ambassador" or "envoy" for "old man" or "aged" (see Amplified, NEB, Chas. B. Williams, Twentieth-Century NT; Goodspeed). Others bracket 1 Timothy 5:23 or place it in a footnote, as though it were not a part of the text. But there is no MS support for this. These examples are sufficient to illustrate the fact that one needs to use a strikingly new element in a passage of a new version with caution.

The OT of most recent versions is based on the traditional Masoretic text. Translations may differ as to the extent of the use of the ancient versions—particularly the Greek, Syriac,

Latin, and Targums—to correct the Hebrew where it appears to be defective. Some also make use of the newly available materials from the Qumran caves. They also differ in the frequency with which they resort to conjectural readings where the Hebrew text does not seem to make sense.

A good translation today should be based on the best Hebrew, Aramaic, and Greek texts available. This means it should be based on the earliest and best MSS that have thus far been found. In the NT there is little need for conjectural changes. Even in the OT the tendency to emend should be curbed unless it is obvious that the text is faulty.

The second criterion for evaluating a version is its accuracy in translation. It is not enough for a version to be based on the best available Greek and Hebrew MSS; one must further ask, "How carefully and accurately have the original texts been translated?" This is, in reality, the most essential test of a satisfactory version. A translator is under a solemn and sacred obligation to reproduce as closely as possible the thoughts, ideas, and sentiments of the original writers, not his own convictions, beliefs, or feelings.

But how is such fidelity to be measured? By what standards is accuracy in translation to be judged? There is no simple answer to this question. There are varying standards of accuracy and differing philosophies of translation. On the one extreme are those who hold that faithfulness demands a literal word-by-word translation that retains, as far as possible, the original grammatical units. Words not actually in the original, but needed to complete the sentence in English, should be indicated by italics or other literary devices. On the other extreme are those who hold that the translator is not concerned with words so much as thoughts and ideas. He should strive for the principle of equivalent effect. The translation should have the same effect on those who read it as the original produced, or produces, on its readers. The translator should seek to grasp the message of the original and then seek to put it into whatever English he feels will express it most accurately and satisfactorily.

These differing concepts of translation have had a long history. In the fifteenth century there were two different versions that circulated under the name of John Wycliffe. The first was an extremely literal translation of the Vulgate, closely following the Latin constructions and Latin word order. The second was a freer, more natural translation made after Wycliffe's death, probably by his secretary, John Purvey. In the prologue to the second version the philosophy of translation employed is explained as follows: "First, it is to knowe, that the best translating is out of Latyn, into English, to translate after the sentence, and not oneli after the wordes, so that the sentence be as opin, either openere in English as in Latyn." By "sentence" is meant "sense," "substance," "general significance." The general significance of the English translation must be as plain as that which is translated. This means it must be idiomatic.

Eugene Nida has given this helpful definition of translation: "Translating consists in producing in the receptor language the closest natural equivalent to the message of the source language, first in meaning and secondly in style. An extremely literal translation is not necessarily the most faithful, for it may actually distort the meaning or even convey no meaning at all. Everyone who has studied languages knows there is often no exact equivalent in a given language for words in another language. Therefore an exact, meaningful word-by-word translation from one language into another is frequently impossible. On the other hand, there must be limits to the freedom the translator exercises. He should use "the closest natural equivalent." We believe that he should stick as closely as he naturally can to the letter of the original, while making sure that he sets forth its spirit. This is the happy median of a good version.

Paul Cauer has succinctly stated what we believe to be the ideal: "So frei wie nötig, so treu wie möglich!" This means that a version should be "as free as necessary, as faithful as possible." Paraphrases are particularly liable to substitute the modern writer's own opinions for the actual teaching of the sacred Scriptures. The paraphraser may feel free to add not only words, but phrases, and even whole sentences to Holy Writ. There is real danger of distortion in such a procedure.

For a translator to be accurate in rendering a passage today means also that he must avail himself of the latest information available regarding the vocabulary and structure of the biblical languages. Significant discoveries in archaeology and linguistics have resulted in meaningful advances in the recovery of the languages and cultures of the Middle East. All of this new information must be brought to bear upon the meaning of a word or a passage of the Bible.

As an added safeguard to accuracy it is helpful to have a committee go over the work of a translator. The checks and balances that are thus brought in serve to smooth out one man's idiosyncracies and result in greater reliability.

The third basic criterion for a satisfactory version concerns the quality of its English. For one thing, it is essential that a good version have clarity of expression. It is possible for a translator to have accurately determined the sense of the original without stating it clearly in English. Accuracy and clarity are related but they are not identical. Clarity has to do with the relationship of the translation to the reader. An ideal version presents the message of the original in language that is clear as crystal.

Among other things, this means that it must use words that are understandable to the reader. The level of understanding of readers, of course, varies with their cultural and educational backgrounds. But if the version uses simple, direct, and common English, it will be understandable to both the learned and those with limited education. For American readers an ideal version should not use words and expressions that have meaning in England or Scotland but are foreign to America.

Although it is desirable that a version have a simple, direct form of English, the language must be dignified and reverent. Slang, colloquialisms, and momentarily popular expressions should be avoided. It should be a worthy vehicle for the expression of the profound truths of the Word of God.

At the same time, the version must have a literary appeal. It must be readable, euphonious, and interesting. It must be clothed in language that will grip the heart. Only then can it speak with full force the words of truth the world needs to hear.

Appendix

An Annotated List of Twentieth-Century English Translations

The translations are arranged under the date the entire Bible was published. Earlier parts of the translation are listed under this date. If only the NT has been translated, it is, of course, listed under its date. If no complete NT or OT exists, then the date of the first portion is used. The compilers are aware that there may be other translations not listed, especially those of individual books, particularly the Psalms. Annotations are included for those that the compilers were able to examine. Reference is made to the appropriate chapter when that translation has been treated in the book. Reprints of pre-twentieth-century Bibles are not included in the list.

The compilers were especially indebted to the following two works in putting together this bibliography: Margaret T. Hills, ed., *The English Bible in America: A Bibliography of Editions of the Bible and the New Testament Published in America, 1777-1957.* New York: The American Bible Society and the New York Public Library, 1961. A. S. Herbert, *Historical Catalogue of Printed Editions of the English Bible, 1525-1961.* London: The British and Foreign Bible Society; New York: The American Bible Society, 1968.

1900   Hayman's Epistles
       The Epistles of the New Testament. An attempt to present them in current and popular idiom by Henry Hayman. London: A. and C. Black.

1901   Modern American Bible
       The New Testament. The Modern American Bible. . . . The Books of the Bible in Modern American Form and Phrase

with Notes and Introduction. By Frank Schell Ballantine. . . . New York: Thomas Whittaker, 1899-1901.

Part I: S. Mark (1899?). Part II: S. Matthew, S. Peter, S. Jude, and S. James (1899?). Part III: S. Luke (Gospel-Acts) (1899?). Part IV: S. Paul (including Hebrews) (1901?). Part V: S. John (Gospel, Letters, Revelation) (1901?). Based on Textus Receptus and later Greek Texts. Preceded this by translation of the Four Gospels (Good News—The Four Gospels in a Modern American Dress, 1897). Revised 1909.

1901   Moffatt's Historical New Testament
The Historical New Testament. . . . A New Translation . . . by James Moffatt. Edinburgh: T. & T. Clark.

The books are chronologically arranged. A different translation from Moffatt's later translation.

1901   Way's Epistles
The Letters of St. Paul to Seven Churches and Three Friends. Translated by Arthur S. Way. London: Macmillan.

Arthur S. Way, a classical scholar, translated the Letters of St. Paul, the first edition of which appeared in 1901, and a second thoroughly revised edition, which included Hebrews, was published in 1906, and reprinted in 1951.

1901   Young People's Bible
The Young People's Bible; or, the Scriptures Corrected, Explained, and Simplified, by Harriet Newell Jones . . . with Introduction by Rev. Malcolm MacGregor. . . . Philadelphia: American Book and Bible House.

1902   Emphasized Bible (Rotherham)
The Emphasized Bible (complete), a new translation designed to set forth the exact meaning, the proper terminology and the graphic style of the sacred originals; arranged to show at a glance narrative, speech, parallelism, and logical analysis, also to enable the student readily to distinguish the several divine names; and emphasized throughout after the idioms of the Hebrew and Greek tongues. . . . By Joseph Bryant Rotherham.

Old Testament (1902), New York, Chicago, Toronto: Fleming H. Revell Company, 3 vols. Vol. I: Genesis-Ruth. Vol. II: 1 Samuel-Psalms. Vol. III: Proverbs-Malachi.

New Testament (1897), is a rewritten edition of the version first printed in 1872, and reissued in a revised form in 1878. Gospel according to Matthew (1868). Greek text of Tregelles.

In 1916, published four volumes in one.

1902?   Godbey's New Testament
Translation of the New Testament from the original Greek. By Rev. W. B. Godbey. Cincinnati: M. W. Knapp, Office of God's Revivalist.

Based on Tischendorf's edition of the Codex Sinaiticus. Dedicated to "The Holiness People of all lands."

1902   Twentieth Century New Testament
The Twentieth Century New Testament. A translation into Modern English. Made from the Original Greek. New York: Fleming H. Revell Company.

Part I: The Five Historical Books (undated, 1898?). Part II: Paul's Letters to the Churches (1900). Part III: The Pastoral, Personal and General Letters, and the Revelation (1901). Based on Westcott and Hort's Greek text.

One volume edition (revised) in 1904. Reprinted frequently. See chapter 1.

1903   Fenton's Bible
The Holy Bible in Modern English, containing the complete sacred scriptures of the Old and New Testaments, translated into English direct from the original Hebrew, Chaldee, and Greek, by Ferrar Fenton.

1882, Romans; 1884, Epistles; 1895, New Testament; 1903, whole Bible. New Testament and four parts of Old Testament.

First ed. of New Testament in Modern English 1895, rev. 1900. Vol. I: Pentateuch, 1901? Vol. II: Joshua-II Kings, 1902? Vol. III: Isaiah, Jeremiah, Ezekiel, Minor Prophets, Prophets, 1902?

Farrar Fenton was a London businessman who devoted some twenty years of his life to fulfill a pledge of making the Scriptures intelligible "through the use of modern English." This work by an amateur was popular for a time, but "its erroneous and inaccurate renderings have rather damaged its earlier favor" (Price).

1903   Weymouth's New Testament
The New Testament in Modern Speech. An Idiomatic Translation into Every Day English from the text of The Resultant Greek Testament by Richard Francis Weymouth.

The text was revised in the 1924 edition by the Rev. S. W. Green, the Rev. Prof. A. J. D. Farrer, and the Rev. Prof. H. T. Andrews, and again in 1929 by the Rev. Prof. James Alexander Robertson.

See chapter 1.

1904   Worrell's New Testament
The New Testament Revised and Translated by A. S. Worrell, with Notes and Instructions designed to aid the earnest Reader in obtaining a clear Understanding of the Doctrines, Ordinances, and primitive Assemblies as revealed in these Scriptures. . . . Louisville, Kentucky: A. S. Worrell.

Based on the Greek text underlying the ERV and on West-cott and Hort as modified by Scrivener and others. "Baptize" is translated "immerse"; "church" is "assembly" or "congregation." Claims great fidelity to the Greek. "To handle the tenses carelessly," writes the translator, "is to trifle with the word of God. . . . It is the business of the translator to translate with scrupulous exactness." Contains some textual variants, alternate renderings, and explanatory notes.

1905 Lloyd's New Testament
The Corrected English New Testament. A Revision of the "Authorized" Version (By Nestle's Resultant Text). Prepared with the Assistance of Eminent Scholars and Issued by Samuel Lloyd, a Life Governor of the British and Foreign Bible Society as His Memorial of the Society's Centenary, 1904. London: Samuel Bagster & Sons, Ltd., 1905.

The corrections are of two kinds: (1) the removal of textual defects in the underlying Greek and (2) a modernization of the English. Because of the large extent to which the AV had failed, Lloyd proposed that the Bible Society produce a new revision as a memorial to its centenary. When this was not accepted, he, with the cooperation of a number of biblical scholars, independently produced this version of the NT as an illustration of the kind of revision needed. He attempted "to show the possibility of popularizing without demeaning the Sacred Scriptures and of correcting without defacing the Version so worthily beloved."

1906 Forster
St. John's Gospel, Epistles, and Revelation, translated by Henry Langstaff Forster. Adelaide: Hunkin, Ellis and King.
The Revelation (1903). Tasmania: Henry Langstaff Forster.

1907 Bourne's Gospels
The Fourfold Portrait of the Heavenly King . . . translated by 'Interpreter' i.e., A. E. Bourne. London: E. Stock.
A new translation of the Gospels.

1907 Moulton's Modern Reader's Bible
The Modern Reader's Bible; the Books of the Bible with Three Books of the Apocrypha presented in Modern Literary Form; edited with Introductions and Notes, by Richard G. Moulton. New York: The Macmillan Co.

1908 Rutherford's Epistles
Paul's Epistles to the Thessalonians and to the Corinthians. A New Translation by W. G. Rutherford, London, 1908.

1909 The Bible in Modern English
The Bible in Modern English. A Rendering from the Origi-

nals by an American, making use of the best scholarship and the latest research at home and abroad. Perkiomen, Pa.

1909   Weaver New Testament
New Testament in Modern Historical and Literary Form for the church, the school, and the home, embracing the life of Jesus Christ in the words of Matthew, Mark, Luke and John, and the Church of the Apostles according to the Acts, the Epistles and Revelation, historically harmonized. Translated by S. Townsend Weaver. Philadelphia: University Literature Extension.

1910   Cunard's
The first Judgment of the Christians by the Spirit, Alpha and Omega. An Authorized Revision of St. Matthew, and the History of this Planet, from the First Strata to the End. Written for the Spirit at Command by F. W. Cunard. Liverpool: Cunard & Sons.

1912   Improved Bible Union Version
The Holy Bible containing the Old and New Testaments. An Improved Edition (Based in Part on the Bible Union Version). Philadelphia: American Baptist Publication Society.

The Bible Union Version was an "immersion" version begun in the middle of the nineteenth century, but of which the OT was never fully completed. The NT of that version used "immersion" for "baptism." The Improved Version has "baptism (immersion)," "baptize (immerse)," and "baptized (immersed)." The poetic portions of the OT, including those of the prophets, are printed in poetic form.

1914   Numeric New Testament
The New Testament from the Greek text as established by Bible Numerics. Edited by Ivan Panin. New Haven: Bible Numerics Co.

Based on the number value of the Greek and Hebrew letters. Awkward in many places.

Second edition, 1935, and reprinted several times.

1914   Cunnington's New Testament
The New Covenant, commonly called the New Testament of our Lord and Saviour Jesus Christ. A revision of the version of A.D. 1611 by E. E. Cunnington. London: G. Routledge & Sons.

Other editions appeared, e.g., in 1919 by T. Fosher Unwin, London, under the title The Adelphi New Testament; and in 1926 with the title The Western New Testament.

1916   McFadyen
The Psalms in Modern Speech and Rhythmical Form by John Edgar McFadyen. London: James Clarke & Co.

The Wisdom Books, also Lamentations and the Song of Songs, in Modern Speech and Rhythmical form by John Edgar McFadyen, 1917. Isaiah in Modern Speech, 1918. Jeremiah in Modern Speech, 1919.

1917 Jewish Publication Society Bible

The Holy Scriptures According to the Masoretic Text. A new Translation with the Aid of Previous Versions and with Constant Consultation of Jewish Authorities. Philadelphia: The Jewish Publication Society.

Jewish Publication Society Version. Psalms, 1903.

See chapter 7.

1918 Anderson New Testament

The New Testament. Translated from the Sinaitic Manuscript Discovered by Constantine Tischendorf at Mt. Sinai, by H. T. Anderson. Cincinnati: The Standard Publishing Company.

1919 The Messages of the Bible

The Messages of the Bible edited by Frank K. Sanders and Charles F. Kent. Twelve vols. New York: Charles Scribner's Sons, 1898-1919.

Brief introductions of each book and free rendering in paraphrase.

1921 Pym

Mark's Account of Jesus. Cambridge: W. Heffer and Sons.

'Common Speech' by T. W. Pym.

1921 Shorter Bible

The Shorter Bible, translated and arranged by Charles Foster Kent . . . with the Collaboration of Charles Cutler Torrey . . . Henry A. Sherman . . . Frederick Harris . . . Ethel Cutler. . . New York: Charles Scribner's Sons.

New Testament, 1918. Old Testament, 1921. About two-thirds of the OT and one-third of the NT are omitted.

1922 Plainer Bible

A Plainer Bible for Plain People in Plain American . . . (New Testament) from the original Greek by Chaplain [Frank Schell] Ballentine. . . . Jersey City, N. J.: Plainer Bible Press.

See 1901, Modern American Bible.

1923 Riverside New Testament

The Riverside New Testament; a translation from the original Greek into the English of today, by William G. Ballantine. Boston: Houghton, Mifflin.

An eclectic rendering of Nestle's Greek text by William G. Ballantine, a former President of Oberlin College, who confesses his indebtedness to other versions, such as Weymouth's, Moffatt's, and *The Twentieth Century New Testament.* Produced in a very readable form with an index, this version was first published in 1923, and revised in 1934.

1923   Robertson
A Translation of Luke's Gospel with Grammatical Notes by A. T. Robertson. New York: George H. Doran Company.

1924   Labor Determinative Version
The New Covenant: a Mutual Arrangement or Testament for a true civilization founded upon brotherly labor, following the Greek title which is usually rendered the New Testament, translated out of the Greek as a Labor Determinative Version, and diligently compared with former translations herein revised for the recovery of Biblical labor standards. Jackson, Mich.: Home of the American Labor Determinative Revision Committee.

1924   Montgomery's Centenary Translation
Centenary Translation of the New Testament in Modern English. Translated by Helen Barrett Montgomery. Philadelphia: Judson Press. 2 vols.

In commemoration of the centenary of the American Baptist Publication Society, Mrs. Helen Barrett Montgomery of Rochester, N. Y., and a graduate of Wellesley College, published this translation. Many of her colloquial paragraph and chapter headings are striking, such as "Play the Game," "A 'Close-up' of Sin," "Paul's Swan Song," and "Orchestrate Your Virtues."

1925   Askwith's Psalms
The Psalms Books IV and V. Rendered into English in Rhythm Consonant with that of the Original Hebrew by E. H. Askwith. London: M. Hopkinson and Co.

1925   People's New Covenant
The People's New Covenant . . . Translated from the Metaphysical Standpoint by Arthur E. Overbury. Monrovia, Calif.: Arthur E. Overbury.

This version is based on the premise of Scientific Statement of Being, as given in Science and Health by Mary Baker Eddy.

1925   Children's Bible
The Children's Bible. Selections from the Old and New Testaments Translated and Arranged by Henry A. Gherman and Charles Foster Kent. New York: Charles Scribner's Sons.

A translation in readable, simple English of selections from the OT and NT. Includes not only narratives, but poetic and didactic selections.

1926 Moffatt
A New Translation of The Bible, Containing the Old and New Testaments, by James Moffatt. New York & London: Harper and Brothers.
New Testament, 1913. New edition, revised, 1917. Old Testament, 1924-1925, in 2 vols. Vol I: Genesis-Esther (1924). Vol. II: Job-Malachi (1925). Revision of complete Bible in 1935.
See chapter 1.

1927 Kent's Student's Old Testament
The Student's Old Testament Logically and Chronologically Arranged and Translated by Charles Foster Kent. New York: Charles Scribner's Sons, 1904-1927.
Six vols. I: Narratives of the Beginnings of Hebrew History from the Creation to the Establishment of the Hebrew Kingdom, 1904. II: Israel's Historical and Biographical Narratives from the Establishment of the Hebrew Kingdom to the End of the Maccabean Struggle, 1905. III: The Sermons, Epistles, and Apocalypses of Israel's Prophets from the Beginning of the Assyrian Period to the End of the Maccabean Struggle, 1910. IV: Israel's Laws and Legal Precedents from the Days of Moses to the Closing of the Legal Canon, 1907. V: The Songs, Hymns, and Prayers of the Old Testament, 1914. VI: Proverbs and Didactic Poems, 1927.

1927 Smith-Goodspeed
The Bible. An American Translation. The Old Testament Translated by J. M. Powis Smith and a Group of Scholars. The New Testament Translated by Edgar J. Goodspeed. Chicago: The University of Chicago Press.
Revised, 1935. The New Testament, An American Translation, 1923. The Old Testament, An American Translation, 1927. The Apocrypha, An American Translation, 1938. Reprinted, with Apocrypha included, 1939.
See chapter 1.

1928 Christian's Bible
The Christian's Bible—New Testament. Strasburg, Penn.: George N. Le Fevre.
A translation from the Greek, chiefly from B and Aleph. Not simply a translation of the Words, but under the guidance of the Holy Ghost, His thoughts as recorded. . . . George Le Fevre is considered the translator as well as publisher.

1928 Czarnomska Version
The Authentic Literature of Israel freed from the Dis-

arrangements, Expansions, and Comments of Early Native Editors, edited with an introduction by Elizabeth Czarnomska. New York: The Macmillan Company, 1924-28.

1928   Spiritualist's Matthew
The Good Message according to Matthew. For the use of Christian Spiritualists . . . an entirely new and accurate translation edited by J. W. Potter. London: Society of Communion.

1929   Gowen's Psalms
The Psalms; or, the Book of Praises. A New Transcription and Translation arranged Strophically and Metrically from a critically constructed text, with introduction, textual notes, and glossary by Herbert H. Gowen. London: Mowbray.

1930   Loux' Mark
Mark: To Every Man His Work, His Pay, His Rest. Translated by DuBois H. Loux. Jackson, Mich.: Privately printed.

1931   Wales' Psalms
The Psalms. A Revised Translation, by Frank H. Wales. London: Oxford University Press.

1932   Chaplain Ballentine
Our God and Godhealth, our Healer. Godhealth's Messenger and Godhealth's Message of Life and Light and Love and Law, the Light of Life and the Law of Love, the wisest wisdom of the wise of all ages: translated from the original Greek, reinterpreted in the thought-forms, language and idioms of America today, and arranged for reading with sustained interest from beginning to end as a modern novel, by Chaplain [Frank Schell] Ballentine. . . . Collegeville, Pa.: The Craigie Publishing Co.

1932   Kleist's Memoirs of St. Peter
The Memoirs of St. Peter, or the Gospel according to St. Mark, translated into English sense-lines. By James A. Kleist, S. J. Milwaukee: Bruce Publishing Co.
Translated into sense-lines, which it is maintained is the form that resembles the original itself.

1933   Torrey's Four Gospels
The Four Gospels, a New Translation by Charles Cutler Torrey. New York and London: Harper & Brothers.
Its purpose is to show that the Gospels of Matthew, Mark, and John were composed in Aramaic.

1934   Royds' Epistles and Gospels
The Epistles and Gospels for the Sundays & chief holy days of the Christian year. A new translation by Thomas Fletcher Royds. Oxford: Basil Blackwell.
New Testament into modern English: "such English as in-

telligent village schoolchildren can understand without much explaining of long words." Nestle Greek text. Not continuous text. Good straightforward translation.

1934 Old Testament in Colloquial English
The Books of the Old Testament in Colloquial English, 1920-34.

Listed in E. H. Robertson's *The New Translations of the Bible*.

1934 Wade
The Documents of the New Testament. Translated and Historically Arranged with Critical Introduction by G. W. Wade. London: Thomas Murby & Co.

Copies of Mark, Luke, and John issued separately in 1936.

Claims to be "an accurate, yet not literal" translation. Avoids ambiguity by presenting what the translator judges to be the most probable meaning. Literary relationships are indicated in the Synoptics, Acts, and 2 Peter-Jude. Westcott and Hort text.

1935 Westminster Version
The Westminster Version of the Sacred Scriptures, general editor, Cuthbert Lattey. Introductions and commentaries with translation.

New Testament, 1935. Smaller edition in 1948, translation with brief introductions by Father Lattey.

New Testament in parts from 1913-1935, edited by Cuthbert Lattey and J. Keating.

Malachi, 1934—Lattey. Ruth, 1935—Lattey. Nahum and Habakkuk, 1937—Bevenot. Jonah, 1938—T. E. Bird. Psalms 1-41, 1939—Lattey. Psalms, 1944—Lattey. Daniel, 1948—Lattey. Obadiah, Micah, Zephaniah, Haggai, Zechariah, 1953—Sebastian Bullough.

An excellent translation by English Roman Catholic scholars under the editorship of Cuthbert Lattey, S. J., based on the original texts in both Testaments. An independent venture; not an "official" translation.

1937 Cornish's St. Paul from the Trenches
St. Paul from the Trenches, translated by Gerald Warre Cornish. Two epistles of Corinthians, part of Ephesians.

1937 Greber's New Testament
The New Testament. A New Translation and Explanation Based on The Oldest Manuscripts, by Johannes Greber. New York: John Felsberg, Inc.

The English translation was made by a professional translator and corrected by a committee of American clergymen. A somewhat eccentric translation. It is based mainly on Codex Bezae, but at times the translator has given a version with no MS authority. Originally published in German but subsequently translated into English. Translator is a former Roman Catholic priest who came to believe in communication with the world of divine spirits.

1937   Martin's New Testament
The New Testament critically reconstructed and retranslated, by William Wallace Martin. Nashville, Tenn.: Parthenon Press.

Epistles in two volumes. Part I: Press of Marshall and Bruce Co., Nashville, 1929. Part II: Press of the Publishing House of the Methodist Episcopal Church, Nashville, 1930.

The twenty-one canonical Epistles have been reconstructed into thirty-six, including as authors Apollos, Barnabas, and John, son of Zebedee (as the writer of the Epistle of James).

> 1928   The Psalms Complete: Their Prayers, their Collects, their Praises, in three Books. Separated, arranged and translated by William Wallace Martin. Nashville, Tenn.: Marshall & Bruce Co.
>
> 1929   The Book of Job in two Versions: a Judean Version, an Ephramaean Version; and The Book of Ecclesiastes. Nashville, Tenn.: Methodist Publishing House.
>
> 1940   Isaian Prophecies. Nashville, Tenn.: Parthenon Press.
>
> 1940   Jeremiah-Ezekiel Prophecies. Nashville, Tenn.: Parthenon Press.
>
> 1941   The Book of Genesis Complete. The Ephramaean Version . . . the Judean Version. Nashville, Tenn.: Parthenon Press.
>
> 1941   Twelve Minor Prophets. Nashville, Tenn.: Parthenon Press.

1937   Spencer's New Testament
The New Testament of Our Lord and Saviour Jesus Christ; translated into English from the original Greek by the Very Rev. Francis Aloysius Spencer, O. P.; edited by Charles J. Callan, O. P., and John A. McHugh, O. P. New York: Macmillan Co.

After publishing a new translation of the Gospels from the Latin in 1898, Father Francis Aloysius Spencer was moved to attempt a new translation from the Greek. The four Gospels were published in 1901 and the rest of the NT finished with notes shortly before Spencer's death in 1913. The whole NT, however, was not published until 1937, under the editorship of Charles J. Callan and John A. McHugh, and has been reprinted several times since. The words of Christ are printed in italics, quotations from the OT are put in small capitals, and Vulgate readings that differ from the Greek are given in brackets or footnotes.

1937 Williams' New Testament
The New Testament; a translation in the language of the people, by Charles B. Williams. Boston: Bruce Humphries. Slightly revised edition, Chicago: Moody Press, 1950. Verse numbers inserted in the text. Westcott and Hort Greek Text.

A Greek professor from Union University (Jackson, Tenn.), Charles B. Williams' aim was to reproduce as far as possible the exact shades of meaning in the Greek tenses. To do this requires the use of auxiliaries and the like in English and can result in overtranslation and in the use of language that is hardly the "language of the people."

1938 Book of Books
The Book of Books. A Translation of the New Testament Complete and Unabridged. London: R.T.S. The Lutterworth Press, The United Society for Christian Literature. R. Mercer Wilson, General Secretary, The United Society for Christian Literature, translated this NT to celebrate the centenary of the *Annotated Paragraph Bible,* which he follows in the arrangement of his text, and the fourth centenary of the setting up of the English Bible in the Churches. Rather straightforward simple translation.

1938 Buttenweiser's Psalms
The Psalms. Chronologically Treated with a New Translation by Moses Buttenweiser, Prof. Emeritus of Biblical Exegesis, Hebrew Union College. Chicago: The University of Chicago Press.

1938 Clementson's New Testament
The New Testament. A Translation by Edgar Lewis Clementson. Pittsburg: The Evangelization Society of the Pittsburgh Bible Institute.

1939 Oesterley Psalms
The Psalms. Translated with Text-Critical and Exegetical Notes by W. O. E. Oesterley. London: S.P.C.K.; New York: Macmillan Co. 2 vols.

1940 Dakes' Gospels
Christ Jesus: The Authentic Story of the Founder of Christianity as told by Matthew, Mark, Luke and John in the Four Gospels translated from the Original Greek by John A. Dakes. Chicago: Avalon Publishing Co.

Dakes was a Greek businessman who felt "that a translation made by a Greek who had learned the original language of the Gospels in the schools of Greece might prove helpful."

Certain Greek words are transliterated, such as *petros* and *petra* in Matthew 16:18, *ecclesia, aeonian,* and *Logos.* A glossary appears at the back of the book.

1940   St. Mark in Current English
St. Mark in Current English. By Mary L. Matheson. Melbourne: National Council of Religious Education of Australia.

1944   Callan's Psalms
The Psalms. Translated from the Latin Psalter, in the Light of the Hebrew, of the Septuagint and Peshitta Versions, and of the Psalterium Juxta Hebraeos of St. Jerome. With Introductions, Critical Notes and Spiritual Reflections by Charles J. Callan. New York: Joseph F. Wagner.

1944   Wand's New Testament Letters
The New Testament Letters, prefaced and paraphrased by J. W. C. Wand. Brisbane, Australia.
Revised edition published in England, 1946.
Romans-Jude. According to the Introduction, the work "may be called either a free translation or a close paraphrase." "I have tried," says Bishop Wand, "to put the Epistles into the kind of language a Bishop might use in writing a monthly letter for his diocesan magazine."

1945   Stringfellow's New Testament
New Testament. A Translation, Harmony and Annotations by Ervin Edward Stringfellow. . . . Planographed by John S. Swift Co., Inc.
Vol. I: The Gospels (1943). Vol. II: Acts-Revelation (1945). Dubuque, Iowa: Wm. C. Brown Co.
Westcott and Hort text.

1946   Lenski
The Interpretation of the [New Testament] . . . R. C. H. Lenski. Columbus, Ohio: Lutheran Book Concern, 1931-46.
Twelve vols. Commentary with independent translation by a noted Lutheran scholar.

1947   Eerdmans' Psalms
The Hebrew Books of Psalms by B. D. Eerdmans. Oudtestamentliche Studien, IV. Leiden: E. J. Brill.

1947   Swann's New Testament
The New Testament . . . Translated from the Greek text of Westcott and Hort. By Rev. George Swann. . . . Louisville, Ky.: Printed by the Pentecostal Publishing Company.
Second ed. (1949)
Third ed.

1948 Letchworth New Testament
The New Testament . . . Letchworth Version in Modern English, by T. F. Ford and R. E. Ford. Letchworth, Herts: Letchworth Printer, Ltd.

A translation of the TR Greek text into current English, mainly using words of Anglo-Saxon origin, and free from colloquialisms and slang expressions. Seeks to maintain in modern dress the simple, dignified style of writing associated with the classical English versions.

1949 Basic Bible
The Basic Bible, containing the Old and New Testaments in Basic English. Cambridge: The University Press and Evans Bros. New York: Dutton.

The New Testament in Basic English, 1940. Whole Bible, 1949. Selections, 1933; Micah and Habakkuk, 1934; Mark, 1945; John, 1938.

Basic English is a system of simplified English with a primary vocabulary of 850 words devised by C. K. Ogden as an international auxiliary language and as an aid in learning English. In 1940 a committee under the direction of S. H. Hooke of the University of London produced an independent translation of the New Testament, using the 850 words in the primary vocabulary of Basic English to which 50 special Bible words and 100 others were added.

1949 Leslie's Psalms
The Psalms. Translated and Interpreted in the Light of Hebrew Life and Worship by Elmer A. Leslie. New York and Nashville: Abingdon-Cokesbury Press.

1951 Authentic Version
The New Testament . . . The Authentic Version. Plattsburg, Missouri: Brotherhood Authentic Bible Society.

Anonymous translator: "Believing that I have been given divine authority through the Holy Spirit to bring the true translation of the original Greek text, and that which has been given me through the inspiration of the Holy Spirit, I have diligently and carefully compared with the original Greek text by the use of the best Greek dictionaries and former translations, some out of the Greek and some Latin: and find that what the Spirit has given me is according to the Original Greek." Modern speech version.

1951 Vernon's Mark
The Gospel of St. Mark: A New Translation in Simple English, translated by Edward Vernon.

For the average intelligent child of twelve years old and upwards.

1952   New Testament in Plain English
The New Testament; a new translation in plain English by Charles Kingsley Williams. London: S.P.C.K., Longmans, Green and Co.

The Life of Our Lord Jesus Christ according to St. Luke, together with some passages from the other Gospels, newly done into very simple English from the Greek of The Revised Version, 1933. Matthew, 1934.

"Plain English" is a simplified form of the English language based on a list of 1,500 "fundamental and common words that make up ordinary English speech," plus some 160 or 170 others that are explained in a glossary at the end of the volume. The translation is based on Souter's Greek Text (Oxford Press, 1910).

1952   Penguin Bible (Rieu)
The Four Gospels, a New Translation from the Greek by E. V. Rieu. London and Melbourne: Penguin Books.

Acts of the Apostles by Saint Luke, by C. H. Rieu, son of E. V. Rieu.

E. V. Rieu justifies his translation on the basis that it is from the literary standpoint more in harmony with the Greek Gospels than the KJV, whose translators "mistook fidelity to the idiom of the Greek for fidelity to its meaning" and "felt the sanctity and importance of the original so keenly that the use of normal language would have seemed a kind of sacrilege." Accurate and readable.

1952   Revised Standard Version
The Holy Bible . . . Revised Standard Version . . . Being the Version Set Forth A.D. 1611. Revised 1881 and 1901 . . . and Revised 1952. New York, Toronto, Edinburgh: Thomas Nelson & Sons.

New Testament, 1946. Old Testament with Complete Bible, 1952. Apocrypha, 1957.
See chapter 2.

1954   Kissane's Psalms
The Books of Psalms. Translated from a Critically Revised Hebrew Text with a Commentary by Monsignor Edward J. Kissane. Dublin: Brown and Nolan, Ltd. Vol. I, 1953; Vol. II, 1954.

1954   Kleist and Lilly's New Testament
The New Testament rendered from the original Greek with Explanatory Notes. Milwaukee: The Bruce Publishing Company.

The Four Gospels translated by James A. Kleist, S. J., and the Acts to Revelation by Joseph L. Lilly, C. M. Made from

1943 Bover Greek Text into modern popular English. An independent modern American translation.

1954 Kleist and Lynam's Psalms
The Psalms in Rhythmic Prose. By James A. Kleist, S. J. and Thomas James Lynam, S. J. Milwaukee: Bruce Publishing Company.

Based on Latin text of the Pontifical Biblical Institute, Rome.

1954 Moore's New Testament
The New Testament. A New, Independent, Individual Translation from the Greek, by George Albert Moore, Colonel, U.S.A. Chevy Chase, Md.: The Country Dollar Press.

Based on Souter's 1950 Greek text. Gospels issued separately in 1953.

1955 Fides Translation (Psalms)
The Psalms. Fides Translation. Introduction and Notes by Mary Perkins Ryan. Chicago: Fides Publishers Association.

Made in accordance with the new Roman Psalter.

1955 Knox
The Holy Bible; a translation from the Latin Vulgate in the light of the Hebrew and Greek originals. Authorized by the hierarchy of England and Wales and the hierarchy of Scotland. Translated by Monsignor Knox. London: Burns and Oates.

Old Testament. New York: Sheed and Ward, 1948-50, 2 vols. Vol. I: Genesis-Esther. Vol. II: Job-Machabees.

New Testament . . . Newly Translated from the Vulgate Latin at the Request of Their Lordships, the Archbishops of England and Wales. New York: Sheed & Ward, British Trial Edition, 1944.

See chapter 3.

1955 Schonfield's Authentic New Testament
The Authentic New Testament, edited and translated from the Greek for the general reader by Hugh J. Schonfield. London: D. Dobson.

This is a work of high quality by the distinguished Jewish scholar, Dr. Hugh J. Schonfield, who approaches these documents "as if they had recently been recovered from a cave in Palestine or beneath the sands of Egypt, and had never previously been given to the public." Much helpful information on the Jewish references in the New Testament is given in the Notes and Introduction.

1956 Laubach's Inspired Letters
The Inspired Letters in Clearest English. Prepared by Frank C. Laubach. New York: T. Nelson.

Romans-Jude. Written in short, clear sentences with a limited vocabulary of about 2,000 words, this translation is intended as a preparation for the reading of the RSV for beginning students of English. The Gospels and Acts, the translator feels, are simple enough in the RSV. By the world's leader in the fight against illiteracy.

1957   Concordant Version
Concordant Version. International Edition. The Sacred Scriptures. An Idiomatic, Consistent, Emphasized Version. . . . Los Angeles: Concordant Publishing Concern.

Old Testament—Half title: Concordant Version of the Hebrew Scriptures. In a Beginning, commonly called "Genesis."

[The New Testament] Concordant Version, 1919-26. One volume reprint, 1931.

This version is based on the belief that "every word in the original should have its own English equivalent." It is said to aim "at truth and accuracy rather than literary elegance." It shows the eccentricities "of a self-taught and opinionated 'one man' translator who has certain peculiar views to proclaim yet is 'reverent, careful, and thorough.' "

1957   Lamsa's
The Holy Bible from ancient Eastern manuscripts. Containing the Old and New Testaments, translated from the Peshitta, the authorized Bible of the church of the East, by George M. Lamsa. Philadelphia: A. J. Holman Co.

The Four Gospels according to the Eastern Version, 1933. The Book of Psalms according to the Eastern Version, 1939. The New Testament, 1940.

George M. Lamsa's translation purports to be produced "from original Aramaic sources." Lamsa's original claims for his work are generally questioned. The Peshitta is not to be identified with the "original Aramaic." Lamsa also adapted some questionable renderings such as "rope" for "camel" in Matt. 19:24, et al.

1958   Hudson
The Pauline Epistles: Their Meanings and Message. Introduction, Translation, Marginal Analysis and Paraphrase by James T. Hudson. London: James Clark & Co., Ltd.

"New translation with the missing steps in Paul's thought supplied in brackets." Omits Hebrews.

1958   Meissner's Gospels
New Testament Gospels, a Modern Translation by Lawrence Meissner. Portland, Oregon.

All the verses, 40 percent fewer words.

1958   Phillips' New Testament
New Testament in Modern English. New York: Macmillan.

Letters to Young Churches; a translation of the New Testament Epistles, by J. B. Phillips; with an introduction by C. S. Lewis, 1951. A corrected edition, 1957. First published in England, 1947. The Gospels, translated into modern English by J. B. Phillips, c. 1951. First published in 1952. The Young Church in Action; a Translation of the Acts of Apostles by J. B. Phillips, 1955. Book of Revelation, 1957. Gospels, a corrected edition, 1958. Four Prophets: Amos, Hosea, First Isaiah, Micah; a modern translation from the Hebrew, by J. B. Phillips, 1963. Second revised edition of the New Testament, 1973.

See chapter 4.

1958   Tomanek's New Testament
The New Testament of Our Lord and Savior Jesus Anointed by James L. Tomanek. Pocatello, Ida.: Printed by Arrowhead Press, 1958.

1959   Cressman
St. Mark. Toronto: Full Gospel Publishing House.
Mark, 2nd ed., 1960. John, American Bible Society, 1962. Simplified English for Liberians by Annie Cressman of the Assemblies of God Mission.

1959   Modern Language Bible (Berkeley)
The Holy Bible, the Berkeley Version in Modern English containing the Old and New Testaments. Translated afresh from the original languages and diligently compared with previous translations, with numerous helpful nondoctrinal notes to aid the understanding of the reader. Gerrit Verkuyl, editor-in-chief and translator of the New Testament section. Grand Rapids: Zondervan Publishing House.
Berkeley Version of the New Testament, 1945. Berkeley, Calif.: James J. Gillick & Co. Zondervan Publishing House, 1950, 1953.
See chapter 5.

1960   The Children's "King James"
The Children's "King James" Bible: New Testament. Jay Green is responsible for the wording; "Peter" Palmer for the stories. Evansville, Ind.: Modern Bible Translations.
Not KJV of 1611, but a modern version using the same text the KJ translation used.

1961   New World Translation—Jehovah's Witnesses
New World Translation of the Holy Scriptures, rendered from the original languages by the New World Bible Translation Committee. Rev. Brooklyn: Watchtower Bible and Tract Society of New York.

The New World Translation of the Christian Greek Scriptures, 1950.

Based on Westcott and Hort, supplemented by Nestle, Bover, Merk.

New World Translation of the Hebrew Scriptures, 1953-1960. Issued in five vols. Genesis-Ruth, 1953; 1 Samuel-Esther, 1955; Job-Song of Solomon, 1957; Isaiah-Lamentations, 1958; Ezekiel-Malachi, 1960. Based on 3rd ed. Kittel. 1951.

See chapter 6.

1961   Noli's Greek Orthodox New Testament
The New Testament of Our Lord and Savior Jesus Christ, Translated into English from the approved Greek text of the Church of Constantinople and the Church of Greece, by Fan S. Noli. Boston: Albanian Orthodox Church in America.

1961   One Way
One Way: The Jesus People New Testament. A Translation in Modern English. Pasadena, Calif.: Compass Press.

This is the same as Norlie's The New Testament in Modern English, 1951.

1961   Simplified New Testament (Norlie)
Simplified New Testament in Plain English for Today's Reader. A New Translation from the Greek by Olaf M. Norlie. With the Psalms for Today, a new translation in current English by R. K. Harrison. Grand Rapids: Zondervan Publishing House, 1961.

Dr. Olaf M. Norlie of St. Olaf College designed this translation particularly for teenagers. It is rendered in plain, lucid and straightforward English.

An earlier translation of Norlie was published by the author in 1951 in Northfield, Minn., with the title: The New Testament... in Modern English translated from the original Greek and supplied with an outline by Olaf Morgan Norlie. Still earlier, in 1943, a translation of the Gospel of John was published in mimeographed form in San Antonio, Texas by the Life Builders Press.

1961   Wuest's Expanded New Testament
Expanded Translation of the Greek New Testament by Kenneth S. Wuest. Grand Rapids: Wm. B. Eerdmans Publishing Co.

Vol. 1: Gospels (1956). Vol. 2: Acts through Ephesians (1958). Vol. 3: Philippians through Revelation (1959).

Kenneth S. Wuest endeavors to reproduce for the English readers the nuances of the Greek text, both philologically and theologically. Bible scholars may feel that he at times overtranslates and finds shades of meaning not actually in the Greek text. He does for all parts of speech what Williams does for verbs.

1962 Children's Version
The Children's Version of the Holy Bible. New York: McGraw Hill.

Printed in large, Caledonia type for easy reading. The text is arranged in paragraphs, though the verse numbers are retained in small type interspersed through the text. Difficult words, names, and places are diacritically marked and some are phonetically pronounced. The text is a simplification and modernization of the KJV. The preface is by Jay P. Green.

1962 New Jewish Version
The Torah: The Five Books of Moses, the first section of A New Translation of the Holy Scriptures according to the Masoretic Text.

Second revised ed., 1973. The Five Megilloth and Jonah; a new translation. Introductions by H. L. Ginsberg, with drawings by Ismar David. Philadelphia: Jewish Publication Society of America, 1969. Psalms, 1972. Isaiah, 1973.

See chapter 7.

1963 Beck's New Testament
The New Testament in the Language of Today, by William F. Beck. St. Louis: Concordia Publishing House.

The Concordia Publishing House produced this version by William F. Beck, a Lutheran scholar. He has produced a refreshing translation in simple, precise English. It is printed in readable type with orderly paragraphing and lively headings.

1963 Gelineau's Psalms
The Psalms: A New Translation. Translated from the Hebrew and arranged for Singing to the Psalmody of Joseph Gelineau. Philadelphia: The Westminster Press.

1963 The Holy Name Bible
The Holy Name Bible containing the Holy Name Version of the Old and New Testaments. Revised by A. B. Traina. Irvington, N.J.: The Scripture Research Association, Inc.

The New Testament of our Messiah and Saviour Yahshua. Sacred Name Version, 1950.

This translation is understood to have been made by A. B. Traina and reprinted at his expense. The version attempts to restore Semitic proper names to their Aramaic or Hebew form and to clear up difficulties in the text in the light of possible Semitic background.

1964   Anchor Bible
Anchor Bible, edited by William F. Albright and David N. Freedman. Individual translators for books. Garden City: N.J.: Doubleday & Co., 1964.

1964   Hadas' Psalms
The Book of Psalms for the Modern Reader: A New Translation by Gershon Hadas. New York: Jonathan David.

1965   Amplified Bible
The Amplified Bible, containing the Amplified Old Testament and the Amplified New Testament. Grand Rapids: Zondervan Publishing House.

The Amplified New Testament. Zondervan Publishing House, 1958-1965. Old Testament: Part I (1964), Genesis-Esther; Part II (1962), Job-Malachi. Zondervan Publishing House. Translation by Frances E. Siewert.

See chapter 8.

1965   Bruce's Expanded Paraphrase
An Expanded Paraphrase of the Epistles of Paul. Printed in parallel with the Revised Version, with fuller references by Drs. Scrivener, Moulton & Greenup, by F. F. Bruce. Exeter: Paternoster Press.

American edition has title: The Letters of Paul: Expanded Paraphrase.

This paraphrase is designed, as he states, "to make the course of Paul's argument as clear as possible." The "expanded paraphrase" is printed alongside the Revised Version of 1881, "for the convenience and interest of readers who may care to compare and contrast two renderings produced on directly opposite principles."

1966   The Bible in Simplified English
Listen . . . The Lord is Speaking: The Bible in Simplified English. Collegeville, Minn.: The Liturgical Press.

The authorized English edition of the Katholische Schulbibel, which is an abridged selection of biblical passages rearranged to provide a chronological history of the biblical period. The poetic books, duplicated historical material, and Epistles are not included. Written in simple English, this is intended for beginners in the study of the Bible.

1966   Burke
God Is For Real, Man; Interpretations of Bible passages and stories as told by some of God's bad-tempered angels with busted halos to Carl F. Burke. New York: Association Press.

1969 edition entitled God Is Beautiful, Man.

Free treatment of selected Bible passages in American downtown slang by young people of the inner city.

1966 Jerusalem Bible
Jerusalem Bible. General editor, Alexander Jones. Garden City, New York, and London: Doubleday and Darton, Longman and Todd.
See chapter 9.

1966 Living Scriptures
The Living Scriptures, a New Translation in the King James Tradition. Edited by Jay Green. Marshatton, DE.: National Foundation for Christian American Bible Society. New York: Macmillan.

1966 Today's English Version
Good News for Modern Man. The New Testament in Today's English Version. New York: American Bible Society. Psalms for Modern Man, 1970. Job for Modern Man, 1971. Wisdom for Modern Man (Proverbs and Ecclesiastes), 1972.
See chapter 11.

1967 Dale's New World
New World: The Heart of the New Testament in Plain English, by Alan T. Dale. London: Oxford University Press, c1967, 1968.

1967 Liverpool Vernacular Gospels
The Gospels in Scouse, translated by Dick Williams and Frank Shaw.
"A rollicking, carefree interpretation of some Gospel passages in the Liverpool vernacular."

1968 Cotton Patch Version
The Cotton Patch Version of Paul's Epistles, by Clarence Jordan. New York: Association Press.
The Cotton Patch Version of Luke and Acts, 1969. The Cotton Patch Version of Matthew and John, 1970. First eight chapters of John only. The Cotton Patch Version of Hebrews and the General Epistles, 1973.
A local dialect version rather than merely an English version. Intended for the South, especially the area around Atlanta. This version goes to the limit of the spectrum in translating ideas and substitutes local place names for biblical ones. Based on Nestle-Aland, 23rd ed., 1957. By the founder of an interracial farming community in Americus, Georgia, with a Ph.D. in Greek from Southern Baptist Theological Seminary.

1968 Hanson's Psalms in Modern Speech
The Psalms in Modern Speech for Public and Private Use, by Richard S. Hanson. Philadelphia: Fortress Press.
3 vols. Vol. 1: Psalms 1-41. Vol. 2: Psalms 42-89. Vol. 3: Psalms 90-150.
A fresh poetic rendering of "the Hymnbook of Ancient

Israel," with special attention to its liturgical usage. Contains an informative "Introduction," introductory notes to many of the Psalms, and footnotes explaining deviations from previous translations.

1968   Restoration of Original Name New Testament
The New Testament of Our Master and Saviour Yahvahshua the Messiah (commonly called Jesus Christ): Restoration of Original Name New Testament. Junction City, Oregon: Missionary Dispensary Bible Research.

Rotherham's version but with changes made principally by returning to the Hebrew form of God's name and by replacing Lord and God in the New Testament by YAHVAH or, for the latter, Elohim when it is used with God.

1969   Barclay's New Testament
The New Testament: a new translation by William Barclay. London, Cleveland: Collins.
Gospels and Acts, 1968. Letters and The Revelation, 1969. See chapter 10.

1969   Children's New Testament
The Children's New Testament. Translated by Gleason H. Ledyard. Waco, Texas: Word Books.

1970   The Mercier New Testament
The Mercier New Testament: A Version of the New Testament in Modern English. Part I: Matthew, Mark, Luke, John. Prepared by Kevin Condon. Cork: Mercier Press. (Identical with The Alba House New Testament.)

A fresh Catholic translation from the Greek in plain, simple, modern English. Patterned after the German Das Neue Testament für Menschen unserer Zeit (1964). Not meant to compete with the standard English versions, but to lead to a greater appreciation and use of them. Illustrated by a hundred carefully selected photographs.

1970   New American Bible
The New American Bible. Translated from the original languages, with the critical use of all the ancient sources, by members of the Catholic Biblical Association of America. New York: P. J. Kenedy.

The New Testament of Our Lord and Savior Jesus Christ translated from the Latin Vulgate. A revision of the Challoner-Rheims Version edited by Catholic Scholars under the patronage of the episcopal committee of the Confraternity of Christian Doctrine. Paterson, N.J.: St. Anthony Guild Press, 1941. (The NT in the NAB is a new translation from the Greek text.)

Genesis, 1948; Vol. I (Genesis-Ruth), 1952; Vol. III (Sapiential or Wisdom Books), 1955; Vol. IV (Prophetic Books), 1961; Vol. II (Samuel-Maccabees), 1969.

See chapter 13.

1970 New English Bible
The New English Bible with the Apocrypha. Oxford University Press and Cambridge University Press.
New Testament, 1961; 2nd ed., 1970. The Old Testament and Apocrypha, 1970.

See chapter 12.

1971 Blackwelder's Exegetical Translation
Letters from Paul. An Exegetical Translation by Boyce W. Blackwelder. Anderson, Ind.: Warner Press.
Based on Nestle's 4th ed., 1904. At times reads more like a condensed commentary than a translation. Sacrifices literary quality for exegetical values. Uses brackets in place of italics to indicate words or expressions that are added to complete the meaning of the Greek. Does not include Hebrews. By the chairman of the Department of NT at Anderson College, Indiana.

1971 Living Bible
The Living Bible, Paraphrased. Wheaton, Ill.: Tyndale House.
Living History of Israel, a paraphrase of Joshua, Judges. 1 and 2 Samuel, 1 and 2 Kings, 1 and 2 Chronicles, Ezra, and Nehemiah, 1970. Living Prophecies: the Minor Prophets paraphrased with Daniel and the Revelation, 1965, 1967. Living New Testament Paraphrased, 1967. Living Letters: the paraphrased Epistles, 1967, c 1962.

See chapter 15.

1971 New American Standard Bible
New American Standard Bible. Carol Stream, Ill.: Creation House.
New American Standard Bible. New Testament Pilot ed., La Habra, Calif. Produced and published by The Lockman Foundation, 1963.

See chapter 14.

1972 The Bible in Living English
The Bible in Living English. Translated by Steven T. Byington. Brooklyn, New York: Watchtower Bible and Tract Society of New York, Inc.

See chapter 6.

1973 Common Bible
Common Bible: The Holy Bible; Revised Standard Version, containing the Old and New Testament with Apocrypha/

Deuterocanonical Books. New York: William Collins Sons. See chapter 2.

1973   New International Version
The Holy Bible, New International Version: The New Testament. Grand Rapids: Zondervan Bible Publishers. See chapter 16.

1973   The Translator's New Testament
The Translator's New Testament. London: The British and. Foreign Bible Society.

Under the direction of W. D. McHardy a team of thirty-five Bible scholars and eighteen missionary linguists prepared this translation in order "to make available, to those translators of the New Testament into their own mother tongue who depend on English for access to the sources of biblical scholarship, such help as is necessary for the making of effective translations in the languages of today." Includes Notes and a Glossary. Based on the United Bible Societies' Greek Text, 1966.

1973   The Better Version of the New Testament
The Better Version of the New Testament based on the Greek text according to eminent scholars and according to certain fundamental principles and rules of biblical interpretation, by Chester Estes. Muscle Shoals, Alabama.

Bibliography

General

Beegle, Dewey M. *God's Word Into English*. Grand Rapids: Wm. B. Eerdmans Publishing Co., 1960.

Beekman, John, and Callow, John. *Translating the Word of God*. Grand Rapids: Zondervan Publishing House, 1974.

Bridges, Ronald, and Weigle, Luther A. *The Bible Word Book, Concerning Obsolete or Archaic Words in the King James Version of the Bible*. New York: Thomas Nelson & Sons, 1960.

Bruce, F. F. *The Books and the Parchments: Some Chapters in the Transmission of the Bible*. 3rd rev. ed. Westwood, N.J.: Fleming H. Revell Co., 1963.

Bruce, F. F. *The English Bible: A History of Translations*. New rev. ed. New York: Oxford University Press, 1970.

Coggan, Frederick D. *Word and World*. London: Hodder & Stoughton, 1971.

Dennett, Herbert. *A Guide to Modern Versions of the New Testament: How to Understand and Use Them*. Chicago: Moody Press, 1965.

Elliott, Melvin E. *The Language of the King James Bible: A Glossary Explaining Its Words and Expressions*. Garden City, N.Y.: Doubleday & Co., Inc., 1967.

Grant, Frederick C. *Translating the Bible*. Greenwich, Conn.: Seabury Press, 1961.

Greenslade, S. L., ed. *The Cambridge History of the Bible: The West from the Reformation to the Present Day*. Cambridge: Cambridge University Press, 1963.

Kenyon, Frederic George. *Our Bible and the Ancient Manuscripts*. Revised by A. W. Adams. New York: Harper & Brothers, 1958.

Levi, Peter. *The English Bible from Wycliff to William Barnes*. Grand Rapids: Wm. B. Eerdmans Publishing Co., 1974.

MacGregor, Geddes. *The Bible in the Making*. Philadelphia and New York: J. B. Lippincott Co., 1959.

————. *A Literary History of the Bible: From the Middle Ages to the Present Day*. Nashville, Tenn.: Abingdon Press, 1968.

May, Herbert Gordon. *Our English Bible in the Making: The Word of Life in Living Language*. Rev. ed. Philadelphia: Published for the Cooperative Publication Association by Westminster Press, 1965.

Nida, Eugene A., and Taber, Charles R. *The Theory and Practice of Translation*. Helps for Translators, 8. Leiden: Published for the United Bible Societies by E. J. Brill, 1969.

Partridge, A. C. *English Biblical Translation*. London: Andre Deutsch, 1973.

Pope, Hugh, O.P. *English Versions of the Bible*. Rev. and amplified by Sebastian Bullough, O.P. St. Louis: Herder, 1952.

Price, Ira M. *The Ancestry of the English Bible*. 3d rev. ed. by William A. Irwin and Allen P. Wikgren. New York: Harper & Brothers, 1956.

Reumann, John H. P. *Four Centuries of the English Bible*. Philadelphia: Muhlenberg Press, 1961.

————. *The Romance of Bible Scripts and Scholars: Chapters in the History of Bible Transmission and Translation*. Englewood Cliffs, N.J.: Prentice-Hall, 1965.

Robertson, E. H. *The New Translations of the Bible*. Studies in Ministry and Worship. Naperville, Ill.: Alec R. Allenson, 1959.

Robinson, H. Wheeler, ed. *The Bible in Its Ancient and English Versions*. Rev. ed. Oxford: Clarendon Press, 1954.

Specht, Walter F. "The Use of Italics in English Versions of the New Testament." *Andrews University Seminary Studies* 6 (1968): 89-109.

Weigle, Luther A. *The English New Testament from Tyndale to the Revised Standard Edition*. New York: Abingdon-Cokesbury Press, 1949.

Wonderly, William L. *Bible Translations for Popular Use*. Helps for Translators, 7. Leiden: Published for the United Bible Societies by E. J. Brill, 1968.

Chapter 1. Early Modern Speech Versions

Clark, Kenneth W. "The Making of the Twentieth Century New Testament." *Bulletin of the John Rylands Library* 38 (1955): 58-81.

Goodspeed, Edgar Johnson. *As I Remember*. New York: Harper, 1953.

————. *New Chapters in New Testament Study*. New York: The Macmillan Co., 1937.

Reumann, John H. P. *The Romance of Bible Scripts and Scholars*. Englewood Cliffs, N.J.: Prentice-Hall, 1965.

Robertson, A. T. *Studies in the Text of the New Testament*. New York: George H. Doran Co., 1926.

Reviews

Bruce, F. F. *Evangelical Quarterly* 34 (1962): 43-44.

Chapter 2. The Revised Standard Version

Bender, Harold Stauffer, et al. *The Revised Standard Version: An Examination and Evaluation*. Scottdale, Pa.: Herald Press, 1953.

Burrows, Millar. *Diligently Compared. The Revised Standard Version and the King James Version of the Old Testament*. New York: Thomas Nelson & Sons, 1964.

Feinberg, Charles Lee. *The Revised Standard Version: What Kind of Translation?* Los Angeles: Bible Institute of Los Angeles, 1953. (Pamphlet)

Huffman, Jaspar Abraham. *The Revised Standard Version, an Appraisal*. Winona Lake, Ind.: The Standard Press, 1953.

An Introduction to the Revised Standard Version of the Old Testament. By Members of the Revision Committee, Luther A. Weigle, Chairman. New York: Thomas Nelson & Sons, 1952.

An Introduction to the Revised Standard Version of the New Testament. By Members of the Revision Committee, Luther A. Weigle, Chairman. N.p.: International Council of Religious Education, 1946.

May, Herbert G. "The Revised Standard Version After Twenty Years." *McCormick Quarterly* 19 (1966): 301-308.

————. "Revised Standard Version Bible." *Vetus Testamentum* 24 (1974): 238-240.

An Open Letter Concerning the Revised Standard Version of the Bible. New York: Division of Christian Education, National Council of the Churches of Christ in the U.S.A., n.d. (Pamphlet)

Swain, Joseph Carter. *New Insights into Scripture: Studying the*

Revised Standard Version. Philadelphia: Cooperative Publication Assn. of the Westminster Press, 1962.

Thompson, Dorothy. "The Old Bible and the New." *Ladies' Home Journal,* March, 1953, pp. 11ff.

Reviews

Allis, Oswald T. *Christianity Today,* 8 July 1957, pp. 6, 7, 21-24.

Black, M. *Journal of Semitic Studies* 4 (1959): 395-397.

Bright, J. *Interpretation* 7 (1953): 338-344.

Gilmour, S. MacLean. *Christianity Today,* 26 September 1960, pp. 6, 8, 10.

Higgins, A. J. B. *Congregation Quarterly* 31 (1953): 173-174.

Ladd, George Eldon. *Christianity Today,* 8 July 1957, pp. 7-11.

McKenzie, J. L. *Catholic Biblical Quarterly* 17 (1955): 88-90.

Major, H. D. A. *Modern Churchman* 44 (1954): 134-135.

Myers, R. *Lutheran Quarterly* 4 (1952): 457-458.

Nesbitt, C. F. *Journal of Bible and Religion* 21 (1953): 33-34.

Peifer, C. *Worship* 47 (1973): 313-315.

Power, A. D. *Church Quarterly Review* 154 (1953): 122-127.

Reider, J. *Jewish Quarterly Review* 43 (1953): 381-384.

Chapter 3. The Knox Translation

Kleist, James A., S. J. "Monsignor R. A. Knox's New Rendering of the New Testament." *Catholic Biblical Quarterly* 5 (1943): 311-317.

Knox, Ronald A. *The Trials of a Translator.* New York: Sheed & Ward, 1949. Published in England under title *On Englishing the Bible.*

Reviews

Cooper, Charles M. *Lutheran Quarterly* 3 (1951): 366-382.

Ellard, Gerald, S. J. *Catholic Biblical Quarterly* 7 (1945): 120-121.

Hooke, S. H. Vol. I, *Church Quarterly Review* 149 (1949): 93-97; Vol. II, 152 (1951): 120-123.

Lussier, J. E., S.S.S. *Theological Studies* 11 (1950): 598-602.

Skehan, Patrick W. *Theological Studies* 10 (1949): 325-332.

Chapter 4. Phillips' Translation

Phillips, J. B. "The Problems of Making a Contemporary Translation." *Bible Translator* 16 (1965): 25-32.

———. "Some Personal Reflections on New Testament Translation." *Bible Translator* 4 (1953): 53-59.

Smalley, William A. "Phillips and the New English Bible: Some Comments on Style." *Bible Translator* 16 (1965): 165-170.

"Translating the Gospels: A Discussion Between Dr. E. V. Rieu and the Rev. J. B. Phillips." *Bible Translator* 6 (1955): 150-159.

Reviews

Andrews, Elias. *Canadian Journal of Theology* 6 (1960): 60-62.

Bratcher, Robert G. *Bible Translator* 10 (1959): 135-143.

Cartledge, Samuel A. *Interpretation* 7 (1953): 366-368.

Danker, Frederick W. *Concordia Theological Monthly* 30 (1959): 541-542.

Englert, D. M. C. *Theology and Life* 7 (1964): 245-246.

Habel, Norman C. *Concordia Theological Monthly* 37 (1966): 246-248.

Hammond, Philip C. *Interpretation* 18 (1964): 230-231.

Harrelson, Walter. *Journal of Biblical Literature* 83 (1964): 210.

Horton, D. *Harvard Divinity Bulletin* 24 (1960): 21-22.

Jones, G. H. *Religious Studies* 9 (1973): 367-368.

Kidner, D. *Churchman* 78 (1964): 63-64.

Maly, Eugene H. *Catholic Biblical Quarterly* 16 (1954): 112-114.

Mitton, C. L. *Expository Times* 84 (1973): 323-324.

Motyer, J. A. *Christianity Today*, 6 December 1963, pp. 38-39.

Petriburg, R. *Church Quarterly Review* 160 (1959): 373ff.

Price, B. F. *Bible Translator* 15 (1964): 98-100.

Robertson, E. H. *Frontier* 7 (1964): 70-71.

Schofield, J. N. *Modern Churchman* 7 (1964): 127-128.

Skilton, John. *Westminster Theological Journal* 21 (1959): 193-196.

Snape, H. C. *Modern Churchman* 5 (1962): 283-284.

Snyder, Russell. *Lutheran Quarterly* 6 (1954): 360.

Chapter 5. The Modern Language Bible

Verkuyl, Gerrit. "The Berkeley Version of the New Testament." *Bible Translator* 2 (1951): 80-85.

Reviews

Anderson, R. A. *The Ministry* 35 (1962): 24-25.

Bratcher, Robert G. *Christianity Today,* 8 October 1971, pp. 16-19.

————. *Bible Translator* 14 (1963): 140-143.

Danker, Frederick W. *Concordia Theological Monthly* 30 (1959): 951-952.

Hull, W. A. *Review and Expositor* 56 (1959): 423-424.

Kerr, David W. *Westminster Theological Journal* 23 (1960-61): 97-100.

Kuist, Howard Tillman. *Interpretation* 14 (1960): 85-86.

Surburg, Raymond F. *The Springfielder* 34 (1970-71): 151-152.

Chapter 6. The New World Translation and The Bible in Living English

Eddy, G. Norman. "The Jehovah's Witnesses: An Interpretation." *Journal of Bible and Religion* 26 (1958): 115-121.

"How Bible Translators Work: Behind the Scenes in the Preparation of a New Version of the New Testament." (Comments on Byington's Review of 1 November 1950 by New World Bible Translation Committee and Byington's Response to this) *Christian Century,* 9 May 1951, pp. 587-589.

Mattingly, John F. "Jehovah's Witnesses Translate the NT." *Catholic Biblical Quarterly* 13 (1951): 439-443.

Metzger, Bruce. "The Jehovah's Witnesses and Jesus Christ: A Biblical and Theological Appraisal." *Theology Today* 10 (1953): 65-85.

Stuermann, Walter E. "The Bible and Modern Religions. III. Jehovah's Witnesses." *Interpretation* 10 (1965): 323-346.

Reviews

Byington, Steven T. *Christian Century,* 1 November 1950, pp. 1295-1296.

Haas, Samuel S. *Journal of Biblical Literature* 74 (1955): 282-283.

Metzger, Bruce. *Bible Translator* 15 (1964): 150-152.

Rowley, H. H. *Expository Times* 65 (1953-54): 41-42.

————. *Expository Times* 67 (1955-56): 107-108.

Chapter 7. The New Jewish Version

Borowitz, Eugene B. "Theological Issues in the New Torah

Translation." *Judaism* 13 (1964): 335-345.

Ginsberg, H. L. "The New Jewish Publication Society Translation of the Torah." *The Journal of Bible and Religion* 31 (July, 1963): 187-192.

———. "The Story of the Jewish Society's New Translation of the Torah." *Bible Translator* 14 (1963): 106-113.

Greenberg, Moshe. "The New Torah Translation." *Judaism* 12 (1963): 225-237.

Jocz, Jakob. "Rabbi, Why Torture the Pronoun?" *Christianity Today,* 12 April 1963, p. 44.

Meek, Theophile J. "A New Bible Translation." *Journal of Biblical Literature* 82 (1963): 265-271.

Orlinsky, Harry M. "The New Jewish Version of the Torah: Toward a New Philosophy of Bible Translation." *Journal of Biblical Literature* 82 (1963): 249-271.

———. *Notes on the New Translation of the Torah.* Philadelphia: The Jewish Publication Society, 1969.

Toombs, Lawrence E. "The Law in English." *Pulpit Digest,* March 1963, pp. 11-14.

Reviews

Dahood, M. *Biblica* 45 (1964): 281-283.

Stinespring, W. F. *Interpretation* 18 (1964): 88-90.

Wegner, Walter. *Concordia Theological Monthly* 44 (1973): 74.

Chapter 8. The Amplified Bible

Reviews

Wegner, Walter. *Concordia Theological Monthly* 34 (1963): 53-54.

Chapter 9. The Jerusalem Bible

Brown, Raymond E. "Recent Roman Catholic Translations of the Bible." *McCormick Quarterly* 19 (1965-66): 283-292.

Danker, Frederick W. "The Jerusalem Bible: A Critical Examination." *Concordia Theological Monthly* 38 (1967): 168-180.

Rhodes, E. F. W. "Text of NT in Jerusalem and New English Bible." *Catholic Biblical Quarterly* 32 (1970): 41-57.

Scobie, Charles H. H. "Two Recent New Testament Texts and Translations." *Canadian Journal of Theology* 14 (1968): 54-63.

Reviews

Archer, Gleason L. *Westminster Theological Journal* 33 (1971):
    191-194.

Child, R. L. *Baptist Quarterly* 22 (1967): 186-187.
    18-20.

Dewitz, L. R. M. *Christianity Today*, 16 January 1970, pp.
    131.

Di Lella, Alexander A., O.F.M. *Catholic Biblical Quarterly*
    29 (1967): 148-151.

Fitzmyer, Joseph A., S. J. *Theological Studies* 28 (1967): 129-
    91-93.

Gold, V. R. *Lutheran World* 15 (1968): 354.

Grant, Frederick C. *Journal of Biblical Literature* 86 (1967):

Harrington, W. J., O.P. *Revue Biblique* 75 (1968): 450-452.

Herbert, Arthur S. *Bible Translator* 18 (1967): 95-97.

Hughes, P. E. *Churchman* 81 (1967): 134.

Kuyper, Lester J., and Oudersluys, Richard C. *Reformed Review*
    21 (1967-68): 22-27.

Landes, George M. *Union Seminary Quarterly* 22 (1966-67):
    280-283.

Metzger, Bruce M. *Princeton Seminary Bulletin* 60 (1967):
    45-48.

Walker, L. L. *Southwestern Journal of Theology* 11 (1968):
    120.

Chapter 10. Barclay's New Testament

Reviews

Bratcher, R. G. *Bible Translator* 22 (1971): 47-48.

Duffield, Gervase E. *Churchman* 83 (1969): 251-254.

Harvey, A. E. *Theology* 72 (1969): 368-369.

Marshall, I. Howard. *Evangelical Quarterly* 41 (1969): 175-
    177.

————. *Evangelical Quarterly* 42 (1970): 114-115.

Chapter 11. Today's English Version

Bratcher, Robert G. "Good News for Modern Man." *The Bible
    Translator* 17 (1966): 159-172.

————. "The Nature and Purpose of the New Testament in
    Today's English Version." *The Bible Translator* 22 (1971):
    97-107.

————. "The T.E.V. New Testament and the Greek Text." *The
    Bible Translator* 18 (1967): 167-174.

Scobie, Charles H. H. "Two Recent New Testament Texts and Translations." *Canadian Journal of Theology* 14 (1968): 54-63.

Reviews

Dahood, M. *Catholic Biblical Quarterly* 34 (1972): 240-242.

Danker, Frederick W. *Catholic Biblical Quarterly* 29 (1967): 257-258.

————. *Concordia Theological Monthly* 39 (1968): 216.

Ebor, D. *Church Quarterly* 1 (1968): 66-67.

Hodges, Z. C. *Bibliotheca Sacra* 126 (1969): 86-87.

Jackson, J. J. *Interpretation* 26 (1972): 95-96.

Metzger, Bruce M. *Princeton Seminary Bulletin* 60 (1966): 67-68.

Reumann, John. *Journal of Biblical Literature* 86 (1967): 234-236.

Chapter 12. The New English Bible

Barr, James. "After Five Years: A Retrospect on Two Major Translations of the Bible." *Heythrop Journal* 15 (1974): 381-405.

Brockington, Leonard Herbert, ed. *The Hebrew Text of the Old Testament: The Readings Adopted by the Translators of the New English Bible.* Oxford: Oxford University Press, 1973.

Dodd, C. H. *The New English Bible; A History of the Project.* Oxford: Oxford University Press. (Brochure)

Driver, G. R. "The New English Bible: The Old Testament." *Journal of Jewish Studies* 24 (1973): 1-7.

Hunt, Geoffrey. *About the New English Bible.* London: Oxford University Press, 1970.

Macintosh, A. A.; Stanton, G.; and Frost, D. L. "The 'New English Bible' Reviewed." *Theology* 74 (1971): 154-166.

Metzger, Bruce M. "Four English Translations of the New Testament." *Christianity Today,* 22 November 1963, pp. 6-10.

Nineham, Dennis Eric, ed. *The New English Bible Reviewed.* London: Epworth Press [c1965].

Pfeiffer, Charles F. "A Highly Readable Translation." *Christianity Today,* 27 March 1970, pp. 13-16.

Rice, G. "Isaiah 28:1-22 and the New English Bible." *Journal of Religious Thought* 30 (1973-74): 13-17.

Stinespring, William F. "Some Remarks on the New English Bible." *Understanding the Sacred Text,* ed. by John Reumann. Valley Forge, Pa.: Judson Press, 1972.

Terrien, Samuel. "The New English Bible with the Apocrypha." *Union Seminary Quarterly Review* 25 (1969): 549-555.

Reviews

Allis, Oswald T. *Westminster Theological Journal* 33 (1970): 81-93.

Bartels, R. A. *Lutheran Quarterly* 13 (1961): 269-271.

Beare, F. W. *New Testament Studies* 8 (1961): 80-92.

Benoit, P. *Revue Biblique* 69 (1962: 147-149.

Boling, R. G. *McCormick Quarterly* 23 (1970): 277-283.

Brown, Raymond E. *Catholic Biblical Quarterly* 23 (1961): 321-324.

Bruce, F. F. *Christianity Today,* 13 March 1961, pp. 5-8.

———. *Christianity Today,* 30 January 1970, pp. 8-11.

———. *Scottish Journal of Theology* 14 (1961): 194-196.

Burrows, M. *Journal of Biblical Literature* 89 (1970): 220-222.

Cadbury, H. J. *Theology Today* 18 (1961): 188-200.

Child, R. L. *Baptist Quarterly* 19 (1961): 52-58.

———. *Baptist Quarterly* 23 (1970): 330-331.

Christianity Today, 30 January 1961, pp. 25-26.

Clements, R. E. *Church Quarterly* 2 (1970): 335-338.

Clines, D. J. A. *Evangelical Quarterly* 42 (1970): 168-175.

Dahood, M. *Biblica* 52 (1971): 117-123.

Davidson, R. *Scottish Journal of Theology* 23 (1970): 231-236.

Davies, P. E. *Interpretation* 15 (1961): 339-344.

Evangelical Quarterly 33 (1961): 112-116.

Goetchius, E. V. N. *Anglican Theological Review* 52 (1970): 167-176.

Gordon, Cyrus H. *Christianity Today,* 27 March 1970, pp. 6-8.

Grant, F. C. *Journal of Biblical Literature* 80 (1961): 173-176.

Hibbitts, J. B. *Canadian Journal of Theology* 7 (1961): 286-290.

Hobbs, E. C. *Anglican Theological Journal* 43 (1961): 413-415.

Howes, J. *Frontier* 5 (1962): 429-433.

Kraus, C. N. *Mennonite Quarterly Review* 45 (1971): 390-391.

Lloyd, G. *Japan Christian Quarterly* 27 (1961): 269-271.

Metzger, Bruce M. *Interpretation* 24 (1970): 375-378.

———. *Princeton Seminary Bulletin* 55 (1961): 56-63.

Meyer, W. F. *Springfielder* 34 (1970): 51-55.

Mitton, C. L. *Expository Times* 72 (1961): 206-207.

Murphy, R. E. *Theological Studies* 31 (1970): 320-321.

Petersen, L. M. *Springfielder* 25 (1961): 65-67.

Petrie, C. S. *Reformed Theological Review* 20 (1961): 57-58.

Robertson, E. H. *Expository Times* 81 (1970): 203-204.

Skilton, J. H. *Westminster Theological Journal* 24 (1961): 70-79.

Stendahl, K. *Harvard Divinity Bulletin* 27 (1962): 25-30.

Summers, R. *Review and Expositor* 58 (1961): 233-237.

Swain, J. C. *Journal of Ecumenical Studies* 7 (1970): 823-824.

Tait, R. C. *Modern Churchman* 14 (1971): 169-170.

Throckmorton, B. H., Jr. *Journal of Bible and Religion* 29 (1961): 193-203.

Vawter, B. *Catholic Biblical Quarterly* 32 (1970): 426-428.

Chapter 13. The New American Bible

Barr, James. "After Five Years: A Retrospect on Two Major Translations of the Bible." *Heythrop Journal* 15 (1974): 381-405.

Reviews

Crim, Keith. *Interpretation* 26 (1972): 77-80.

Danker, Frederick W. *Catholic Biblical Quarterly* 33 (1971): 405-409.

Expository Times 82 (1970-1971): 381.

Metzger, Bruce M. *Princeton Seminary Bulletin* 54 (1971): 90-99.

Reumann, John. *Journal of Biblical Literature* 92 (1973): 275-278.

Sabourin, L. *Biblical Theology Bulletin* 2 (1972): 206-208.

Stagg, Frank. *Review and Expositor* 68 (1971): 400-402.

Chapter 14. The New American Standard Bible

Reviews

Alden, R. L. *Westminster Theological Journal* 34 (1972): 217-223.

Bratcher, Robert G. *Bible Translator* 13 (1962): 234-236.

Hodges, Z. C. *Bibliotheca Sacra* 121 (1964): 267-268.

Peifer, C. J. *Worship* 45 (1971): 102-113.

Chapter 15. The Living Bible

Bowman, R. C. "The Living Bible: A Critique." *Brethren Life and Thought* 18 (1973): 137-144.

Neufeld, Don F. "Will the New Bibles Let You Down?" *Insight*, 29 February 1972, pp. 14-18.

"The Story of the Living Bible." *Eternity*, April 1973, pp. 64-65, 74-75.

Reviews

Bratcher, Robert G. *Bible Translator* 20, no. 3 (1969): 36-39.

Houston, Jack. *Moody Monthly*, November 1971, pp. 28, 68, 69.

Leaney, R. *Church Quarterly Review* 167 (1966): 255-256.

Waltke, B. K. *Bibliotheca Sacra* 125 (1968): 73-74.

Chapter 16. The New International Version

Harris, R. Laird, and Hardwick, Stanley E. "Do Evangelicals Need a New Bible Translation?" *Christianity Today*, 27 September 1968, pp. 10-15.

Linton, Calvin D. "NIV Style." *Christianity Today*, 28 September 1973, p. 41.

Paine, Stephen W. "Why We Need Another Translation." *United Evangelical Action*, October 1967.

Reviews

Bruce, F. F. *Christianity Today* 17 (1973): 25-31.

Ludlow, William L. *Church Management: The Clergy Review*, January 1974, pp. 23-25.

MacRae, George W. *America*, 23 November 1974, p. 330.

Miller, Donald G. *Eternity*, March 1974, pp. 46-47, 50, 52.

Moody, Dale. *Review and Expositor* 71 (1974): 397-398.

Scholer, David M. *Journal of Biblical Literature* 93 (1974): 591-594.

Chapter 17. Guidelines

Fee, Gordon D. "The Text of the New Testament and Modern Translations." *Christianity Today*, 22 June 1973, pp. 6-11.

Hawthorne, Gerald F. "After the King James Version, What?" *Eternity*, September 1973, pp. 29-33.

Kubo, Sakae. "What Should I Look for in Choosing a Bible Version?" *These Times*, Special Issue, June 1974, pp. 30-33.

"Which Bible Is Best for You?" *Eternity*, April 1974, pp. 27-31.